Prosperity *with* Purpose

Prosperity *with* Purpose

A Muslim Woman's Guide to
Abundance and Generosity

Nausheena Hussain

© 2025 by Daybreak Press

All rights reserved. No part of this book may be reproduced or transmitted in any form or by any means, graphic, electronic or mechanical, including photocopying, recording, typing, or by any information storage retrieval system, without the permission of the publisher.

Daybreak Press
3533 Lexington Avenue North, Arden Hills, MN 55126
www.rabata.org/daybreakpress | daybreakpress@rabata.org

ISBN (print): 978-1-7368031-0-3
LCCN: 2024945594

Cover design and typesetting: Katrina Kuzyk | www.katrinakuzyk.com

Printed in the United States of America

Dedicated to my mother, Razia, my first philanthropy mentor.

Contents

Introduction 1

Chapter 1: Blossoming Where You're Planted:
The Power of a Mother's Journey 7
    Mamma Arrives 9
    The Side Hustle 12
    Nurturing and Providing 15
    Mamma's Generosity 16

Chapter 2: We Don't Talk About Money 21
    Babba 21
    Differentiating Between a Retirement Plan
    and a Child's Obligation 24
    Money Talk 25
    Talks About Charity 31

Chapter 3: Values, Goals, and Dreaming Big 34
    Values 37
    Starting with Essential Values 39
    Intentions, Clarifying Personal Values,
    and Creating Goals 41
    My Personal Roadmap 43
    Mapping Out Your Personal Goals 63

Chapter 4: Myths about Women and Money 69
    Myth #1: Women Aren't Good at Math 72
    Myth #2: Women Aren't Smart Enough to Understand
    Finances and Investing 75
    Myth #3: Boys Invest, Girls Save 79
    Myth #4: Women Are Bad with Money 81
    Myth #5: It Is Taboo to Earn More than Your Man 85

Chapter 5: Gender Inequities 91
    The Pink Tax 91

The Gender Wage Pay Gap............................92
The Funding Gap 100
Workplace Environments.............................100

Chapter 6: How Do You Define Wealth? 111
Knowledge and Education 117
Relationships and Social Connections...................117
Health and Well-Being 118
Time 118
Personal Values and Beliefs 119
Spiritual Wealth 119

Chapter 7: Shifting Mindsets: You Are Wealthier than You Think................................... 123
The *Rizq* Factor.......................................123
The Gardener..127
The Scarcity Mindset.................................129
What Is the Abundance Mindset?.....................134
Tips for Developing an Abundance Mindset.............136
The Minimalist Lifestyle 140

Chapter 8: Connecting the Economic Empowerment Dots. 147
Divorce..148
Death 150
Single Women..153
Women and Inheritance 155
Bringing Joy to Others................................156
Building Generational Wealth 158

Chapter 9: Assessing My Financial Situation 161

Chapter 10: Just Start..................................... 169
Optimize Your Credit Cards 170
Credit Scores..177
Banks 183

Chapter 11: Interest, Taxes, Inflation, and Financial Advisers 187

Alternatives 189
Taxes 192
Inflation 194
Investment Management Firm 197
Should You Pay for a Financial Adviser? 200

Chapter 12: Halal Investing 101 .... **205**
What Is Halal Investing? 208
Example: 211
Diversifying Your Stock Portfolio 212
Owning Company Stock Is Not the Same as Gambling 218
Saving for College 223

Chapter 13: Retirement Plans, 401(k)s, and IRAs **227**
SEP IRA 230
Rollover IRA and SEP IRA 231
Roth IRA 232

Chapter 14: Wills—Do You Have One? **235**

Chapter 15: Secrets to Financial Freedom **241**
Secret #1: Pay Yourself First—Put Yourself First 241
Secret #2: Don't Budget—Spend Consciously 244
Secret #3: Live Rich Now 247

Chapter 16: Philanthropy and Gratitude **265**

Chapter 17: Muslim Philanthropy **273**
Zakat 276
Ṣadaqa 283
Awqāf 287

Chapter 18: My DAF as My Philanthropic Tool **295**

Chapter 19: Giving Circles **301**

Chapter 20: Muslim Women Philanthropists **309**
Islam's Philanthropic Roots 311
Muslim Female Philanthropists 320
The Rest of the Ts 325
How Am I a Philanthropist Through the Five Ts? 331

Chapter 21: Transfer of Wealth to Women in 2030 337
Conclusion 341
Glossary 349
    Non-English Terms 349
    Financial Terms 355
Bibliography. 363
Index 375

Introduction

The year 2020 threw the world into a state of frenzy. Entire countries were shutting down. Food and basic necessities were flying off shelves as the international supply chain was severely impacted. Government and health care systems faced a global crisis never before experienced in living memory, as the coronavirus (a.k.a. COVID-19) spread voraciously through the world. Life as we knew it screeched to a halt.

In March 2020, Minnesota governor Tim Walz declared a state of emergency and issued a stay-at-home order to curtail the spread of the COVID-19 virus. Other states followed suit. Many of us who were not frontline workers closed our offices and began to work from home. Our children started distance learning as schools shut down. Remote work and a pod lifestyle became a way of life. From our homes, we fearfully watched the virus consume the world and take a destructive toll on our health care systems. We watched helplessly as loved ones succumbed to the virus. We lost human connection, watched businesses close, and figured out creative ways to avoid becoming bored out of our minds. We binge-watched television series, read mountains of books, baked tons of bread, and picked up new hobbies to fill the extra time.

About halfway up my mountain of books, I happened upon *The Latte Factor* by David Bach and John David Mann, a financial advice book for novices. I devoured it in a day, while nerding out and taking notes in a Google Slides document that evolved into a presentation on Canva. My inspiration knew no bounds and, along with a colleague, I cocreated an entire series of workshops on economic empowerment for Muslim women at Reviving Islamic Sisterhood for Empowerment (RISE), the nonprofit organization I founded. I named the first workshop "The *Rizq*[1] Factor," a play on the title *The Latte Factor*. While the title was similar, the workshop was original. I infused many Islamic values and concepts into my financial explanations and advice. The series incorporated topics such as managing personal finances, halal investing, how to buy a house, understanding credit scores, understanding zakat,[2] and making use of donor-advised funds for charitable giving. The series also included an interactive panel featuring Muslim women entrepreneurs, following their journey into the world of running a business and becoming financially independent.

This book turns that first Canva presentation into a financial management guide for Muslim women. It is my attempt to honor them, especially the immigrants among them, who work hard to restart life in a new environment, while also struggling to understand a different culture and language, and prosper within a new infrastructure and financial system. These challenges all intersect in the immigrant experience.

Immigrating to the United States requires learning about banking practices, credit scores, taxes, and investment options. Understanding financial terms and banking procedures while navigating paperwork can be overwhelming. Cultural and religious differences around financial practices can also create confusion and require adjustment. One of the aims of this book is to help immigrants acquire the financial literacy crucial to making informed decisions about managing money and building a secure financial future for the next generation.

---

1 *Rizq* is an Arabic term that refers to the provisions that Allah (God) provides to His creation. It's a multifaceted concept that encompasses all forms of sustenance necessary for human survival and well-being, including food, water, clothing, shelter, health, knowledge, time, opportunities, love, and relationships.

2 Zakat is a mandatory act of charity in Islam that involves donating a portion of one's wealth to those in need. It is one of the five pillars of Islam and is required annually from every Muslim who has the minimal amount of savings.

Introduction

This book is also my attempt to honor and validate the experiences, stereotypes, and obstacles that Muslim women face. Gendered Islamophobia, lack of representation, money myths, and gender inequities have all played roles in impeding economic stability for Muslim women. And usually, no one talks about all of this. People are unsure about how to manage their money and even more unsure about how to discuss it. I hope this book will help you start that conversation.

I am writing this book primarily for my Muslim sisters. There is a lack of literature written by us and for us about finance. I hope my journey resonates with you enough to help you leap into action.

The beginning of the book will help you understand your why and then provide you with a slate of options to choose from and action steps to follow in order to build your wealth. It will weave in philanthropy and charitable giving, as wealth building and charitable giving go hand in hand. I draw a lot from our *deen*[3] as I explain things and share my stories. This is not a book on the *fiqh*[4] of finance, but rather a guidebook to managing money with an Islamic attitude.

Sometimes money is a welcome guest that shows no sign of leaving, and other times it stays for too short a period, wreaking havoc in every aspect of our lives. I hope reading this book changes your relationship with money for the better and deepens your relationship with Allah ﷻ[5] and that you find yourself seeking His pleasure as you manage your finances and give generously.

---

3   This Arabic term is often translated as "religion" or "faith." However, the concept of deen encompasses much more than just a belief system or set of practices; it more accurately translates as a comprehensive way of life based on beliefs and ethical principles.

4   *Fiqh* is Islamic jurisprudence. It is often described as the human understanding of the divine Islamic law as revealed in the Quran and the Sunna.

5   ﷻ is an Arabic honorific for God that is said or written after the mention of Allah by name or pronoun. It ﷻ reads *subḥāna wa taʿāla*, which means "the Most Glorified, the Most High."

Allah ﷻ is the ultimate source of wisdom and guidance; may He provide you with divine guidance in this journey, bless your every step, and accept your generosity. Inshallah you will gain financial control and independence, create a rich and meaningful life, and give back, storing mountains of blessings for the next life through your *ṣadaqa jāriya*.[6]

Whatever good comes out of this book is from Allah. Whatever is wrong or incorrect is from my personal shortcomings. May we always do what is pleasing to Him; may He increase our *rizq*; and may He help our *ummah*[7] be legendary. *Ameen!*

Your sister in Islam,

NAUSHEENA HUSSAIN

---

6   *Ṣadaqa jāriya* is a form of continuous charity in Islam whereby the benefits of a good deed continue to accrue even after the giver has passed away.

7   The *ummah* is the global community of believers.

Part I: Finances

The ultimate goal of Part I is to educate and empower Muslim women to achieve financial literacy and realize their economic impact while upholding the intrinsic values of their faith. In my own personal journey, I struggled to work within the confines of a capitalistic framework devoid of Islamic values, but that didn't stop me from learning or pursuing solutions to those challenges. I found resources, experts, and sharia-compliant tools to accomplish my goal of becoming economically empowered. Here, I share the tale of my financial odyssey, and I hope to empower and guide you on your own journey toward stability and prosperity.

The goal is not to help you make more money or get rich quick. Of course I want you to earn more money and build your wealth, but beyond that, I want Muslim women to level up our impact. I want us to become stronger and more confident in understanding and managing our money. I want us to take control of our lives and claim our right to financial freedom, to build a life full of joy and financial abundance. You will learn to leave behind habits that don't serve you and form new ones that do. You will learn to prioritize, budget, analyze, invest, and give back. You will learn to discipline yourself financially. You will learn ways to balance financial sacrifice and generosity. It's not just about giving something up. It's about understanding what's most important to you and prioritizing that. Let's get started!

Chapter 1

Blossoming Where You're Planted: The Power of a Mother's Journey

A used white envelope hangs between a wall calendar and the kitchen phone. Our family's budget for the month is scrawled in my mother's handwriting in black ink on its back. Rent: $300. Electricity. Gas. Phone. I can't remember what each utility cost, but there is a total down at the bottom. The calendar shows due dates for the bills as well as our birthdays, family dinners, and other social events. This was my mother's budgeting planner. She managed our household expenses, kept track of monthly bills, and knew how much to budget for each expense. She was responsible and frugal. She was thrifty and careful.

Fareeda Begum Ali was born to Ahmed Abdul Haleem and Abida Unisa Begum on March 21, 1951, in the village of Nalgonda in India. She was the fourth daughter after four sons. Her mother passed away a year later due to pregnancy complications. With seven children and a teacher's salary, my grandfather remarried. Mamma graduated with bachelor's degree in arts from Vanitha Degree College for Women. In 1975, she married my father, Mir Muzaffer Ali, and migrated alone to the United States in 1976. Three months later, I was born.

My dad arrived a year later and eventually got a job at Sherman Hospital on the east side of Elgin, Illinois. We were proud when he was promoted to chief engineer. Every time the hospital was renovated, my dad took the opportunity to bring home the stuff the hospital was throwing out. And Mamma put it to use. I didn't realize we couldn't afford anything brand new or expensive. I had no idea what discretionary spending money was or that we didn't have any of it.

Our dinner table had a metal frame with a wooden top surrounded by six metal chairs that had leather seats and backings. *A conference table.* We had a large, makeshift *takhat.* In India, a *takhat* is an intricately-carved wooden daybed, piled with velvet throws, colorful blankets, silk sheets, and embroidered pillows. Our "modern" *takhat* was covered with foam and white sheets. *A physical therapy platform.* Instead of brightly colored fabrics, our *takhat* was covered with crisp white linens with "Sherman Hospital" imprinted on the borders. *Hospital sheets.*

The basement had a TV with our Nintendo, and it doubled as our playroom. We would watch evening sitcoms but couldn't change the channel unless we got up, crawled to the TV, and manually pushed the buttons because there was no remote. *Hospital room TV.* I remember making dinner using recipes from a children's cookbook while the four of us siblings watched TGIF—Thank God It's Friday. TGIF was a programming block on the American television network ABC that aired on Friday evenings during the 1990s. It featured a lineup of family-friendly sitcoms with shows like *Full House, Family Matters, Step by Step, Perfect Strangers,* and my favorite, *Just the Ten of Us.*

As kids, we felt we had everything in that basement. Using our imaginations, we created haunted houses and winter sleds out of old cardboard boxes. We held Eid[8] parties featuring piñatas with our cousins. We ruled that little world when Mamma was working the second shift at Hoffer's Plastics, a local factory.

---

8   Eid, in Arabic, is defined as "celebration" or "festival." Muslims celebrate two Eids: Eid al-Fitr, which marks the end of Ramadan, and Eid al-Adha, the feast of sacrifice marking the end of the holy pilgrimage, Hajj.

Blossoming Where You're Planted: The Power of a Mother's Journey

MAMMA ARRIVES

My mom arrived at O'Hare International Airport in Chicago, Illinois, in the summer of 1976, pregnant with me, while my dad was still in India. His paperwork didn't come through, or maybe they couldn't file it until she got here, so Mamma moved in with her sister, Auntie Mamma,[9] and her brother-in-law, Ishaq Uncle. Mamma had brought my cousin Asra, their eldest daughter, with her from India. Auntie Mamma was also pregnant. Their due dates were a few days apart.

Mamma had no job, so she had no health insurance. When she went into labor, Ishaq Uncle had to take her to a public hospital. And so it was that I was born in Cook County Hospital. Two weeks later, Auntie Mamma delivered my cousin, Ashfaq. We were born only fifteen days apart. We grew up like twins. He was my first brother and my best friend. Ishaq Uncle was my first father figure. He gleefully shares that "Two stars were born in my home in October of 1976." It's endearing, but then I jokingly counter with "Then why did you give me away?!"

The six of us continued to live together until my father arrived in the United States a year later. Eventually, my parents moved into their own apartment. My father found a job, and shortly after, my mother began her very first job. They were officially a two-income household. The idea of a Muslim woman working outside of her home was a foreign concept for families in India. Yet in the United States, the idea of a two-income household was becoming a natural way of life. With her away from home, my parents needed to find a babysitter to watch me during the day. I am sure many first-time mothers find this to be one of the hardest things to do. And I can only imagine how my immigrant mother felt leaving her little brown girl at a white, non-Muslim, unrelated person's home for at

---

9 In our family and culture, your mother's sisters are like your mothers. So, we affectionately call them aunts and moms. Hence, Auntie Mamma.

least forty hours a week. But to afford their new place, a car, food, and basic necessities, she had to make this sacrifice.

My parents worked hard and lived frugally. A few years later, my brother was born. We moved into a two-bedroom apartment that was on the bottom floor of a three-story apartment building. And when I say bottom floor, it wasn't the first floor or the ground floor. It was literally a floor in the ground, a walkout basement. Our living room had a sliding door out to a patio. It had stairs that you walked up to get out to the driveway. The kitchen had a door that led to the rest of the building's basement and laundry room. The basement was large enough that in the winters, my brother and I would ride our Big Wheel and bicycle down there. It was so much fun! We had a cat, black with white paws. We named him White Sox.

Mamma became pregnant again. My little sister was born two months premature, tiny and not fully developed. She was rushed to a children's hospital via ambulance and grew in a little incubation crib for the first few weeks. The doctors said we had to make a few changes in our lives in order for her to survive and thrive. My dad had to quit smoking. We had to give up our cat (devastating!). And we needed to move out of that basement.

We moved into a three-bedroom apartment a neighborhood away. Now we were up on the third floor, which was the top floor of that building. What a view! And not three months later, my mother was pregnant again! My baby brother was born almost exactly one year after my sister. My mom quit her job. It was in this home that I recall the makeshift budget on the wall. But soon there were four little kids running around, and our neighbors down below weren't too happy. It was time to move again.

My father had moved up in rank at the hospital, which meant that he had more professional stability and we had more income. As for my mom, she was the primary caretaker and household manager, and she continued to move from one minimum-wage job to the next. My parents worked hard and saved money. Truth be told, my father might have been earning more, but my mother was much more financially responsible. Together, they were able to purchase a duplex home in South Elgin, the next town over. Although this wasn't too far out, moving there meant moving away from the masjid (mosque) and a lot of my mom's side of the family, including all of our cousins. But it was a house! A house we *owned*. The American dream. My mom went back to work. My father worked first shift and she worked second. As the eldest daughter, I often played a role second to that of my mother.

That house had only two bedrooms, one full bath, and one half bath. Six of us shared one shower—in a bathroom with a door that didn't lock! But necessity is the mother of invention, and we figured out that we could pull the vanity drawer out to block the door from opening. My dad and his coworker, who happened to be his best friend, renovated the basement, allowing me and my siblings to have a playroom once again.

My sister and I took the second bedroom. Back then, every girl dreamt of having a canopy bed. At least two of my cousins had this furniture set. For Mamma, the canopy bedroom set was not just furniture for her daughters, but rather a symbol of social status. Ours was a second-hand set and we couldn't afford the fancy canopy drapery, but we loved it.

That *takhat* (a.k.a. physical therapy bed) out in the living room became my brothers' bed. My mother kept their personal belongings in her bedroom—making space for them as she continued to try to build a better life for all of us. One summer, my father converted the laundry room into a third bedroom for my brothers by moving the washer and dryer down into the basement. Imagine a tiny laundry room with no windows or closets. That was their new room. They didn't like it, so they continued to sleep on the *takhat*.

Our American dream had been realized! We had two cars, and the second one was a brand-new yellow Ford Escort for Mamma. Brand-new! I mean, having two cars was a significant sign of prosperity in the 80s. But a brand-new car? That's called living the high life of luxury. It was the perfect vehicle for my mom. My dad parked his used station wagon outside on the street, in front of our house, and our single-car garage housed mom's new yellow car. All four of us kids had bicycles, and mine was bought at a garage sale.

We outgrew this house, and as financial stability grew for my parents, we moved from our duplex back to Elgin and the rest of the extended family. There, we built our first single-family home. It had four bedrooms, two-and-a-half bathrooms, a two-car garage, a basement, and a huge backyard.

Financially, life was on an upswing for our family. My parents were diligently investing in their 401(k)s for retirement, demonstrating their commitment to long-term financial security. At the same time, our day-to-day circumstances were improving. Mamma worked for an employee-owned company that offered profit sharing, which boosted our household income. This additional money, separate from their retirement savings, allowed us to furnish our home with brand-new items. The family room and living room boasted new furniture, we got a brand-new dining table, and my brothers each enjoyed new bedroom furniture in their own rooms. My mom discovered the glory and convenience of bed-in-a-bag sets, ensuring all our beds had matching linens and blankets. She even had time to garden in the backyard. In our neighborhood, we were keeping up with the Joneses—or, rather, the Ahmeds.

THE SIDE HUSTLE

My mom was the queen of the side hustle before there was even a term for it. She became an Avon sales lady and went door-to-door to sell makeup and cosmetics. She struggled to communicate with new clients using her beginner's-level English, which made it a hard gig, so she moved on to a new one.

Devon Avenue in Chicago was where we Desis[10] could find and stock up on our culturally affirming groceries, entertainment, clothing, and everything else we needed. My mom loved watching Bollywood movies, and the only place to rent a Bollywood movie was from Devon Ave. Since it was in the city, though, far from a lot of the suburban Desis, Mamma saw an opportunity. She started a side business in our house. Once a month, we would take a day trip out to Devon Ave. While buying all of our *zabiha* (Islamically slaughtered/halal) meat and Indian groceries, Mamma would invest in a couple of Bollywood movies on VHS. These were not original tapes. These were copies of copies. She brought them back to our suburban home and converted our dining room into the community's Bollywood Blockbuster! She rented the movies out to the local Desis, most of whom were Muslims. She charged two dollars to rent a movie and recorded their "memberships" in a red spiral notebook. Patrons were expected to return the movie in two days, but of course, no one followed any of her business rules. She didn't implement late fees or place "Be kind, please rewind" stickers on the tapes. We had one auntie who tried to exercise her bargaining power and wanted to pay only one dollar because the tapes were copies of the originals. Mamma was too nice. She should have told her to drive to Chicago and get her own rentals!

Bollywood Blockbuster got a little boring for Mamma, so she created a new side hustle: catering. You could enlist her culinary skills to cook delicious, traditional Hyderabadi dishes like

---

10   A Desi is a person of South Asian birth or descent who lives abroad.

mutton biryani,[11] *mirchi ka salan*,[12] and chicken korma[13] for your newborn's *'aqīqa*,[14] your child's *ameen*,[15] or a family *dawat*.[16] I only recall her filling one order, so that business didn't last very long. I'm guessing Mamma realized she didn't include her labor costs when calculating her net profits.

The one side hustle that drove me crazy was her Desi Claire's boutique. I remember my mom purchased all this fake Indian jewelry to sell at local bazaars hosted by different Islamic centers. Although there weren't enough Islamic centers or bazaars to sell at, she continued to buy more and more of this fake jewelry. And when the Muslims and the Desis didn't buy it, she tried to sell it to her coworkers. This didn't last long either, and she still has boxes, Tupperwares, and bins of this fake jewelry in her current apartment. At least she's wearing the stuff now.

Mamma's side hustles were really more like hobbies for her—a way to stay busy and connected with people—than a secondary source of income. She loved these gigs, always getting excited over sales, and she enjoyed meeting people and bargaining with them. I inherited her sense of serial entrepreneurship, but my entrepreneurial drive manifested in establishing nonprofits and community service projects.

---

11   Mutton biryani is a delicious rice and meat dish of India. It's made with lamb, goat, or chicken along with yogurt and spices layered with rice.
12   *Mirchi ka salan* is a famous Hyderabadi chili and peanut curry that accompanies biryani.
13   Chicken korma is a Mughali gravy dish made with yogurt, nuts, onions, and spices.
14   *'Aqīqa* is an Islamic ritual after a baby is born that includes shaving the baby's head, sacrificing an animal, and cooking and serving the meat in a celebration to welcome the newborn.
15   *Ameen* is a rite-of-passage celebration when a young Muslim completes their first full reading of the Quran in Arabic.
16   *Dawat*, in Urdu, means "party."

NURTURING AND PROVIDING

Mamma never made us feel like we didn't have enough. As kids, we felt we had everything. Every Eid she made sure we had brand-new outfits. Every birthday, she threw me a party, dressed me up as a *dulhan*,[17] and invited all my friends and cousins over. She cooked scrumptious food and decorated our home.

Every August we would go back-to-school shopping with Mamma and get new clothes, new backpacks, and new school supplies. We would be ready for a new school year. We never felt like we didn't have enough. It was only later that I realized how hard it must have been on Mamma. She was working a full-time job, raising four kids, and taking care of a household. She cooked our meals before she left for work. When we came home from school, there was always a fresh, hot Hyderabadi meal waiting for us on the dinner table. Our laundry was washed and put away. Our home was clean. And she never looked tired or complained. She was a super-shero!

I went to public school and then community college on a full, merit-based scholarship. The only things I had to pay for were books and lab fees. My parents dreamed of me becoming a doctor. My mom understood the economic stability that a career in medicine would provide. So after two years at community college, I transferred to a private university to continue my premed track. The tuition was $25,000 per year. I had a scholarship that covered $15,000 each year, and I took out $6,500 in student loans. I was short $5,000 for tuition. Mamma knew I couldn't take out any more loans, so her hard work stepped in. She worked a minimum-wage job to cover the gap. She saved $500 per month from her weekly paycheck to pay for my tuition.

After my third year in college, I got married. Mamma was the ultimate wedding planner, as she had been planning for my

---

17   *Dulhan,* in Urdu, means "bride."

wedding by investing in gold jewelry since I was born.

Throughout millennia and across cultures, gold has been considered a sign of wealth. It is a stable investment that provides financial security and is even a strong marker of the global economic state. Why? Gold is rare—a limited natural resource—so it increases in value. In Desi wedding culture, gifting gold to newlyweds, mostly in the form of wearable jewelry, provides a little financial nest egg. Savings to begin a new life together. The bride receives gold from her family and her husband's family as a form of personal financial security. My mom didn't receive any gold from her own family or her in-laws when she got married, so as soon as she began earning money, she began to slowly invest her money in buying gold. For twenty years, she bought gold bangles, earrings, and rings, investing her earnings into a future for her two daughters. At my wedding, my mom gave me six different sets of jewelry and two sets of gold bangles. She gave me everything she had and then began to rebuild her wealth for my sister.

MAMMA'S GENEROSITY

Despite raising a growing family on a tight budget and saving whatever was left, my mom was incredibly generous. Whenever we went to a new masjid, she would place a few dollar bills in the donation box. She wanted to support every mosque she ever prayed in. Every year, around Ramadan, she would pool money and send it back home to cousins and distant relatives in Hyderabad. And when I started to earn money, she would remind me to set aside an amount for giving. Her guiding value was that we were blessed and we should share our blessings with others. She taught me not to worry that giving would leave us with less. She was my first example of abandoning a scarcity mindset and confidently seeking an abundance mindset through faith in Allah ﷻ.

It wasn't just money that Mamma gave. She made a point to help others in any way possible with the resources she had available. She would pack the clothes we had outgrown and pass them on to my cousins here in the States. I remember her packing up a *janimaz* (prayer rug), a few pots and pans, some dishes, and other household things and giving them to her friend's family when they immigrated to the US. When someone was sick, she made food and sent it over. I remember when my dad and brother would go to the local masjid to pray Maghrib[18] during Ramadan, she would send her famous fruit *chaat* (salad) to share. She sent a dish of food each night so that not only my father and brother, but anyone at the masjid would be able to break their fast together. My lessons around charitable giving began with watching my mom.

After they retired, my parents became Desi snowbirds, traveling back to India and spending winters there. While they were visiting India one Ramadan, my siblings and I sent a portion of our zakat to my mom. (Zakat is the obligatory charitable giving required of Muslims. I'll discuss this more in Chapter 19.) Mamma created food baskets using our donation money and distributed them to the local needy. She enjoyed this act of giving immensely; the active physical labor that went into selecting goods, arranging and delivering the food baskets, and the joy and relief she saw on people's faces were a profound experience for her.

Mamma's generosity has always humbled me. The more she had, the more she gave. As our household income grew, she recognized the blessings she was receiving and continued to share them. She showed me the strong connection between financial stability and charitable giving. She taught me that the goal of economic empowerment and financial freedom isn't just to have lots of money and be rich. The goal of having more is so that we can give more to make the world a better place, whether it's to eliminate poverty,

---

18 The Maghrib prayer is the fourth of the five daily obligatory prayers performed by Muslims. It occurs just after sunset.

provide food security, help a family stay in their home, support survivors of domestic violence or sexual assault, or challenge gendered, anti-Muslim hate. Money helps us do all these things.

All main characters have an origin story, and this was mine. It began with my childhood memories of Mamma's wisdom and faith. Her influence during our humble beginnings shaped my views on the importance of financial stability and generosity. She lived a life full of abundance and never succumbed to a scarcity mindset, and her example taught me to trust in Allah's provision while also working diligently and giving generously. I will forever be grateful to her—my real super-shero—who guided me on this path. May Allah ﷻ always preserve our mothers. *Ameen.*

Reflection Exercise

1. What is a memory that you recall from your childhood that has shaped your understanding of money?

2. Describe a time as a child when you felt abundance, as if you had everything. What did it feel like, smell like, taste like, sound like, and look like?

3. Is there someone in your childhood who shaped your relationship with money? Who was that and how did they influence you?

Chapter 2

We Don't Talk About Money

Like many immigrant children, I began my relationship with money with my parent's perspective—a focus on having enough and securing financial stability. Unfortunately, I can't remember having actual conversations about money. We never discussed money in my family. In this chapter, I explore the complex relationship families have with money and why. I invite you to do the same if you and your family struggle to acknowledge finances.

BABBA

My grandfather died when my father was very young, thrusting their family into a spiral of poverty and scarcity. To this day, I only know vague bits and pieces of my father's family life and experiences. Like many men of his generation, he doesn't share much about his past. It's as if he struggles to find the right words to express himself without stirring up the repressed trauma of his childhood. This reticence might be cultural, or it could stem from his belief that since the hardship happened in the past and he eventually overcame it, there's no need to dwell on it. Despite the lack of details, I can only imagine how difficult and stressful life must have been for him and his family.

My paternal grandmother was not formally educated and was unable to earn a living. During the 1950s in India, when a husband passed away, the expectation fell on immediate male relatives—father, brothers, brothers-in-law, and sons—to take on the financial responsibility of caring for the widow and remaining children. Unfortunately, this was not an option for my grandmother and her five children. My grandfather had no brothers, and his father had passed away more than a decade before he did. My father and his older brother took on the responsibility, lying about their ages so they could support the family. My uncle increased his age by a few years so he could join the Indian military and collect a salary to send back home, and a distant uncle helped my dad get a job at Nizam College in Hyderabad. My dad took college courses in the evening and worked in an administrative position at the college during the daytime. He made just enough to cover tuition and provide for his family. He graduated with a bachelor's in commerce. He and his siblings had heard about the "land of opportunity" in the US and set their sights on immigration.

By then, the United States had passed the Immigration and Nationality Act of 1965. This public policy abolished that era's race-based immigration quota system and replaced it with a system that prioritized refugees, people with special skills, and those with family members living in the United States. In the sixties and seventies, India began what we called the "brain drain," where everyone in India with a college degree wanted to move to the United States for a better life. The American dream felt like a real possibility for escaping the cycle of poverty. In 1975, when it was time for my father to get married, he was adamant about finding a spouse who was heading to the United States.

In my mother's family, the same sentiment was building. My mom's engineer brothers were migrating to the US in the 1970s and taking their advanced degrees with them. My mother received her visa to immigrate to the States after one of her brothers sponsored her. She practically had one foot on the plane in 1975 when my very traditional and conservative grandfather objected to sending his unwed daughter to a foreign land without a husband to protect her. And so, in a time and place where arranged marriages were the norm, a matchmaker by the name of Azam Nawab brought a proposal to my maternal grandfather, Nana Ba. Nana Ba accepted, and my parents were married on December 15, 1975.

My mother immigrated to the United States in the summer of 1976 (without her husband after all, at first). I was born in October of 1976, and it took an entire year for the immigration paperwork to go through for my father for him to receive his visa. He joined us in the fall of 1977.

My dad struggled with managing money and understanding how money worked in the new system. He never budgeted or planned for expenses. When I got married, Babba withdrew money from his 401(k). My wedding needed to be paid for, and with no savings account to withdraw from, he tapped into his 401(k). Thus, it turned into my wedding budget. And that was fine by Babba, as he had never really considered the 401(k) a retirement plan to begin with.

My father's true retirement plan, like that of many in his generation and those before them, consisted of relying on his children to support him in his old age. This approach reflects a long-standing tradition in much of the Muslim world: For centuries, children have relied on their parents during their youth, with the understanding that they would reciprocate this care when they became adults and their parents entered old age. This cycle of intergenerational support has been a cornerstone of our cultural and familial values. While this system has its merits in fostering strong family bonds and ensuring eldercare, I've often wondered about its sustainability in our rapidly changing world. The financial burden on adult children can be significant, potentially impacting their own ability to save and plan for the future. Moreover, this traditional approach doesn't account for those who don't have children, or for families with only daughters in cultures where sons are expected to be the parents' primary maintainers. As we age, it becomes increasingly clear that a more comprehensive approach to retirement planning is necessary—one that combines familial support with personal savings, investments, and consideration of professional eldercare options.

As my parents entered retirement, they found themselves relying primarily on Social Security checks, Medicare, and the support of their children. Without substantial retirement savings or 401(k) funds, their monthly Social Security benefits often fall short of covering their living expenses. My siblings and I are blessed to be in a position where we can provide additional financial support, and we each contribute in our own ways, helping with various living expenses, utilities, and occasional larger purchases or unexpected costs. While we're grateful for the opportunity to care for our parents, their situation underscores the importance of early retirement planning. It's a reminder of how crucial it is to prepare for the future, not just for oneself, but to ease the potential burden on loved ones. Our family's experience has taught us valuable lessons about financial foresight and the complexities of eldercare in today's economic landscape.

DIFFERENTIATING BETWEEN A RETIREMENT PLAN AND A CHILD'S OBLIGATION

Many of us are familiar with the hadith of the Prophet ﷺ that advises us to both trust Allah ﷻ and be responsible. In a hadith narrated by Anas ibn Mālik, there was a Bedouin man who was leaving his camel outside without tying it to a secure post. The Prophet ﷺ asked, "Why don't you tie down your camel?" The man answered, "I put my trust in Allah." The Prophet ﷺ replied, "Tie your camel and put your trust in Allah."[19] I have complete trust in Allah's plan for my later years, and I know that Allah ﷻ will

---

19 *Sunan al-Tirmidhī*, no. 2517.

provide for me in my retirement. However, financial planning is a way to put faith into action. We are tying our financial camels while maintaining complete trust in Allah's provision.

In Islam, it is indeed the child's responsibility and duty to care for their parents. This expectation should be seen as an honor and a blessing. But not every person has children to fulfill that caretaker role, and not everyone has living parents to care for when they come of age. In light of that, creating a retirement plan and managing one's finances is a way for parents to care for their children and for children to care for their parents (and their own future children). We're both "tying our camels."

Watching my elderly parents struggle to make ends meet every single month is difficult. It is an unspoken consequence of the financial illiteracy that many first-generation immigrants experience. I knew I never wanted to be in that predicament. That is why it was so important to me to pursue my educational goals and find a career that had the potential to earn a livable wage. A wage that would enable me to save money and invest. I want to live a joyful life right now and have a plan for the future when I retire. I want to be financially independent and avoid becoming a burden to my children. I know you're thinking, "But Nausheena, in Islam, isn't it a blessing that your children take care of you? Your children are required to take care of you!" To which I reply, "Yes, of course. But I'm tying my camel."

MONEY TALK

My younger sister is a brilliant CPA and earns three times as much as I do. When we discuss money, she says, "I spend a lot because I want to enjoy my life right now." She loves to travel and plans to retire early. At first I laughed at her, but then I wondered about her budgeting process, savings, and retirement plans. When I asked, she was happy to share. She's the one who taught me about different credit cards and mobile banking. Now, every time we see each other, we share a little bit more about what we are doing in relation to our investments and retirement planning. And of course, traveling to our next big adventure. Having healthy financial conversations is an important part of your journey to financial empowerment.

When my siblings and I were growing up, our parents didn't discuss money, expenses, or the future of our finances with us. When it was time to open a savings account or checking account at the bank, I don't remember my parents helping me or guiding me through the process. No one explained the concept of balancing a checkbook or saving money. No one explained the purpose of having a credit card, how to pay off the balance, or what interest rates were. My parents never spoke of investing in real estate, the stock market, or any other investment strategy.

The result was that we siblings developed a complicated relationship with money. Since we did not discuss money management, we had no concept or comprehension of investing at all. I don't think my mom or dad understood stocks or investment accounts. If you couldn't learn from your parents, then you would think public school would provide financial management classes and teach you how to save for the future. But you would be wrong. I don't recall learning any of that in my public school, nor do I remember my children learning financial management at their private Islamic school.

Well, then there's college. The only time I recall talking about money at university was when we discussed how we would pay for college, which turned out to be taking out student loans. Only people who majored in business, accounting, or finance had any chance of acquiring a financial education, leaving the rest of us with no option but to learn about money management on our own.

Unfortunately, to this day, my other siblings and I are uncomfortable discussing money together. We don't talk about future finances; we don't even talk about finances in the present, unless it has to do with how we can help Mamma and Babba. This is not something I want for my children—especially not for my daughter. I want to empower her to understand money and have a positive relationship with it. I want her to use money as a tool to do good, and I want her to be able to ask questions about finances and investments. I want her to come to me with questions and for advice, and I want to be able to provide her with solid answers!

I have open conversations about money with my kids. A detailed conversation around salary negotiations was helpful to my daughter, Arshia, as she moved from internships to starting her career. We spoke about salary ranges, how to be transparent in the salary conversation, and how to negotiate. After they graduated from high school, my husband sat both kids down and explained the importance of setting up a retirement savings account, planting the seeds for their early retirement. My daughter is now researching credit cards. I'm talking to her about building her credit, while she explores which credit card will offer her the most benefits, accumulate the most miles, and feed best into her travel budget. After my mother-in-law passed away in 2022 (may Allah ﷻ bless her soul), we discussed the importance of family inheritance and making a will, specifically from an Islamic perspective (more details in Chapter 14: Wills—Do You Have One?).

Talking to kids about money, savings, budgeting, and investing in retirement plans requires a thoughtful and age-appropriate approach. Here are some tips for how to effectively engage kids in these important financial topics:

1. **Start early.** Introduce basic financial concepts from a young age. Use everyday situations to teach simple ideas like counting money, understanding the difference between needs and wants, and making spending choices.

2. **Use real-life examples.** Incorporate real-life scenarios to explain financial concepts. For example, when shopping, discuss how budgeting helps you make informed choices and prioritize needs over wants. I always compared the prices of different brands of things we were buying. I pointed out to my children things that were on sale or were a better deal. I also made sure they understood the amount we could spend.

3. **Keep it simple.** Tailor your explanations to their age and comprehension level. Use clear and straightforward language, avoiding jargon or complex terms. How you talk to your five-year-old will be different than how you talk to your fifteen-year-old.

4. **Make it practical.** Give kids an allowance or help them earn money through chores. This provides a hands-on opportunity to learn about earning, saving, and spending. When I was in middle school, my dad would pay me a weekly allowance to tutor my brother in math. It taught me discipline and showed me how hard a "job" is, because my brother was such a brat to tutor!

5. **Teach savings.** Help kids set savings goals, whether it's for a toy, a game, or other items. Give your child a savings goal for something they want and create a piggy bank or a savings jar to visually represent their progress. It will allow them to physically see their money grow.

6. **Show them the budget.** Introduce the concept of budgeting by showing them how you plan your household finances. Explain the importance of allocating money for different categories like groceries, bills, and savings. You can start out by sharing what expenses your family has, but be ready to talk about what it takes to cover those expenses.

Prepare yourself to have a meaningful conversation about your salary.

7. **Introduce investing.** As they get older, explain the concept of investing and how it can grow their money over time. Use relatable examples like planting seeds that grow into trees or allowing money to "work" for them. We waited until high school to introduce our kids to stocks.

8. **Use visual aids.** Be a nerd. Charts, graphs, PowerPoint presentations, and Excel spreadsheets can all help make abstract financial concepts more tangible and engaging for kids.

9. **Share stories.** Tell stories or anecdotes of how your grandparents or elders saved, invested, or planned for their future—or how they weren't able to. This makes the concepts more relatable and memorable. It also helps your kids connect with you and helps them understand your own journey in financial acumen and freedom.

10. **Involve them in decisions.** When making financial decisions as a family, involve your kids in age-appropriate ways. This could include comparing prices, discussing options, or choosing family activities that fit within the budget. When my kids were in high school and college, I involved them in planning our vacations, which included researching flights, hotels, and excursions. They learned how to look for deals, cheaper days to fly, and other ways to stretch the budget to have a great vacation.

11. **Discuss retirement.** As they grow into young adults, introduce your kids to the concept of retirement planning. Explain that adults save money over time to ensure they have enough for when they're no longer working. We

began this conversation with our daughter when she started her first job after graduation and it offered a 401(k) benefit.

12. **Encourage questions.** Create an open environment where your kids feel comfortable asking questions about money. Address their curiosity and provide clear, honest answers. I feel this is the most important piece of advice I can give to parents. Your conversation should not be a speech or one-way communication. The more curious they are, the more questions they ask, the better their chances of understanding financial concepts and becoming financially empowered.

13. **Be a role model.** Model the behavior that you want your kids to follow. Your financial habits and attitudes influence your kids. So show them how to responsibly manage money. Show them how you save, budget, and make informed financial decisions. You are your children's first role models.

14. **Gradually introduce new concepts.** As your child matures, gradually introduce more complex financial concepts. For instance, you could begin with the benefits of a savings account, talk when they're a bit older about how to check their credit score, and address retirement accounts when they get their first job.

Remember, the goal is to empower kids with the knowledge and skills they need to make informed financial decisions as they grow. And different children respond differently. One kid might love this and another might abhor it! It's OK. Approach these conversations with patience, understanding, and a willingness to adapt your approach to your child's individual needs and learning style. Make it a fun experience. But please make sure to have this conversation early and often.

Because I didn't have conversations with my parents about money, I struggled with financial literacy and acumen. I made mistakes—costly ones. It took me time to learn about different financial instruments and tools. If you haven't had these conversations, then take the time to have them now. Start planning your future. Just as we teach our children life skills from a young age, it's important we teach them the value of money, saving, investing, and giving. There's so much we continue to learn as parents and so much to teach our kids. This is just the beginning.

TALKS ABOUT CHARITY

Along with saving money, we have conversations about charitable giving. I'm teaching my kids about zakat and *ṣadaqa*.[20] I'm tying it to causes that matter to them. This is a good conversation to have with your children. Ask them what bad things they see happening in the world or in the community. Ask them what changes they would like to see and how they can donate their time or their money to make the world a better place.

One of the most beautiful things I've learned about generosity in Islam is that when life is hard or you've hit a rough patch, give. When you are having a great day and life is just beautiful, give! This is something I'm instilling in my kids as well. I've watched my daughter give *ṣadaqa* when she's facing a challenge. Helping someone else while you're also struggling gives you hope in overcoming your challenge. And when life is going splendidly, I've seen Arshia pay it forward like an act of gratitude. She is a budding young philanthropist, and I want to show her examples of more Muslim women philanthropists changing the world.

---

20   *Ṣadaqa,* in Arabic, is defined as "voluntary charitable giving."

Reflection

1. From your childhood, do you recall conversations about money? What did you hear your parents discuss? Did they share anything about the household finances with you?

2. What is one thing you wish you could have learned about money while you were growing up?

3. Who is someone in your family or friend circle that you would like to have a money conversation with, and what would you share or ask?

Chapter 3

Values, Goals, and Dreaming Big

Where do you spend money? Do you buy a daily coffee? Do you buy gold and store it in the bottom drawer of your dresser? Do you buy expensive groceries? Do you upgrade your plane tickets? How do we make these decisions about when to spend, when to save, and when to give?

The Latte Factor revolves around the idea that small, everyday expenses, such as buying a daily latte, can add up over time and prevent people from achieving their financial goals.

The main character in the book is a young woman named Zoey Daniels, who is struggling to make ends meet despite having a good job in the publishing industry. With the help of a wise old man named Henry, Zoey learns about the concept of the latte factor and how small changes in her spending habits can lead to big changes in her financial situation. The book stresses three key concepts for economic empowerment.

First, small, everyday expenses can have a big impact on your overall financial situation. By paying close attention to your spending and cutting back on unnecessary expenses, you can save money and work toward your financial goals. I don't believe the authors are telling you to literally stop buying lattes, but to find and cut the places where you may be spending mindlessly.

Second, the book emphasizes the power of long-term investing. By investing your money wisely and letting it grow over time, you can build wealth and achieve financial security. I wish I had read a book like this when I was twenty-two years old and just starting my career! But that's OK—it's never too late to start.

Finally, the book stresses the importance of long-term financial planning and creating goals for your future. It helped me think about my retirement and how I want to spend it. Create a plan. Stick to it. You will make progress toward your financial goals and achieve the financial freedom you desire.

Overall, *The Latte Factor* offers a simple but powerful message about the importance of paying attention to your spending habits and taking small steps toward your financial goals. The book is a very fast read at only 121 pages. I read it twice, once in 2021 and then again in 2022. What I liked about this book was the storytelling approach and how Bach and Mann drew the reader into the financial lives of the characters. Zoey works long hours, barely makes enough, and has never traveled outside the US. She cannot afford it. She meets Henry, a barista at the coffee shop (spoiler alert: he's the owner of the coffee shop, living his best life because he's financially stable) where she purchases her daily morning latte. (I prefer mochas, but I digress...) They enter into a conversation that changes her frame of mind around money and gives her ideas for how to gain financial independence.[21]

One day, on Zoey's way to work, she sees a message on a giant LED screen, "If you don't know where you're going, you might not like where you end up."

This quote prompted me, just like it prompted Zoey, to reflect on where I wanted to see myself in the near future and also in the long term. I gave myself permission to dream big. And as I thought about these things, foremost in my mind was how does my Islamic faith influence my financial journey?

---

21 David Bach and John David Mann, *The Latte Factor: Why You Don't Have to Be Rich to Live Rich* (Atria Books, 2019).

I also read Bach and Mann's other book *Smart Women Finish Rich*—a 1999 *New York Times* bestseller. *Smart Women Finish Rich* is a personal finance book geared toward women that focuses on empowering them to take control of their financial futures. I polished it off in two days.

These were the major themes and takeaways of the book for me:

1. **The importance of taking responsibility for your financial future.** Bach and Mann emphasize the idea that financial security and independence is something that almost every woman can achieve, regardless of her current financial situation. I understood that by taking responsibility for my financial future, I could achieve my goals and live the life I want. We are all responsible for our future!

2. **The need for a long-term financial plan.** Like *The Latte Factor*, *Smart Women Finish Rich* stresses the importance of having a long-term financial plan and setting goals for your future. I created my own plan using their tools and am finding them useful. Writing out my plan, setting goals, and journaling were all tools that helped me visualize a future with financial freedom.

3. **The power of investing.** The book also emphasizes the power of investing and encourages women to begin to invest as soon as possible. By investing in the stock market and other assets, I am building my wealth and achieving financial security. It takes time, but I've enjoyed watching that growth over the years.

4. **The importance of negotiating and advocating for yourself.** Bach and Mann encourage women to negotiate

for better pay and benefits and to advocate for themselves in all areas of their lives. By standing up for ourselves and demanding what we deserve, we can increase our incomes and improve our financial situations.

I've provided you with summaries of these books because I am using many of their themes as guideposts throughout this book. I felt motivated and empowered by *Smart Women Finish Rich*. It encouraged me to take control of my financial future and work on my financial goals. It offered practical advice and actionable steps for me to take, with lots of storytelling. And it wasn't complex; there was so much power in taking a few small steps and achieving big results. The *Latte Factor* and *Smart Women Finish Rich* were the beginning of my financial assessment journey. Unfortunately, when I was looking for a personal finance book that incorporated an Islamic lens for Muslim women, I couldn't find one. As much as I enjoyed Bach and Mann's books, they contained advice (about things like interest) that was in direct conflict with Islam. So I wrote the book I needed when I started out.

VALUES

One thing I loved about *Smart Women Finish Rich* was the section on values. Values are the guiding principles that influence or inform the way we behave. We can care about a lot of issues, but intrinsic values define the type of person we aspire to be, and that cannot be taken away from us. For example, some common values are honesty, generosity, trustworthiness, empathy, and compassion. When I list these out, I am reminded of the characteristics of our beloved Prophet Muhammad ﷺ,[22] who was known as al-Ṣādiq, the truthful one, al-Amīn, the trustworthy one. As Muslims, we strive to be like the Prophet ﷺ by following his sunna (his way of life) and

---

22 ﷺ is a symbol that stands for the Arabic phrase, "*Ṣallā Allāhu 'alayhi wa sallam.*" It translates to "Peace and blessings be upon him," and Muslims use this phrase to send salutations to Prophet Muhammad after mentioning his name.

attempting to embody his *shamā'il*[23] (virtues and mannerisms) in every endeavor. This holistic approach to following the Prophet's example ensures that our values guide us not only in our spiritual lives but also in our financial decisions and practices.

These values guide and influence our interactions with money. Our faith constantly reminds us to pursue a halal livelihood. But what does it mean to earn a halal livelihood? It means seeking and engaging in employment or business activities that are permissible according to Islamic principles and that are pleasing to Allah. We are also encouraged to ensure our source of income is not polluted by haram sources. These sources can include prohibited industries such as gambling, alcohol, pork production, interest-based financial institutions, or any other business that promotes or involves activities that are considered sinful or harmful.

Honesty, fairness, and a strong moral compass should always guide our business dealings. As Muslims, we believe we are accountable to Allah ﷻ for our actions and conduct, including our earnings, financial management, and investing. Acting with honesty and fairness is a means of earning the pleasure of Allah ﷻ and fulfilling the ethical responsibilities placed upon us as believers. We view wealth and resources as blessings from Allah ﷻ and are expected to be good stewards of these resources. Acting with honesty and fairness in business is a way of fulfilling this responsibility, ensuring that wealth is acquired and utilized in a manner that aligns with our ethical principles and is utilized to benefit society. Islamophobes wrongfully perpetuate the trope that Islam was spread by the sword,[24] but the truth is that it was our honesty and mannerisms

---

23 *Shamā'il* is an Arabic word that means "characteristics" or "features" of a person that define who they are. It can also mean a description of a person's beauty.

24 Hassam Munir, "Did Islam Spread by the Sword? A Critical Look at Forced Conversions," Yaqeen Institute for Islamic Research, May 12, 2018, https://yaqeeninstitute.org/read/paper/did-islam-spread-by-the-sword-a-critical-look-at-forced-conversions.

in the souk[25] that attracted and invited people to our *deen*, Islam.

I want to dive a little deeper into Islamic values when it comes to money and finances. Our *deen* teaches us the value of generosity and giving to those who are poor and in need. If we define *'aqīda*[26] as the underlying beliefs that determine how we behave, then money and charitable giving is certainly an *'aqīda* issue.

Imam Al-Ghazali, one of the most prominent and influential scholars in Islamic history, defines the purpose of sharia as connected to five principles—the *maqāṣid al-sharī'a*.[27] Imam Al-Ghazali says:

> And the purposes of sharia are five, which are to protect religion, life, intellect, lineage, and property.[28]

What does it mean to protect and preserve your wealth? As a Muslim, it means that how we earn, spend, grow, manage, and give money must all comply with Islamic guidelines.

STARTING WITH ESSENTIAL VALUES

Make it halal. As you build your wealth, be vigilant in making sure it is from lawful and halal sources. Work in places and companies that are not producing haram things. If you are a small business owner or a solo entrepreneur, provide goods and services that are halal.

Focus on generosity. Remember that the goal is not to accumulate wealth for only yourself; giving is an essential part of accumulating wealth. Avoid being greedy or wasteful; protect and grow your

---

25 Souk is an Arabic word that means "marketplace."
26 *'Aqīda*, in Arabic, is defined as "creed" or "belief."
27 *Maqāṣid al-sharī'a*, in Arabic, is defined as "objectives of Islamic law."
28 Abu Amina Elias, "Sharia, Fiqh, and Islamic Law Explained," September 7, 2021, https://www.abuaminaelias.com/shariah-fiqh-qanun/.

wealth through proper financial planning using halal investing tools and faith-compliant channels. Allah ﷻ says in the Quran:

$$وَٱلَّذِينَ إِذَآ أَنفَقُوا لَمْ يُسْرِفُوا وَلَمْ يَقْتُرُوا وَكَانَ بَيْنَ ذَٰلِكَ قَوَامًا ۝$$

They [are] those who spend neither wastefully nor stingily, but moderately in between.

Quran 25:67

Consider Islamic values. Performing virtuous deeds is tied to our *imān*.[29] One of the names of Allah ﷻ is al-Karīm, the Giver. And Prophet Muhammad ﷺ was known as "the most generous." These two qualities—giving and generosity—should be part of our personal values and belief system. We should be generous givers, and inshallah our *rizq* in this life will increase.

Fulfill duties. As in all matters, Islam asks us to follow the middle way with our wealth. We are taught to both give of our wealth to others and save some of it for our families. So purify your wealth by calculating and paying your zakat. Give *ṣadaqa* by sharing your wealth with those in need. But also reserve some for your children to inherit.

Stay focused on the end. Accountability is a crucial Islamic value that one must consider when it comes to our wealth. In the next stage of our life, on the Day of Judgment, Muslims will be asked about their wealth. Ibn Masʿūd ﷺ narrated that the Messenger of Allah ﷺ said:

> The feet of the child of Adam shall not move from before their Lord on the Day of Judgment until they are asked about five things: their life and what they

---

29   *Imān*, in Arabic, means "faith."

did with it, their youth and what they wore it out in, their wealth and how they earned it, their wealth and how they spent it, and their knowledge and how they acted upon it.[30]

INTENTIONS, CLARIFYING PERSONAL VALUES, AND CREATING GOALS

Set your intention, make note of the most important values you want to fulfill, and formulate your financial goals. Then consider the necessary steps to reach those goals and decide how you will track your progress. Setting my intentions in financial planning was a key component to achieving financial stability and creating a secure and stable financial future.

Here's how I set my intentions.

What is my *niyya*? First and foremost, my intentions for pursuing financial stability are to do so for the sake of Allah, to please Him. When I know that I'm doing this with Him in my heart and mind inshallah, I am confident that He will guide me through the entire process. I am a true believer that one of the best ways to serve Allah ﷻ is to be of service to others. I aim to forge my path to financial independence and philanthropy through serving my community and serving Allah. Once I set this intention, I wrote it down so I could read it again and again, to remind myself why I was taking control of my financial situation. It helped keep me grounded and focused as I created my goals.

Clarifying your personal values is a crucial step in financial planning. Your values are the principles and beliefs that guide your decisions and actions. When it comes to finances, understanding your values helps ensure that your financial choices align with what truly matters to you.

---

30   *Sunan al-Tirmidhi*, no. 2416.

Values, Goals, and Dreaming Big

To clarify your values, consider what's most important to you in life. Is it family security, personal growth, community service, or environmental stewardship? Perhaps it's a combination of these and other principles. Once you've identified your core values, you can use them as a compass for your financial decisions.

For example, if one of your key values is environmental sustainability, you might prioritize investing in eco-friendly companies or allocating funds for energy-efficient home improvements. If family security is a top value, you might focus on building a robust emergency fund or increasing your (well-researched, halal) life insurance coverage.[31]

In my own journey, I realized that serving Allah ﷻ and my community were core values that deeply influenced my financial goals. This led me to prioritize halal investments and plan for charitable giving through my stock portfolio. By aligning my financial choices with these values, I found greater purpose and satisfaction in my financial planning process.

By setting goals, you create a sense of urgency and feel driven to take action toward achieving them. This can help you overcome any procrastination or lack of momentum that may be holding you back from making progress. Goals also help you track progress. When you have a goal, you have a framework for measuring your success. This can help you stay motivated and make any necessary adjustments to your financial plan along the way. It also provides a sense of accomplishment, which can help boost your confidence and improve your overall well-being.

In 2021, I set a goal of diversifying my stock portfolio with the intention of growing it. I knew that I wanted to use my stocks as the source of my giving. I wanted the ability to donate appreciated

---

31 Joe Bradford, "Video: Is Life Insurance Halal?," Joe Bradford, April 10, 2019, https://joebradford.net/video-is-life-insurance-halal/.

stocks to nonprofits I believed in. My guiding values focused on ensuring my current stock holdings were halal and investing in other halal or sharia-compliant companies (I'll share my steps in Chapter 12: Halal Investing 101).

The investment account I have provides me with a report—a pretty pie chart—that shows the breakdown of the types of stocks I have invested in. At the start of 2021, that pie chart did not have many "slices." By the end of the year, I saw my efforts reflected in a more colorful chart. I'm not done, of course. I continue to track my progress every few months, making sure the portfolio includes different types of stocks.

In 2022, I set a new goal. I wanted to invest more money in my retirement account, and I did it! When I was setting my intention for this goal, I had to reflect a great deal to figure out why I wanted to do this. I thought about the cost of health care if I lived to be over seventy years old, the price of the drugs, doctors' bills, hospital bills, and surgeries that come with old age. I intended to have a safety net in case something happened to my husband. The values that informed my goal were about "tying my camel." The first step I took was to assess the current value of my retirement account. The second step was to explore options for contributing more to it. And finally, I took one of those options and made it actionable. By the end of 2022, I had contributed more to my retirement plan and had planned steps for future contributions. I track my progress by reviewing my retirement plan's annual statement. By setting financial goals and working toward them, I am able to increase my financial security and stability over time.

MY PERSONAL ROADMAP

I use the SMART goals technique to help me write goals that are clear, attainable, and meaningful. This technique gives me clarity in my goal setting, which provides me with the motivation and focus

I need to be successful. SMART goals are specific, measurable, achievable, relevant, and time-bound. As much as I love the SMART goals framework, it's missing the financial element. We're talking here about goals that have a financial implication, so I'm going to add a letter to the SMART framework: C for cost-conscious. SMART-C (pronounced "smartsy").

The cost-conscious addition emphasizes the crucial financial dimension of goal setting. This extra element encourages individuals to thoroughly consider the monetary aspects of their objectives. When setting SMART-C goals, you are prompted to evaluate three key financial factors.

First, you must identify and estimate the costs directly associated with achieving your goal; second, you need to assess whether these costs align with your current budget and financial situation; and third, if the costs exceed your present means, you must develop a concrete plan for financing your goal. This approach ensures that goals are not just well-defined and achievable but also financially viable, thereby increasing the likelihood of successful implementation and reducing potential financial stress.

Career

I started Reviving the Islamic Sisterhood for Empowerment (RISE) in September 2015. I was disturbed by the number of hate crimes that were being perpetrated against Muslim women. It seemed that every time a Muslim woman was mentioned, it was in the context of being oppressed or a victim of hate. *She was targeted because of her hijab...Her civil rights were being violated in the workplace or at school...*So I gathered a group of Muslim women to talk about these issues.

We had honest conversations about our lack of leadership opportunities in both the nonprofit and business sectors. We talked about civic engagement and what it meant to participate in our democracy, as the 2016 presidential elections were coming up. One recurring theme I heard from my Muslim sisters was that while they were all contributing to their communities in one way or another, they didn't feel connected to other Muslim women and what they were doing. I realized we needed to build something. We couldn't wait for someone else to do it. We were who we were waiting for.

I left my job at another nonprofit at the end of that year and officially incorporated RISE in January 2016. RISE's mission is to amplify the voice and power of Muslim women through narrative change, cultivating leadership, civic engagement, and advocacy. RISE imagines a better world where Muslim women are connected, reflected, celebrated, and emboldened to make change in their communities.

Many of us aspire to be promoted and reach a higher position in our companies. For me, I wanted to start a nonprofit organization. I wanted to create a place for Muslim women to achieve work-life balance and well-being. *I* wanted a healthy work-life balance and to prioritize my personal well-being! I was able to do that at RISE.

Founding RISE allowed me to fulfill another personal goal as well—that of doing meaningful work that had a social impact. I wanted a career that made a positive difference in society and that aligned with my personal values and passions. I wanted to make the world a better place—especially for Muslim women.

After five years of laying the groundwork, building a network, and developing and leading RISE, however, I understood that good leadership meant passing the baton at the right time. I was ready to exit.

Our personal career goals can evolve over time as circumstances change and new opportunities arise. It's been helpful for me to

Values, Goals, and Dreaming Big

reflect on my personal career goals as my interests change and the world changes. Like when the pandemic hit us in 2020.

As I reflected on my career goals in 2021, I realized how much I had grown in my career as an entrepreneur, a nonprofit leader, and a supervisor. It was time for me to move on, and I imagined myself pushing deeper into the philanthropic world. I wanted to "decolonize wealth," as Edgar Villanueva described in his book *Decolonizing Wealth: Indigenous Wisdom to Heal Divides and Restore Balance*.[32] I wanted to help Muslims build a philanthropic legacy and move money into our communities. From the nonprofit sector, philanthropy was calling me to make my next career move.

I wanted Muslim-led nonprofits to benefit from my skills and expertise. I wanted to be able to pay that forward and share those learnings, best practices, and tips to help strengthen the infrastructure of the nonprofit sector, specifically within the Muslim community.

In the fall of 2021, I re-evaluated my personal career goals and decided RISE was ready for a new executive director to take the organization to new levels with fresh and innovative ideas. I approached the board with my resignation letter as well as a timeline for the executive search. I slowly began conversations with my staff. We hired a search firm, who advised us to first communicate with our most important stakeholders: donors and funders. In the first week of January, we made the public announcement that I was stepping down. Six months later, we hired my successor. On August 31, 2022, I said goodbye. And then I said hello to developing my next set of career goals.

---

32   Edgar Villanueva, *Decolonizing Wealth: Indigenous Wisdom to Heal Divides and Restore Balance* (Berrett-Koehler Publishers, 2018).

> ### SMART-C Goal for Career
>
> **Specific:** By August 31, 2022, hire a new executive director and complete onboarding.
>
> **Measurable:** Create a list of ten potential candidates to tap and invite into the interview process.
>
> **Achievable:** Work with board and executive search firm on recruitment and interview process.
>
> **Relevant:** Hire the right candidate as selected by staff and board.
>
> **Time-Bound:** Complete transition of executive director by August.
>
> **Cost-Conscious:** Allocate $5,000 for the executive search process. Allocate additional $8,000 for 2.5 months of overlap between two EDs. Ensure this fits within the current annual budget by reallocating funds from the temporarily vacant executive director salary.

But first, I took a radical sabbatical. During the last month of my transition, I planned out what I would do for the next four months. I traveled, spent time with my mom, and took care of my sister after my niece was born. I wrote. I upped my *tahajjud*[33] game. I read so many fun books. I binged on way too many Netflix series. I cooked healthy meals. I worked out. I was drinking seventy-two ounces of water a day by the end of the sabbatical. It was such a wonderful time that I debated taking early retirement and living happily ever after as a homemaker.

---

[33] *Tahajjud,* also known as the "night prayer," is a voluntary prayer performed in the last third of the night. It is not an obligatory prayer.

Now you're probably thinking, "How does taking a sabbatical help in achieving your career goals?" For starters, it provided me space for a renewed perspective. The sabbatical gave me the opportunity to step away from one job before I took on another. This time helped me think, clear my brain, and gain a fresh perspective on my career and life. It allowed me to reflect on my previous career goals and accomplishments, reassess my next set of priorities, and explore new directions in philanthropy. This renewed perspective helped me clarify my career objectives and informed my decisions moving forward.

Taking a sabbatical contributed to my overall work-life balance and well-being, which is crucial for long-term career success. I was able to rest, recharge, and address personal needs and priorities that were being neglected due to work commitments. By taking time off to focus on my self-care and personal fulfillment, I was able to return to my career path with renewed energy and motivation.

SMART-C Goal for Sabbatical

Specific: Enhance my personal growth and well-being by focusing on self-discovery, skill development, and meaningful experiences.

Measurable: Engage in at least three structured activities each month that contribute to my personal growth, such as networking, building relationships, reading and writing, participating in workshops, and pursuing hobbies.

Achievable: Allocate time and resources to prioritize self-care, learning, and experiences that align with my sabbatical goals.

Relevant: The sabbatical will provide me with the opportunity to recharge, explore my new interest in philanthropy, and invest in my overall well-being.

Time-Bound: Over the course of four months, from September 1, 2022, to December 31, 2022, I will consistently engage in activities that contribute to my personal growth and well-being.

Cost-Conscious: Budget $6,000 for the four-month sabbatical period, allocating funds for books, conference attendance fees, workshop registration fees, self-care, and any other unexpected opportunities.

My sabbatical provided the time and flexibility necessary for me to focus on learning opportunities within the world of foundations and build a new network of professionals in that field. Knowing that building a strong network can open doors to new career opportunities, collaborations, and mentorship relationships, I used my sabbatical to connect with Muslim women in philanthropy. I also read the latest literature on the future of philanthropy. This gave me the ability to figure out what I wanted to do next in my career. I was in a career transition and exploring a new sector. Taking time off to research my options facilitated a more informed transition. My next career goals included becoming a published author and recognized expert in the nonprofit field. I also wanted to start a consulting firm that would upskill Muslim women to strengthen their nonprofits. And I wanted to pursue a doctoral degree in philanthropic leadership.

Family

My husband and I celebrated twenty-five years of marriage in 2022. My children were graduating and moving out. Things were drastically changing in our household. My husband and I were becoming empty nesters (or, as I prefer, "free birds"). I wondered what it would be like for my husband and me to live as a couple again—just the two of us. We no longer had children to run around after. His parents were no longer living with us. His extended family, who had immigrated to Minnesota from India, were all independently living in their own homes. We really weren't sure how we would function with just each other.

Our goal as a couple was to rediscover ourselves outside our roles as parents. We thought about the activities and hobbies we had enjoyed before becoming parents and the new ones that piqued our interest that we wanted to explore. Our aim was to nurture and deepen our relationship. As free birds, it really did feel like we were dating again! Now that we are seasoned parents and professionals, we're a little bit wiser because of our lived experiences, and we are enjoying dinner conversations about philosophical ideas and our vision for the future, as well as many getting-to-know-you-better moments. We're taking leisurely walks on the river and exploring the world together. My husband is my travel buddy, and we are planning our next adventure! Many of our conversations are about our retirement and financial planning. We recognize that this free birding phase isn't just about not having kids at home; it's also about finances and money. We have to plan for both this current phase and the retirement phase that will follow, ensuring our financial stability for the years to come.

SMART-C Goal for Rediscovering Self and Nurturing Relationships

Specific: Over the next year, I am committed to rediscovering my individual passions and interests beyond the role of a parent while nurturing and deepening my relationship with my husband, embracing our newfound free bird status.

Measurable: Engage in at least two activities or hobbies each month that I enjoyed before becoming a parent, and explore one new activity quarterly that piques our mutual interest. Allocate dedicated time for quality conversations with my husband and schedule regular leisurely walks and outings.

Achievable: Prioritize self-care and time for personal exploration by setting aside specific hours for activities and scheduling date nights with my husband.

Relevant: As we transition into the free bird phase, focusing on self-discovery and nurturing our relationship is essential to maintaining a fulfilling and meaningful life together.

Time-Bound: By the end of the next year, I will have reconnected with past hobbies, explored new interests, and strengthened my relationship with my husband.

Cost-Conscious: Budget $3,600 for the year ($300 per month) to support this goal, allocating funds for date night activities and spontaneous opportunities to explore.

SMART-C Goal for Financial Planning

Specific: In the next two years, my husband and I will actively engage in comprehensive financial planning to ensure our retirement and long-term financial stability as free birds.

Measurable: Collaborate with a financial adviser to create a detailed retirement plan that encompasses investment strategies, savings goals, and post-retirement income projections. Review and adjust the plan annually to stay on track.

Achievable: Dedicate time to research, attend online financial workshops, and seek guidance from professionals to make informed decisions about our retirement.

Relevant: As we embark on this new phase of life, securing our financial future is crucial to living comfortably and pursuing our retirement dreams.

Time-Bound: By the end of the two-year period, we will have a well-established and regularly reviewed retirement plan in place, providing us with financial confidence for the years ahead.

Cost-Conscious: Budget $4,000 over the two-year period for financial planning activities, including hiring a financial adviser and fees for financial tool subscriptions.

Another family goal I have is spending more time with my parents, which has become increasingly important as I've entered the free bird phase of my life. This transition coincided with my aging parents' growing need for care, particularly after my mom's recent dementia diagnosis. Watching her progress through the stages of deterioration has been incredibly challenging, as has seeing my dad shift into a caretaker role. I've come to understand that caretaking isn't just a physical action; it requires emotional, mental, and intellectual strength as well. Recognizing the preciousness of this time, I've made it my mission to be there for them as much as possible in this last stage of their lives. To achieve this, I've implemented concrete strategies: Every month, I block out time on my calendar for a trip to Chicago. During these visits, I am Mamma's caretaker, taking her shopping, accompanying her to visit relatives, praying at the mosque, and cooking meals together—activities that allow us to connect and create memories. In the summer months, we plan for my parents to visit us in Minnesota, providing a change of scenery and extended family time. These intentional efforts to be with my parents during this time are profoundly important to me, allowing me to offer support, cherish our relationship, and make the most of our time together.

Born and raised in the Chicago suburbs, I grew up around twelve sets of aunts and uncles, and thirty cousins. Having an extended family guaranteed so many birthdays, anniversaries, religious celebrations, graduations, and weddings within the family that there was never a need to make new friends. I did have one friend from high school who lived in the same neighborhood. She became my college roommate, and we remain friends to this very day. But I miss Chicago and being around my family, immediate and extended, and being a part of milestones and celebrations. It's difficult to coordinate out-of-town visits with a full-time job and a family to take care of. Now, as a free bird, my goal is to visit more often and be a part of their lives again. How does this tie into my financial goals? Money pays for my travel to Chicago, the gas in my car, the tolls, and any other expenses. Being financially stable lets me be with Mamma and the rest of my family more often.

SMART-C Goal for Spending Time with Mom

Specific: In order to provide emotional and physical support to my mom during her journey with dementia, I am committed to spending quality time with her through regular visits and activities.

Measurable: Block out one weekend every month on my calendar for trips to Chicago, allocating at least three to four days for each visit. Engage in activities such as shopping, visiting relatives, attending the mosque, and cooking together.

Achievable: Plan travel logistics in advance, coordinate with family members for visits, and ensure my work and school commitments allow for the scheduled trips.

Relevant: Given my mom's diagnosis and my desire to be present during this phase of her life, spending time together is crucial for both of us.

Time-Bound: Maintain this monthly visitation schedule for the next two years, reassessing as needed based on my mom's condition.

Cost-conscious: Budget $12,000 annually ($1,000 per month) for these visits, including air travel, meals, transportation to the airport and home, and any other extra expenses.

Self

I enrolled in a master's degree program during the pandemic, recognizing that women often need higher education and degrees to compete and flourish in a patriarchal society. According to a 2018 report from the Georgetown Center on Education and the Workforce, "A woman with a master's degree earns $61,000 per year on average, roughly equivalent to that of a man with an associate's degree." Despite this persistent gap, attaining higher degrees has been making a difference. In fact, higher educational attainment has narrowed the gender wage gap by 7%. While this progress is encouraging, it also underscores the ongoing need for women to pursue advanced degrees to achieve pay parity with men.

Advanced degrees contribute to women's success and advancement in leadership positions. How? An advanced degree can help women counter the gender biases and stereotypes that exist in the workplace, as it provides an objective qualification that underscores their competence and expertise. This additional degree can set women apart from other candidates and demonstrate their commitment to continuous learning and professional development, while also breaking glass ceilings. My favorite reason to pursue an advanced degree is because it inspires little girls to dream big. By sharing my journey, I hope to inspire and encourage women and girls to see the limitless opportunities the future holds for them.

Doctoral degrees signify an even deeper level of expertise and specialization in a specific field, which gives a woman added credibility when discussing complex topics or making decisions related to her area of study. Having that expertise also means getting a higher-paying job. Many higher-paying positions, particularly those in management, leadership, and specialized fields, require or prefer candidates with advanced degrees. Having the necessary qualifications can make a woman eligible for these roles, potentially leading to increased earnings. Increased earnings help you on your financial empowerment journey.

I had spent the last ten years in the nonprofit sector and wanted to pursue a career in philanthropy, specifically in growing Muslim philanthropy. After speaking to a colleague in the field, I decided a doctoral program was the way to go. I love school. I am a learner and I wanted to be in a classroom setting to get a solid understanding of philanthropy and earn the highest degree in that field. With an MBA in marketing and master's degree from the Lilly School of Philanthropy at Indiana University (IUPUI), I felt that further education in philanthropic studies would help me understand the history, current state, and future of philanthropy. And that knowledge would help me structure my focus on building philanthropy within the Muslim community.

SMART-C Goal for Doctoral Program

Specific: Pursue a doctorate in philanthropic leadership to deepen my understanding of philanthropy, particularly in the context of building Muslim philanthropy.

Measurable: Successfully enroll in Indiana University's doctoral program by May 2023, complete coursework and research milestones, and attain a doctoral degree by May 2026.

Achievable: Research and identify suitable doctoral programs; gather application materials; allocate time for coursework, research, and writing; and leverage my passion for learning to excel in the program.

Relevant: Aligns with my career goal of becoming a scholar in philanthropy and contributing to the development of Muslim philanthropy.

Time-Bound: Enroll in the doctoral program by May 2023 and consistently progress through coursework, research, and applied research project requirements. Obtain the doctoral degree by May 2026.

Cost-conscious: Budget $100,000 for the entire doctoral program over three years.

I continued my educational journey and started my doctorate in philanthropic leadership in May 2023. This opened up many opportunities for me. I am seen as a scholar in the field, often invited to participate in new research, write white papers, consult for other nonprofits, and speak on various topics. My consulting fees increased. My honorarium rates went up. Learning more led to earning more. Earning more meant I could invest more and give more.

My personal roadmap also includes traveling more. I'm not sure how I will be doing that while in a doctorate program, but I shall try! My goal is to plan for moments of respite, recovery, and rest in between classes. This is my version of self-care: being out in nature and witnessing Allah's many creations. It is incredibly healing and energizing for me to see the beauty in our world.

Of course I have a travel spreadsheet! I budget out costs for flights, hotels, food, cars, and activities. I plan out destinations I want to explore. Here's the thing—I'm not getting any younger, and comfort matters more to me now. I don't want to be crammed into an economy seat at the back of the plane and be sore from the flight once I land; I'm aiming for those upgrades. I want to stay in nice, bougie hotels with beds that feel like clouds and views that'll make me appreciate the world Allah created for us. I'm all about savoring delicious gourmet cuisine at upscale restaurants and really diving into different cultures, including my own heritage. It's not just about the luxury—it's about making these trips count, y'know? Learning, growing, and coming back feeling refreshed and inspired.

But here's the kicker: The only way to do all of that without breaking the bank is to budget like a boss, be super conscious of my spending habits, and plan, plan, plan. It's all about making smart choices so I can have these amazing experiences while still being responsible with my money. Trust me, it's worth it!

SMART-C Goal for Travel Planning and Self-Care

Specific: Incorporate self-care and travel experiences into my doctoral program journey by planning and budgeting for moments of respite and exploration.

Measurable: Plan and execute at least two travel experiences each year during breaks (summer and winter), allocating a specific budget for flights, accommodation, meals, transportation, and activities.

Achievable: Create a dedicated travel fund, research cost-effective options, prioritize destinations that align with my rejuvenation goals, and utilize planning tools to maximize enjoyment within the allocated budget.

Relevant: Balances the demands of the doctorate program with self-care through travel, providing opportunities for relaxation, inspiration, and connection with nature.

Time-Bound: Plan and execute the first travel experience within the next six months, followed by another travel experience during the subsequent break.

Cost-conscious: Budget $4,000 annually for two travel experiences ($2,000 per trip).

Health

My college roommate is my accountability partner when it comes to working out. I first saw her dedication and discipline with her workout routine on Snapchat. She posted her workout outfits, her post-workout glow, and her Friday Fitness instructor pushing her to her limits. I wanted that! So she said, "Let's do it together! Every day, send me a picture on Snapchat of your workout." Since 2019, Sabiha and I have been exchanging our workout pictures. She keeps me on track and accountable. I'm heart healthy and I sleep great!

I want to exercise every day, keep my heart healthy, and have a body that can endure all the traveling I want—you can't scale a volcano or hike a mountain if your body is not fit. I'm perimenopausal, which means my body is changing along with my mood. Adopting a healthy lifestyle will help me embrace this next stage with a little more dignity and control. I look back and cringe at the bad food choices I made in the past: all those sodas, processed foods, and sugar! Sugar—the enemy of all enemies. Now my goal is to fill my plate with fresh vegetables, cook my own meals, and track my water intake. How could I not understand that I was always dehydrated?

SMART-C Goal for Health and Fitness

Specific: Commit to a daily exercise routine and adopt a healthier lifestyle to support heart health, improve overall fitness, and prepare my body for active travel.

> **Measurable:** Engage in a minimum of thirty minutes of exercise each day, logging and sharing workout pictures with my accountability partner on Snapchat. Monitor water intake and ensure at least eight glasses (sixty-four ounces) of water daily. Transition to a diet rich in fresh vegetables and more home-cooked meals.
>
> **Achievable:** Incorporate workouts that align with my fitness level and preferences, gradually increasing the intensity. Create a meal plan and prioritize home cooking using nutritious ingredients. Use a water tracking app to monitor daily water consumption.
>
> **Relevant:** Addresses my goal of maintaining heart health, improving fitness for travel, and embracing a healthier lifestyle during perimenopause for enhanced well-being and control.
>
> **Time-Bound:** Sustain this routine for the next year, reviewing progress and making adjustments as needed.
>
> **Cost-conscious:** Budget $1,200 annually ($100 monthly) for this health goal for gym membership, workout clothes, and any home equipment.

I see being healthy as connected to my financial goals in many ways. The first is that it will reduce my health care costs. Maintaining good health through preventive measures, like exercising and eating better, along with regular medical check-ups, can help minimize health care expenses. Lower medical costs can free up resources for other financial goals. Did you know that the less sick you are and the fewer times you go to the doctor or hospital, the lower your health insurance premiums will be?!

Health and financial well-being are both closely tied to managing stress. Poor financial health can lead to stress, which in turn affects physical health. Conversely, managing stress through healthy habits can positively impact both domains.

Spiritual and Charitable Giving

I would love to walk into a Ramadan banquet dinner of a Muslim-woman-led and Muslim-serving nonprofit and when they say, "Our goal tonight is to raise $xyz," I raise my hand and give them a check for that entire amount. A pleasant but shocking surprise. I know how much work it takes to raise money for a nonprofit organization. I also know how uncomfortable guests feel when they can't raise their hand for the $10,000 donation at the banquet/beatdown/fundraiser. Imagine being able to eliminate both those challenges in one night! How beautiful for everyone to enjoy achieving their fundraising goals while enjoying the food and good company of the evening. May Allah ﷻ permit me and you to be able to do this one day. *Ameen!*

Until then, I'm creating my giving plan, and yes, it's in a spreadsheet. I'm looking at all the wonderful organizations in my community that are doing really great work—from alleviating poverty to housing the homeless, uplifting women and girls, and creating spaces for spiritual growth. Looking at the spreadsheet, I've noticed that every year is different. When I first started to donate money, it was to a handful of nonprofits. Now, my list has grown to almost one hundred organizations. The amounts vary, but to be a part of the missions of all these organizations gives me a stronger sense of purpose. My current goal is to be a better donor and to increase my donations to these organizations little by little. Maybe the one I gave $25 to this year will get $50 next year.

SMART-C Goal for Charitable Giving and Spiritual Growth

Specific: Enhance my philanthropic impact and strengthen my spiritual growth by gradually increasing my donations to a diverse range of women-led and Muslim-serving nonprofit organizations in my community.

Measurable: Review and update my giving plan spreadsheet quarterly to track donations made to each organization, noting the specific amounts and any adjustments to future giving plans.

Achievable: Dedicate a portion of my budget (zakat and ṣadaqa) to charitable giving and allocate incremental increases to organizations I've supported. Research and learn about the impact of each organization to make informed decisions.

Relevant: Aligns with my desire to contribute to positive community change, support meaningful causes, and grow spiritually through impactful giving.

Time-Bound: Over the next two years, consistently increase donations to the organizations listed in my giving plan spreadsheet in gradual increments based on my financial capacity.

Cost-conscious: Set an annual charitable giving budget of $10,000, increasing by 5% each year. Allocate 70% to established organizations and 30% to new or smaller nonprofits.

I have many other goals. They include taking my parents on a vacation, taking my dad to Hajj,[34] paying for grad school, paying

---

[34] Hajj, or the pilgrimage to Mecca, is prescribed as a duty to all Mulslims who are able to make the trip.

off the house, and living *ribā*-free![35]

Sharing Knowledge and Philanthropy

One thing that I've been really struggling with in writing this book is understanding why I am writing it and what its purpose is.

This book is for a niche audience—my Muslim sisters. It will inshallah serve as *ṣadaqa jāriya* for me. It was narrated from Abū Hurayra that the Messenger of Allah ﷺ said:

> When a person dies, all their good deeds come to an end except three: ongoing charity [*ṣadaqa jāriya*], beneficial knowledge, and a righteous child who prays for them.[36]

So these are the only three things that we leave behind that we can receive continuous benefit from, even in the hereafter:

1. A continuous charity: something that lives beyond you, like a mosque you helped build, a well you helped establish, or a tree you planted.

2. Beneficial knowledge from which others continue to learn, such as a class you taught, a book you wrote, etc.

3. A pious child who, in their prayers, makes sincere *dua*[37] for you.

I hope that this book will serve as beneficial knowledge for my community. The knowledge I have gained around finances, money, investing, and philanthropy has been beneficial to me, and I want to share it with others so that they can also benefit and create their

---

35 *Ribā* is the Arabic word for "interest."
36 *Sunan al-Nasāʾī*, no 3651.
37 *Dua* is an Arabic word meaning "prayer or supplication to God."

own continuous charity. I want to learn how to give back and give back even more! If this book can empower Muslim women to increase their financial well-being, charitable giving, and generosity, imagine the positive impact we could have on our communities and the abundant rewards from Allah, the Most Generous.

SMART-C Goal for Sharing Knowledge

Specific: Write and publish a book aimed at providing beneficial financial knowledge and guidance for Muslim women, with the intention of promoting increased financial literacy, generosity, and charitable giving within the community.

Measurable: Complete the book manuscript by September 1, 2023, ensuring it covers key topics related to finances, money management, investing, and philanthropy relevant to the target audience.

Achievable: Dedicate focused time each week for writing, research, and content development, leveraging personal expertise and experiences in finance and philanthropy.

Relevant: Aligns with the goal of empowering Muslim women with valuable financial knowledge, encouraging philanthropic endeavors for the betterment of the community, and creating beneficial knowledge for the community that will outlive me.

Time-Bound: Complete the book manuscript and submit it for publishing by December 31, 2023, ensuring timely availability for the intended readership.

Cost-conscious: Budget $1,000 for travel for a writer's retreat and $500 for additional research materials or resources not covered by the publisher.

MAPPING OUT YOUR PERSONAL GOALS

After you spend time setting your intentions and understanding your values, then you can start to set goals. Some will be short-term goals, and some will be long-term goals. Remember to review your goals to see how you are tracking. Your goals will change—they may get bigger or smaller, or be deleted. Your goals are also going to cover different aspects of your life, such as career, family, spirituality, personal development, and wealth. I find the exercise of reflecting and writing out goals to be affirming and therapeutic. It further supports your intentions and purpose. I created goals last year, and now this year, I'm reviewing those goals and writing some new ones.

I also started a new practice last year of using vision boards, or in my case, a vision book. A vision board is a visual representation of your goals, desires, and aspirations. It is typically created by compiling images, quotes, words, and other visual elements that represent the things you want to achieve or experience. My vision book began as a gift from a friend—a blank black scrapbook that became the canvas for my dreams and aspirations. I filled its pages with a collage of magazine cutouts, stickers, handwritten notes, and drawings, each element representing a goal or dream. At the end of the year, I looked at all the things in my book I had imagined for myself at the beginning of that year and noted what progress I had made. Then at the beginning of the new year, I re-evaluated those visions for the months ahead. I noticed I started out with big-picture views and somewhat vague goals, and now have added more detail. The vision book provided me with a tangible visual reminder of my goals, helping me maintain my focus and motivation. It also gave me a sense of accomplishment when I reflected back on the year and what I had achieved. The tactile nature of creating and revisiting this book made my goals feel more solid and achievable.

When you clarify and map out your goals, you are able to reflect and realize that being financially stable is one of the tools you will need to succeed. So, what are your goals?

Goals Reflective Exercise

1. *Niyya.* Set your intentions of pleasing Allah ﷻ as you embark on this journey.

2. Reflection Exercise: Why is money important to you?

3. What resonated with you after reading about how to protect or preserve your wealth?

4. How does Islam inform your financial goals?

5. What are your goals? As you write these goals out, jot down what the financial implications will be. Create a rough estimated budget.

CAREER

Specific → What will you achieve? What will you do?

Measurable → What data will you use to decide whether you've met the goal?

Achievable → Are you sure you can do this? Do you have the right skills and resources?

Relevant → Does the goal align with your values? How will the results matter?

Time-bound → What is the deadline for accomplishing the goal?

Cost-conscious → What will it cost?

FAMILY

Specific → What will you achieve? What will you do?

Measurable → What data will you use to decide whether you've met the goal?

Achievable → Are you sure you can do this? Do you have the right skills and resources?

Relevant → Does the goal align with your values? How will the results matter?

Time-bound → What is the deadline for accomplishing the goal?

Cost-conscious → What will it cost?

SELF

Specific → What will you achieve? What will you do?

Measurable → What data will you use to decide whether you've met the goal?

Achievable → Are you sure you can do this? Do you have the right skills and resources?

Goals Reflective Exercise

Relevant → Does the goal align with your values? How will the results matter?

Time-bound → What is the deadline for accomplishing the goal?

Cost-conscious → What will it cost?

HEALTH

Specific → What will you achieve? What will you do?

Measurable → What data will you use to decide whether you've met the goal?

Achievable → Are you sure you can do this? Do you have the right skills and resources?

Relevant → Does the goal align with your values? How will the results matter?

Time-bound → What is the deadline for accomplishing the goal?

Cost-conscious → What will it cost?

RELATIONSHIPS

Specific → What will you achieve? What will you do?

Measurable → What data will you use to decide whether you've met the goal?

Achievable → Are you sure you can do this? Do you have the right skills and resources?

Relevant → Does the goal align with your values? How will the results matter?

Time-bound → What is the deadline for accomplishing the goal?

Cost-conscious → What will it cost?

FINANCIAL

Specific → What will you achieve? What will you do?

Measurable → What data will you use to decide whether you've met the goal?

Achievable → Are you sure you can do this? Do you have the right skills and resources?

Relevant → Does the goal align with your values? How will the results matter?

Time-bound → What is the deadline for accomplishing the goal?

Cost-conscious → What will it cost?

SPIRITUAL/RELIGIOUS

Specific → What will you achieve? What will you do?

Measurable → What data will you use to decide whether you've met the goal?

Achievable → Are you sure you can do this? Do you have the right skills and resources?

Relevant → Does the goal align with your values? How will the results matter?

Time-bound → What is the deadline for accomplishing the goal?

Cost-conscious → What will it cost?

Chapter 4

Myths about Women and Money

Right after I finished reading *The Latte Factor*, I came across the article "Myths Women Are Fed About Money: Just Buy the F...... Latte," written by Sallie Krawcheck, a former Wall Street executive and the CEO of Ellevest, a financial investment platform aimed at helping women invest more effectively. The article challenges common misconceptions about women and money and offers practical advice for women on how to take control of their finances. Krawcheck challenges the idea that women need to give up small luxuries like buying a latte in order to save money. She argues that this advice is often given without considering the broader financial context, and that small indulgences can actually help women feel happier and more motivated to achieve their financial goals.[38]

Krawcheck encourages women to take risks when it comes to investing and career advancement. She argues that women are often socialized to be risk-averse, which can hold them back from achieving their full potential. By taking calculated risks and embracing uncertainty, women can build wealth and achieve financial security. She also emphasizes the importance of financial education for women, particularly when it comes to investing. She argues that many women lack confidence in their financial knowledge, which can prevent them from taking control of their finances and making informed investment decisions.

---

38 Sallie Krawcheck, "Just Buy the F...... Latte," *Ellevest*, June 7, 2019, https://www.ellevest.com/magazine/personal-finance/just-buy-the-f-ing-latte.

My favorite part of her article was where she talks about the importance of advocating for yourself. Krawcheck encourages women to advocate for themselves in all areas of their lives, including their finances. She argues that women often face systemic barriers and biases that can make it harder for them to achieve financial success, but that by speaking up and demanding what they deserve, women can overcome these obstacles and achieve their goals. Her article was provocative and empowering and offered practical advice and actionable steps for women to achieve their financial goals.

I'll be honest, though. When I first came across Krawcheck's article, I was disheartened because I truly loved reading *The Latte Factor*. As I continued my research, I found a lot of criticism of Bach and Mann's book, and many financial advisers and gurus shared, "Drink all the lattes you want." Bach and Mann's perspective was that you are wasting money by buying expensive coffee drinks. Instead, make your coffee at home. Making coffee at home will save you money, and that money will help you get out of debt. Or, save that coffee expense money and invest it while you are young in order to become rich later when you're old. Critics like Krawcheck argue that the math doesn't add up: if you saved or invested your five daily latte dollars for forty years, the market would not yield a million dollars. The latte example is patronizing, referring to only women buying lattes. Why not, "Hold off on the rib-eye steak" or some other stereotypically male food reference?

I personally felt that the latte was just a metaphor to help you shift from a scarcity mindset to an abundance mindset. Bach and Mann helped me understand that I have money. You have money. You are already rich, and you just don't realize it.

But I also appreciated Krawcheck's critique. She made me realize that money talk is often masculinized and that we need to address the root causes as to why women are not financially knowledgable and economically stable.

I realized that I had often operated from a scarcity mindset. And my own personal journey in financial literacy has helped me move to an abundance mindset. If we recognize the value of what we already have and move away from focusing too much on what we do not have, we may find out we have the resources we need. Let's not compare ourselves to others who have more. This is a way of encouraging you to appreciate and make the most of what Allah ﷻ has blessed you with rather than constantly striving for more material possessions or wealth.

The more I researched, the more I came across fascinating articles on money and women. So many negative myths and stereotypes persist about how women view money, don't understand how to invest, or outright waste money—and we are socialized and manipulated into believing that they are true. The archaic belief that women are inferior and too simple-minded to comprehend numbers and finances is deeply ingrained in our patriarchal culture.[39]

In 2022, after another polar vortex, my husband and I deemed Minnesota winters too much for our aging bodies, aching muscles, and soon-to-be-out-of-commission joints. We had enjoyed our trips to Houston and Dallas, mainly because we have friends down there who are members of phenomenal Muslim communities and also because we could eat almost anything and everything because of the expansive halal foodie scene.

During one of our trips we visited one of my husband's friends and somehow the topic of investing came up. The friend commented

---

39 Kathy Pierre, "Women Aren't Bad with Money. Society Just Made Them Think They Were," *Relevant*, March 16, 2018, https://relevantmagazine.com/life5/career-money/women-arent-bad-money-society-just-made-think/.

on how the markets had tanked and stocks were down. I so proudly responded, "Oh, but this is the best time to buy! When the market is crashing, it's time to invest."

He turned to my husband and said, "Well, you've got her trained well." I was not pleased.

This is what I mean, ladies. The pervasive stereotype that women are clueless about money, math, and investing is embedded in our society.

The mindset that women can't manage money because we don't understand it is demoralizing. It boggles my mind that, even at this time, some women don't realize their potential and continuously perpetuate these stereotypes. Thinking about it riled me up so much that this chapter is dedicated to understanding how our society perpetuates these false beliefs and unsubstantiated claims. Grab your latte and join me on an adventure in destroying myths about women and money!

MYTH #1: WOMEN AREN'T GOOD AT MATH

Society perpetuates the myth that young girls are not good at math, which can lead them to avoid higher level math classes.[40] We need to disrupt this misconception and shift the paradigm to empower girls to become more confident in their mathematical abilities. This confidence boost, coupled with continued skill development, will positively impact their economic stability. Harvard Business School Assistant Professor Katherine B. Coffman emphasizes that this lack of confidence in math often holds women back from pursuing careers in science, technology, and math.

How can we build confidence in our girls? First off, as parents and

---

[40] Dina Gerdeman, "Bad at Math: How Gender Stereotypes Cause Women to Question Their Abilities," *Forbes*, March 8, 2019, https://www.forbes.com/sites/hbsworkingknowledge/2019/03/08/bad-at-math-how-gender-stereotypes-cause-women-to-question-their-abilities/.

as educators, we can encourage girls' interest in math at an early age by providing opportunities to explore and learn about math in fun and engaging ways. This can include playing math games, reading math-related books, and participating in math-related activities. Sudoku was, and still is, one of my favorite math brain challenges.

Girls also need to see women who excel in math and science to help shift the stereotype that women are not good at math. When they are exposed to women who have achieved success in math-related fields, girls can see that it is possible for them to do the same. Do you know about Muslim Women Mathematicians? Their website hosts profiles and stories on some of the most impressive Muslim women and their contributions to math and science, including a Nobel Prize winner, Maryam Mirzakhani, and Roya Beheshti, a silver-medal International Math Olympiad![41]

If your girl is struggling in math, find a tutor or a coach. According to research conducted by EdResearch for Recovery, students who receive support and mentorship from teachers, peers, and family members are more likely to succeed in math-related subjects. Teachers can also work to create a supportive classroom environment that encourages girls to ask questions and participate in class discussions.

The impact of supportive educators on girls' confidence in math cannot be overstated, as I experienced firsthand. My seventh- and eighth-grade math teacher was fantastic. Not only did I appreciate her teaching style—it was empathetic and personalized—but when I was struggling with any concept, she noticed and provided more instruction. I felt she genuinely cared about me as a student, and that helped me succeed in my math class. This personal experience underscores the crucial role that educators play in fostering

---

41 Muslim Women Mathematicians, https://muslimwomenmathematicians.org/Mathematicians.html.

girls' skills and confidence in mathematics. It also highlights the importance of creating supportive learning environments that can counteract societal myths and empower young women to pursue their interests in STEM fields.

Growing up, I loved math and excelled at it. I used to set the curve in many of my math classes and was usually a year ahead of my peers. As a freshman in high school, I took geometry with a bunch of sophomores and juniors and even a senior. In my junior year of high school, I took the ACT, which is a standardized test used for college admissions in the United States. It measures a student's academic readiness for college-level coursework and assesses their skills in English, math, reading, and science reasoning. These sections are scored on a scale from 1 to 36, with the average score being 20.6. When I took the exam, I scored a 32 on the math section. Because I understood math early on, accounting, financial management, and economics classes made more sense to me. When I began to learn about investing, I could understand balance sheets, income statements, and various ratios as I selected stocks.

If you didn't experience the concern and support that I benefited from and that I aim to provide to my children, that doesn't mean you're sunk. Though math skills are important for making informed decisions, understanding your finances and mastering basic money management skills does not require Einstein-level math; you don't need advanced calculus or geometry to take control of your finances and begin investing. Knowing how to add, subtract, and multiply, however, will up your game. Knowing percentages and ratios is a bonus. In addition to honing your math skills, take advantage of user-friendly technological tools and incorporate built-in programs to help you understand and track your finances. Here are some examples:

> **A basic calculator.** A useful tool for performing quick calculations, such as adding up numbers, calculating change,

or determining a tip at a restaurant. It can also be used for simple budgeting and financial calculations.

Google Sheets. A free, web-based spreadsheet program that is part of the Google Drive office suite. Sheets allows users to create, edit, and collaborate in spreadsheets online using a web browser or mobile app, and features formulas, functions, and charts.

Microsoft Excel. A popular spreadsheet program developed by Microsoft as part of the Microsoft Office suite of productivity tools. It allows users to create and manipulate data in a tabular format, which can then be used to perform calculations, generate charts and graphs, and create pivot tables to analyze complex datasets. Requires purchasing a license.

Personally knowing and tracking your numbers will give you the ability to make investment decisions with speed and confidence. You will then have the freedom to grow your wealth at your own pace.

MYTH #2: WOMEN AREN'T SMART ENOUGH TO UNDERSTAND FINANCES AND INVESTING

A multiyear national study of female clients by New York Life Investments found that 40% of women feel their financial advisers are dismissive and patronizing.[42] I have seen and experienced this firsthand. When I first began exploring my own finances and investment strategies, I rarely encountered female financial advisers. It was mostly male advisers leading and controlling the vast field of financial management.

Now picture this: In walks a hijab-clad, brown-skinned woman,

---

42 R. J. Shook, "Women Feel Ignored by Advisors, Study Says," *Forbes*, August 7, 2020, https://www.forbes.com/sites/rjshook/2020/08/07/woman-feel-ignored-by-advisors-study-says/.

wanting to initiate a dialogue on how to manage her money. After the initial shock of hearing my fluent English wore off, the male advisers were further shocked to learn that I wanted to invest my own personal wealth. Double-whammy shocker when they asked if I had my husband's permission. I used this opportunity to explain that as a married couple, we discussed finances, but as a Muslim woman, I had the right to spend, manage, and invest my personal wealth as I saw fit. The level of ignorance and condescension blew my mind. They didn't outright say it—brown-skinned, covered female equaled uneducated, oppressed, inferior—but their body language conveyed the message. The lack of eye contact, multitasking while talking, and generally impolite behavior made me feel unwelcome, like I was intruding on their precious time. Needless to say, they failed to earn my business.

The Learning Curve and Holding onto Self-Confidence

In order to get started with my investments, I had to learn financial terms and develop a new framework. There were so many concepts and regulations in the investment world that I'd just never heard of. But I want to point out that my lack of financial education wasn't due to being a woman. Everyone needs more financial education. When Sallie Krawcheck ran Merrill Lynch, the "research showed both genders could stand for more financial education. But the men invested regardless (and profited from it), and the women were less likely to."[43]

And as if starting from scratch wasn't hard enough, I soon realized that things change and evolve constantly. I still discover new information, just when I think I have something figured out.

I was recently talking to my cousin about pension plans—I thought

---

43 Sallie Krawcheck, "8 Myths that Hold Women Back from Investing," *Ellevate*, August 9, 2023, https://www.ellevatenetwork.com/articles/7138-8-myths-that-hold-women-back-from-investing.

they were a thing of the past. Didn't 401(k)s replace pension plans? Apparently not. I thought pension plans were only for factory or government workers, who became eligible to receive a pension after spending their entire career in the same company. Actually no, that is not the only way to set up a pension plan. (I will share SEP IRA deets in Chapter 13: Retirement Plans, 401[k]s, and IRAs.)

The information overload can be overwhelming. Start out small and learn at your pace by reading some books and articles and searching the internet. When it starts to become a little too much, that's when you start to talk to friends or family. Finally, seek out a financial adviser who acknowledges and aligns with your requirements. It is very demoralizing to work with a financial adviser who is completely clueless about your goals, assets, and interests in investing. Having a financial adviser who is competent and aware from a cultural, social, and racial standpoint ensures a positive investment experience.

I am bicultural, multilingual, and hold several academic degrees, but trust me, financial advisers—mostly male—have often made me feel incapable and inept by treating me like a little child, covertly implying that I couldn't possibly comprehend or learn big-boy finance terms or culture. This is why it was so important for me to find a financial adviser who looked like me: a woman, preferably a woman of color, and a Muslim—winner, winner, chicken dinner! But...hello haystack, where is the needle? Many Muslim sisters have told me that it's immensely challenging to find someone who empowers them to achieve economic financial freedom.

But if there's any piece of advice that I would like to share with you, it is that you are smart. Don't be intimidated by those who would make you feel that that's not true. You can design your own journey from not knowing to learning and feeling confident, just like I did. You can start slowly and figure this out, beginning with the basic things. Even after finishing this book, you should have enough of a foundation of knowledge to embark on further research. When you're ready to level up, shop around and look for advisers who make you feel important and valued and who believe in your ability to invest and gain financial freedom.

Picture me setting out on a journey through the forest of financial education. In the beginning, I found myself beneath the expansive canopy of financial concepts with a sense of unfamiliarity. It was as though I was standing in a forest of knowledge, each tree representing a different facet of finances. I was nervous; I was scared.

With my first steps, I realized that this forest held a treasure trove of knowledge waiting to be discovered. I began to explore and engage with resources, asking questions and seeking guidance. It was akin to nurturing the tender sapling of my knowledge—providing it with sunlight and water, watching it grow and unfurl its leaves.

With each new piece of information I absorbed, my self-confidence began to take root. Just as a sapling extends its roots deeper into the soil, I felt a growing connection to the subject matter. The seemingly complex terms and concepts started to make sense, and I found myself becoming fluent in the language of finance. As time progressed, I went even further into the forest. I encountered challenges along the way, much like a young tree might face storms or poor soil. Nevertheless, I persisted. I learned from my experiences and, gradually, my financial knowledge branched out. My understanding became stronger and more resilient, mirroring the growth of a young tree with sturdy branches that could endure the elements.

And then, a remarkable transformation occurred. My self-confidence took root and matured. I could now navigate the forest of financial concepts with ease, understanding, and—most importantly—self-assurance. My ability to budget, save, invest, and plan for the future had evolved from mere attempts into practical skills I could apply in real life. My journey showcases the transformative power of knowledge and persistence. Just as the oak's branches spread wide to offer shade and shelter, my newfound financial confidence empowers me to make informed decisions and secure my future. I hope my story inspires you to embark on your own journey toward self-assured financial literacy.

MYTH #3: BOYS INVEST, GIRLS SAVE

Groan. Part of this third myth was affirmed in my case, growing up in an Indian immigrant household. We learned the importance of saving from my mom. She taught both her sons and her daughters the importance of saving money and how to do it. Growing up we saved money in both piggy banks and, later, in savings accounts. When I began working, Mom taught me to transfer 20% from every weekly paycheck into savings.

It's crucial to understand that savings accounts and investment accounts serve different purposes. Traditional savings accounts often come with interest rates, but this presents a dilemma for Muslims who cannot use interest-based financial products. Here's the eye-opening reality: banks offer interest on savings accounts because they use your deposited money and invest it into the market, which generates profits. They then share a small portion of these profits with you in the form of interest. For Muslims avoiding interest, an interest-bearing savings account is problematic. Also, you have no control over where the bank is investing, and most likely it will be in non-sharia-compliant investments. Even if you find a bank that allows you to save in a non-interest-bearing account, you are losing! Money sitting idle in such an account actually loses value over time due to inflation. This means your hard-earned savings are quietly diminishing in purchasing power. The solution? Invest that money! By exploring sharia-compliant investment options, you can potentially grow your wealth while adhering to Islamic principles, rather than watching it slowly erode in a standard savings account.

Unfortunately, my siblings and I weren't taught how to invest. My brothers were not taught any more than my sister or I, despite the fact that boys are often encouraged to invest their money, while girls are expected to save theirs. According to a study conducted by Giftcards.com, girls had on average $693 in savings versus $645 for boys.[44] These numbers seem comparable; however, girls were more likely to be instructed on matters of fiscal restraint, including budgeting, saving, and tracking spending. Boys were more likely to receive advice related to credit scores, taxes, and bank accounts—topics related to investing.

My husband and I have been teaching our daughter and son how to invest. We didn't want to wait until they graduated college and had full-time jobs, so we planted the seed of financial independence while they held internships and summer jobs by creating investment accounts for them.

Instead of giving them seed money, we wanted them to have some skin in the game. We had them invest $1,000 of their savings from their summer earnings into an investment account, and we added $5,000. It's been fascinating to see how differently they invest and interact with their accounts. Both notice that the stock market fluctuates. They see how the value of the stocks they own are affected by world events, inflation, and election results.

When we opened these investment accounts for the kids, the world was entering the third year of the pandemic, inflation rates were

---

[44] "Adolescent Income and Financial Literacy," Giftcards.com, accessed August 18, 2023, https://www.giftcards.com/adolescent-income-and-financial-literacy?utm_source=rakuten&utm_medium=affiliate&utm_campaign=2116208&utm_content=686295&ranMID=44432&ranEAID=TnL5HPStwNw&ranSiteID=TnL5HPStwNw-GYenFuvsd1Ee79UsNbOcVA.

at a record high, economists were talking about a recession, and America was in the midst of midterm elections. All of these events had an impact on the stock market. Most of the time, my kids were just freaking out that they were losing money. I had to teach them that, especially considering how young they are, this is all about the long term.

My husband and I are guiding them in doing the research, growing their portfolios, and being smarter investors. We spend time with them explaining how investing today grows the portfolio in the future. We teach them the importance of investing little by little and building their portfolios one stock at a time. That way, our children will experience the forest of finance as a familiar place where they're knowledgable and confident. By nurturing their financial literacy from an early age, we're helping them develop the skills and mindset to navigate the complex world of investing with ease and assurance.

MYTH #4: WOMEN ARE BAD WITH MONEY

I find this stereotype oppressive and offensive. I hate the notion that women only want to spend money—and that spending money means we are wasting money. This perpetuates the myth that we are incapable of managing money, irresponsible with our finances, and spending our money on frivolous things. This is such an upsetting, misogynistic, and patriarchal stereotype.

It's also wrong on multiple levels. According to Suze Orman, an author, television host, and financial adviser, the primary difference between men and women in terms of personal finance lies in their perceptions of ownership over their money. "Women will always think, especially if they have children, that their money is for their parents, their spouses, their brothers, their sisters, their pets, and everybody but them, because a woman's nature is to nurture," Orman told Fast Company. "Men, on the other hand, know absolutely that the money that they make is for them. They don't have trouble saying 'no,' they have no problem keeping it for themselves, investing it for themselves, and not sharing it with their spouses."[45] This seems to directly contradict what Islam teaches us about men's financial responsibility for their family members and women's role as the caretakers of their husband's money.

So let's debunk this myth! Fidelity Investments' "2021 Women and Investing Study" found that women tend to be more focused on long-term goals, with 67% of women citing retirement savings as a top priority, compared to 61% of men.[46] The study also found that women tend to be more proactive about seeking financial advice, with 72% of women seeking out professional financial guidance at some point, compared to 62% of men. A 2017 study by Vanguard found that female investors tend to have more diversified portfolios and are less likely to take risks than male investors. The study found that female investors held more balanced portfolios with a greater proportion of bonds, while male investors were more likely to hold concentrated portfolios with a greater proportion of stocks. We are not bad with money! We are diligent, thoughtful, and strategic!

And what's more, women carry less credit card debt than men. According to Brianna McGurran's blog, "Women and Credit 2020: How History Shaped Today's Credit Landscape," men carry 20% more personal debt than women.[47] Women also spend less money than men, and it's because we know how to shop for deals and sales. A consumer expenditure survey by the Bureau of Labor Statistics

---

45 Jared Lindzon, "How Parents Talk about Money Differently to Their Sons and Daughters," Fast Company, accessed August 18, 2023, https://www.fastcompany.com/90283344/how-parents-talk-about-money-differently-to-their-sons-and-daughters.

46 Fidelity Investments, "2021 Women and Investing Study," https://www.fidelity.com/bin-public/060_www_fidelity_com/documents/about-fidelity/FidelityInvestmentsWomen&InvestingStudy2021.pdf.

47 Brianna McGurran, "Women and Credit 2020: How History Shaped Today's Credit Landscape," *Experian* (blog), February 28, 2020, https://www.experian.com/blogs/ask-experian/women-and-credit/.

found that men spent an average of $41,203 a year as opposed to $38,838 for women.[48] We must be fabulous with managing money since we also give at a higher rate.[49] Generosity precedes prosperity. All of these statistics prove that women are downright marvelous with money!

My mom was far better at managing our household finances than my father was. Even though my father earned more than she did, she was the one who knew how to manage our bills, save money, and still be able to buy everything we needed to live life with dignity. She managed all of our expenses, and she was very methodical, organized, and thoughtful in how she did it. My father was just a big spender. He didn't plan. He didn't look at prices. He didn't look for sales or find the best price in town. He bought whatever he wanted, while Mom cut coupons.

I remember my mom sitting every week with the Sunday paper, reviewing all the sales, clipping coupons for whatever groceries we were going to purchase, and making her shopping list. I remember her going through all the sales papers, comparing the prices of everything in multiple grocery stores—Jewel, Gromer's, Venture, Zayre, and Butera. It is because of my mother's frugality and her savings routine that my parents were able to save enough money for a down payment on that brand-new house in the 90s.

Coupled with being bad at managing money is the harmful stereotype that women are wasteful. "She's a frivolous spender, a shopaholic, spends all her money on shoes and clothes." These pervasive stereotypes not only portray women as ignorant and self-centered but also undermine their financial capabilities and

---

[48] "Consumer Expenditure Surveys: Tables," U.S. Bureau of Labor Statistics, accessed September 2, 2023, https://www.bls.gov/cex/tables.htm.

[49] Leslie Albrecht, "Who Donates More Time and Money to Charity—Men or Women? Here's Your Answer," MarketWatch, accessed September 2, 2023, https://www.marketwatch.com/story/wealthy-women-give-away-their-money-and-time-more-than-rich-men-2018-10-24.

autonomy. Such misconceptions dismiss women's ability to make sound financial decisions and ignore the complex economic realities many women face. These stereotypes can have real-world consequences, potentially influencing everything from personal relationships to professional opportunities in finance-related fields.

There's a well-known saying: If you give a man a fish, you feed him for a day. If you teach a man to fish, you feed him for a lifetime. In the humanitarian aid world, there's another saying: If you teach a man to fish, you help a man. If you teach a woman to fish, you help her whole community.

Ritu Sharma chronicled her travels across four different countries illustrating how women are overcoming poverty. Her book, *Teach a Woman How to Fish*, helped me expand upon the fishing adage.[50] A woman learns how to fish to feed her children and share with the village. She will build a fish pond to ensure a sustainable food source, making sure everyone else learned how to fish along the way and helping people land a job in the fishing industry—all while teaching them different ways to cook fish! By the end, she will have built up an entire community. She was the spark in revitalization. Women tend to think of collective benefit.

Women are not bad with money, as anecdotally evidenced by my own mother and by the research that shows they simply have different—even superior—approaches to managing money and budgeting.

Take a moment to think about who controls this narrative. Who benefits from Islam continuously prolonging this stereotype? Ladies, do not buy into these tropes. You are capable of managing your money, and don't let anybody tell you otherwise.

---

50   Ritu Sharma, *Teach a Woman to Fish: Overcoming Poverty around the Globe* (Palgrave Macmillan, 2014).

MYTH #5: IT IS TABOO TO EARN MORE THAN YOUR MAN

In *Gender Identity and Relative Income within Households*, coauthors Marianne Bertrand, Jessica Pan, and Emir Kamenica uncovered that marriage rates decline when a woman has the potential to outearn her husband. A married woman earning more than her spouse increases the probability of unhappiness in her union, and wives who earn more often end up doing more of the household chores, not less.[51] Their research also shows that when women have the potential to earn more than their spouses, some women will opt out of working outside of the home altogether.

Between 1970 and 2010, there was a significant increase in divorce rates in the United States. The divorce rate in 1970 was 29%, and by 2010 it had climbed to 49%.[52] While the exact percentages can vary depending on the source and methodology, researchers have all noted a substantial rise during this period. Some studies suggest that changes in gender roles and economic dynamics within marriages have contributed to this trend.[53] For instance, as women's workforce participation and earning potential increased, it challenged traditional marital dynamics. Some researchers propose that marriages where wives earn more than their husbands may face unique stressors, potentially contributing to marital instability in some cases. However, it's important to note that the relationship between women's earnings and divorce rates is complex and influenced by many factors, including societal attitudes, individual circumstances, and broader economic trends.

Bertrand, Pan, and Kamenica also uncovered that when a woman earns more than her husband, she is more likely to be unhappy

---

51 Marianne Bertrand, Jessica Pan, and Emir Kamenica, "Gender Identity and Relative Income within Households," *National Bureau of Economic Research*, May 2013, https://doi.org/10.3386/w19023.

52 Bertrand, Pan, and Kamenica, "Gender Identity and Relative Income."

53 Bertrand, Pan, and Kamenica, "Gender Identity and Relative Income."

in her marriage.[54] When women work outside the home, you would think that household chores would evolve to be more equally divided. But while men in their study spent 20.8 hours on household chores and childcare, women spent 33.5 hours.[55] Why the discrepancy? A wife making more money can end up doing more chores to alleviate her husband's unease. Being the primary breadwinner and the primary homemaker is stressful, and that—along with a husband's potentially insecure response to his wife's status—often leads to unhappiness and divorce. As a result, many women make the choice to forgo their own earnings in order to preserve their marriage.

In some cases, the finances of a higher-earning wife are managed by the husband. All the financial decisions and investment strategies are determined by him, without any input from her. This behavior perpetuates all kinds of unhealthy dynamics, including the stereotype that women aren't smart with money and can't understand finances. It perpetuates the belief that while women can bring in big bucks, the only thing they will do with said big bucks is spend them frivolously.

And finally, there are some women who are taking on the husband's traditional responsibility of being the sole breadwinner for the family.

In Islam, many traditional interpretations advocate for distinct gender roles within a marriage. In this paradigm, the husband is responsible for providing financially for the family. This includes the family's shelter, food, water, and clothing. Men are the providers and protectors of the family, while the wife's role is often defined as the caretaker of the household and the family. In every marriage, there should be mutual consent and understanding, even in matters of financial responsibilities. When a wife takes on her

---

54 Bertrand, Pan, and Kamenica, "Gender Identity and Relative Income."
55 Bertrand, Pan, and Kamenica, "Gender Identity and Relative Income."

husband's financial responsibilities, what happens to the balance of the traditional roles? What type of internal or societal pressure, criticism, or stigma does she face?

Look, attitudes and practices regarding gender roles within our Muslim families and communities are diverse and, in many cases, changing. A good proportion of Muslim women are actively involved in the workforce and contribute to their family's finances. Some are actively managing their homes and raising their children. Some are doing both. Today, there is a growing recognition and realization that, Islamically, there is flexibility in how we divide our roles and responsibilities and, as spouses, we should be able to have conversations about these topics together. Share your preferences with your partner, have open conversations about what you are good at and what you enjoy, and find a balance in your roles. Play to both your strengths!

Furthermore, this is not about competing to earn more than men.[56] Don't compete with them or with other women. Compete with yourself, because that is what will help you grow and improve yourself. In terms of financial acumen and money, push yourself to be better and look at it as the Islamic concept of *iḥsān*.[57] Allah ﷻ loves those who strive for excellence in all their deeds, so that should be your game plan. When you focus on yourself, you avoid falling into the comparison trap. It makes it easier to remember that our *rizq* is promised by Allah. This saves us from jealousy, unhealthy comparisons, and a sense of inadequacy. It'll also reduce the stress and anxiety of feeling like you have outperformed someone else or vice versa.

Instead, focus on yourself. You are your biggest supporter and

---

56 In Islam, men have a God-given financial responsibility over the household (Quran 4:34).

57 *Iḥsān*, in Arabic, is defined as "spiritual excellence."

cheerleader. Embrace your strengths. Celebrate your wins, no matter how small they seem. Set your own goals and foster that internal motivation. When you compete with yourself, you also build your resilience and ability to adapt. Focusing on self-improvement prepares you to face any challenges or changes in life.

Now, interestingly, I personally know a few women who earn more than their husbands. Women are pursuing higher degrees (outnumbering men in universities by 3.1 million in the US)[58] and because of that, they are getting higher-paying jobs and earning more than men.

I know a sister who earns significantly more than her husband. I used to wonder how he felt about that. Recently, she was promoted and, as with most promotions, she received an increase in pay. He was proud of her, supportive, and genuinely happy. We all went out to dinner to celebrate her hard work. Their bank accounts are combined to run their household, and they have a real partnership approach to their budgeting, spending, and giving. Do you know how they manage this? They communicate! They talk about their financial situation; in other words, they have financial transparency. They talk about their income, expenses, debt, savings, and investments. Yes, she makes more, but because they share information on everything related to money, they are able to make informed financial decisions together. They discuss their financial goals and priorities. For the past three years, they've been planning for Hajj and taking care of their elderly parents. They're on the same page and working together toward those goals. I also notice that they talk openly about the differences in their income. Instead of harboring resentment and allowing a power imbalance to take hold, their open communication has helped prevent

---

58 Michael T. Nietzel, "Women Continue to Outpace Men in College Enrollment and Graduation," *Forbes*, August 7, 2024, https://www.forbes.com/sites/michaeltnietzel/2024/08/07/women-continue-to-outpace-men-in-college-enrollment-and-graduation/.

negative emotions from impacting their relationship. I can't say the conversations are easy. I'm sure they are hard. Yet they strive to understand and support each other. Together, they enjoy life. She is a great example of how earning more money than your partner does not have to be a problem.

With all that being said, I'd like to remind you of another Islamic provision for women. In Islam, our money is our money. We are given a right from Allah ﷻ to have agency over our wealth. He didn't place the task of being financially responsible for our families on us. So don't allow yourself to be unfairly burdened with the financial support of your family. Making more than your husband is one thing. Contributing along with your husband to your family's financial needs is also great as long as it's done with kindness and cooperation from both sides. But being forced to turn over your paycheck or support the family on your own is not healthy unless it's something you've agreed to with gusto.

So with the money we earn or the wealth we inherit and accumulate, let's be responsible in spending, investing, and giving in ways that please Allah. Take ownership of this financial privilege and responsibility.

Now that you understand what these myths are, don't get caught up in them. Challenge them, disrupt them, and take care of your money!

Understanding and Challenging Myths Exercise

1. What were your thoughts about and reactions to the myths you just read about? How did they make you feel?

2. What is one way you will challenge these myths?

3. Are there other myths and stereotypes you've been exposed to? What are they? Why do you consider them myths? How will you disrupt these myths?

Chapter 5

Gender Inequities

Women face multiple inequities in their lives, which can have tremendous negative impacts on their journey to financial stability and freedom. You may experience one, while someone else experiences another. There are some of us who face all of these inequities at once or throughout our lives. Understanding these inequities and how to counter them can feel overwhelming. With so much stacked against us, it's no wonder women are behind in taking action and demanding reform. Let's shift the focus from (perhaps unknowingly) perpetuating these myths and inequities to instead centering the narrative on empowering women to cultivate a strong sense of confidence in their financial skills. Together, we can work toward replacing the myths with truths, dismantling fact from fiction, and disrupting an often oppressive reality, one successful story at a time.

Let's begin by exploring some inequities.

THE PINK TAX

"The pink tax" is not an actual tax on menstrual products or lipstick and makeup. The pink tax refers to the fact that women have to pay more money for products that are designed for women compared to the same product designed for men. This is a form of discriminatory pricing also known as gender-based pricing.

What are some examples of "pink-taxed" products? Think about your last haircut. When I go to the salon, I pay a minimum of $55 for my haircut. My son or my husband get the same type of services

I do, a wash with shampoo and conditioner, haircut, and styling. My son even gets a beard trim—and they pay $30 each. When's the last time you went to the dry cleaner's? How much more expensive is it to dry clean a woman's blouse than a man's shirt? Have you gotten clothing alterations? How much did you pay for altering your dress compared to your brother's suits getting fitted to him? Did you know the government imposes import tariffs on women's clothing and products for women? Hence, our clothes are more expensive. And sisters, don't get me started on car repairs! How many times have you gone for an oil change and they try to sell you a hundred other things that are unnecessary?

This difference in pricing of goods and services designed for women is what is known as the pink tax. The discrepancy in the cost of services and products for women versus men has real effects on women's lives. If we have to spend more on certain things, we have less discretionary funds. Less money to save. Less to put into an investment account. (See how much of our spending isn't frivolous or even a choice?)

Multiple states have introduced legislation to address this gender-based pricing discrepancy. However, nothing has passed. Surprised? We don't have gender equity in our legislative bodies. Perhaps things will change as more women run for office and win their elections. In the meantime, talk to your legislators about this nonsense and demand pink tax reform.

THE GENDER WAGE PAY GAP

Research shows that for every dollar that a man earns, on average, a woman earns eighty-two cents. Latinx women earn fifty-four cents, Native American women earn fifty-seven cents, Black women earn sixty-two cents, and Asian American Pacific Islander (AAPI) women earn ninety cents on the dollar of a white man. Unfortunately, there isn't enough data or the ability to disaggregate the data to show what Muslim women earn, but overall, women are paid less for the same work as men. When we earn less than men for the same job, we are at a disadvantage in achieving financial stability and financial freedom. Earning less also impacts our ability to invest. And even when we do invest, we are unable to invest the same amount or at the same rate as our male counterparts.

There are many reasons this disparity exists. I have observed that women do not talk about money, salary, or income with each other or anyone else. Therefore, we end up with little-to-no guidance on salary expectations. We aren't researching equitable pay. We haven't mastered the art of salary negotiation. We undervalue our work and worth and accept lower pay. If we can learn to have transparent and vulnerable conversations, we will be able to shift the power dynamic in these crucial situations.

Personally, I had no idea how to negotiate a salary. When I entered the workforce, I did what every other woman was doing and checked the published salary range for the job title before applying for the position. Thus armed, I thought I had done my research on salary compensation—until I learned the hard way.

One of my biggest salary negotiation regrets is when I was pursuing a new position at my then-current company. At the time, I had a lucrative offer from a previous employer. I planned to leverage the job opportunity and higher salary range of the position I was being offered by my previous employer in my negotiation with my current employer. But when the hiring manager made me an offer and wrote an amount in my offer letter, I froze. I didn't know what I was supposed to do next and simply accepted it. I didn't even try to write another number down—I didn't negotiate.

As years passed, I learned from that mistake. First, I learned that although I regretted not negotiating, the fact was that that particular money wasn't meant for me. I had to trust in Allah ﷻ as the Ultimate Provider. I was meant to start my salary at that rate. Allah ﷻ had a plan, and the plan included me learning the art of negotiation. Second, as I developed my own knowledge, I learned how important it was to reach out to other young women and help them access the tools and techniques necessary to confidently negotiate a higher salary and better work benefits for themselves. Third, I learned the value of salary transparency, particularly in the nonprofit sector.

In the nonprofit sector, we have to report the compensation of executive directors and top leadership administrators. This ensures that nonprofits are responsible for using the nonprofit's resources as they have committed to and it helps maintain the public's trust in charitable organizations. Remember, the funding for nonprofits comes from the public, unlike for-profit businesses. That salary transparency helped me devise my own compensation package when I was at RISE. I was able to benchmark figures to compare against other executive director roles. This helped me determine if my salary expectations were in line with industry standards and if I was being compensated fairly.

Women need to be more open and confident about money and personal worth and need to make sure we are not being underpaid. Having your salary publicly available can feel risky, especially if you fear it may cause people to be jealous. Some fear that publicizing their salary may come off as bragging. We need to reframe this mindset. Salary transparency addresses gender disparities and advocates for equality in the workplace. When we normalize this conversation by regularly sharing our experiences and insights, it'll become less of a taboo subject. Hopefully others won't react with jealousy, but this isn't about individual responses. This is about the bigger picture. When you learn about what I make and other women in your profession make, I hope it helps you negotiate a better salary for yourself.

Do your part in narrowing the gender pay gap. Salary transparency can help us identify and address systemic issues and promote change. And don't forget to celebrate Muslim women earning what they are worth! Be proud and happy about that. That's success, so say mashallah![59]

Overcoming the Need for Unhealthy Self-Sacrifice

When I cofounded RISE, I put off giving myself a salary until there was enough money in the business account. I was being noble and working for the cause. I worked over forty hours a week and on weeknights and weekends. I sacrificed family time and time with friends. Even my own mental health and self-care went out the door. I hired and paid staff before I was pushed to take a salary for myself.

At that time, RISE had a fiscal sponsor: Propel Nonprofits. Propel Nonprofits managed our finances. It was a great partnership. The fiscal sponsor manager, Danielle, was meticulous and diligent with our budgeting and financial reporting. She knew our numbers better than we did. It was probably in the second year of RISE that Danielle encouraged me, or rather gave me the green light, to get paid. "You know it's OK for you to start taking a salary now." She was so gentle about it. I smiled and felt uncomfortable. I wasn't ready yet. A few months went by, and we started to work on the next fiscal year's budget. Danielle reminded me again, but this time with assertiveness: "You should pay yourself too."

I had to reassure myself that I deserved to be paid. Working up the courage to go for it, I was faced with, "Well, what should my salary be?" So I went on a mission and gathered intel. I spoke to twelve different executive directors at a range of organizations—

---

59 Mashallah is an Arabic phrase that means "God has willed it." It is often used to acknowledge something praiseworthy.

ones with similar budgets, larger budgets, startups, scale-ups, and established nonprofits. I chatted with one man, and the rest were women. It was all over the place. The disparity in their salaries made my eyeballs bug out to the size of saucers. The range was staggering: from executive directors who worked for free out of passion for their cause, all the way up to those commanding six-figure salaries. This vast spectrum highlighted not only the complexity of nonprofit compensation but also the potential for significant undervaluation of leadership roles, especially for women.

After careful consideration, I decided on a salary request that matched what I had been earning in my corporate job six years prior. The corporate position had not only provided a substantial income but also came with excellent benefits: a 401(k) match, an employee stock purchase plan, stock options, health care, dental, and professional development stipends. For the first six years at RISE, I had toiled, sacrificing all these employee benefits and denying myself even a basic salary. I mistakenly believed that accepting monetary compensation for nonprofit work—which I saw as God's work—would somehow diminish the *ajr*[60] I would gain in the afterlife. I now understand that we can pursue both fair compensation and spiritual rewards; they are not mutually exclusive.

In Urdu, we call the idea that nonprofit leaders shouldn't get paid *bakwas*—absolute nonsense. I didn't tie my camel. Make sure you tie your camel. To all nonprofit executives who don't pay themselves or their staff what they are worth—you are oppressors. Little pharaohs of the nonprofit world. You might be offended by this, and I may sound harsh. But as nonprofit professionals, we are dedicating our time, skills, and expertise to our work. Our efforts should be appropriately compensated. Everyone should be

---

60 *Ajr* in Arabic means "reward."

appropriately compensated. We need to be able to recruit and retain talent. Nonprofits are part of our economy and should constitute a viable professional pathway. How can we live and afford our expenses without an income? How can we give zakat or *ṣadaqa* without the ability to earn? Providing fair compensation respects our contributions and promotes a healthier work environment. Don't put financial stress on people working in this field. Empower them to earn and create a more sustained commitment to the cause, whatever that may be.

The reality is that, by refusing compensation, executive directors and their employees inadvertently contribute to the gender wage gap. Working for a nonprofit without fair pay impacts one's overall financial stability, retirement savings, and ability to invest—factors that disproportionately affect women in the sector. This practice not only harms individual financial health but also perpetuates the perception that women's contributions are worth less than those of men, regardless of intention. When women work for free or for lower wages in nonprofits, it skews overall wage statistics and reinforces systemic undervaluation of women's work. This cycle can have long-lasting effects on career progression and lifetime earnings. To address the gender wage gap effectively, it's crucial that women in nonprofit leadership roles advocate for and accept fair compensation, setting a standard that values their work appropriately and challenges the notion that passion for a cause should come at the cost of financial security.

Don't put yourself and others on the path to burnout by shorting salaries. Grow your budget or increase your fundraising efforts. You will get the *ḥasanāt* [61] for this work, and it's OK to get paid.

Back to the salary—could I ask for $100,000? Was I bringing enough to the nonprofit table in terms of skills, leadership, and

---

61 *Ḥasanāt* is an Arabic term that refers to the reward or merit that comes from performing good deeds and being pious.

business acumen? I called up my friend Kate to get her thoughts. I met Kate in my early days of transitioning into the nonprofit world. She advised me during the startup phase of RISE and introduced me to philanthropy. Kate ran her own consulting agency, providing organizational change management, leadership development, strategic planning, and cultural and organizational transformation, with a particular emphasis on creating inclusive and equitable workplaces. She has always provided honest advice and feedback.

Me: "I want to ask for [a competitive amount]."

Kate: (*silence that spanned a lifetime*)

Me: (*thinking, "Oh no, it's too much!"*)

Kate: "DO IT!"

Now came the challenging part: drafting my own contract. While the board was certainly capable of handling this task, I felt compelled to take the initiative. I wanted to ensure that the terms aligned perfectly with both the organization's needs and my professional goals. With careful consideration, I drew up a three-year, tiered compensation plan for myself. This plan included gradual salary increases over the three-year period, contingent upon meeting our fundraising goals. By structuring it this way, I aimed to demonstrate my commitment to the organization's growth while also securing a path for my own professional development.[62] When I approached the board, I led with a conversation on pay disparities and the gender pay gap. We, as an organization that uplifts Muslim women, could not be contributing to this gap. We needed to lead in narrowing it. My all-female Muslim board met and unanimously approved my contract, embodying the concept of women supporting women.

---

62 According to the Association of Fundraising Professionals and Nonprofit Law, you cannot tie performance goals to fundraising goals. After learning this, we changed our policy at RISE.

Did you know there is also a disparity in the amount of overall debt women have compared to men? Think about it. Women are paid less, so they have less money with which to pay off their debts. For example, women have student loans just like men have student loans. But it takes longer for women to pay them off because they have to make smaller payments.[63] Another example? Women often face higher interest rates than men when taking out loans to buy a house or a car, due to various systemic factors in the lending industry.[64] This disparity in interest rates can negatively impact their credit scores. Lower credit scores, in turn, lead to even higher interest rates on future borrowing. It creates a vicious cycle that can be difficult to break. This systemic bias in lending practices puts women at a financial disadvantage, making it harder for them to build wealth and achieve financial stability. It is such a vicious cycle.

The other day, I spoke with a friend who is a volunteer board member for a local nonprofit and whose story reflects this systemic cycle. She casually mentioned that she has over $250,000 in student loan debt. I was flabbergasted. Although she is making repayments, the interest is killing any effort to lower the entire repayment amount. How was she ever going to pay it off? Today, my friend is applying for student loan refinancing with interest-free payments through Defynance.[65] This is an Islamic organization that buys people's student loans and helps them repay the loans interest-free!

The second thing my friend is doing is finding a job that matches her degrees. She currently works part-time for a nonprofit. She's looking for work that will pay more and that matches what she studied with those student loans! And finally, she's working on

---

[63] Melanie Hanson, "Student Loan Debt by Gender," EducationData.org, July 16, 2023, https://educationdata.org/student-loan-debt-by-gender.

[64] Ben Guess, "Women Pay up to $37,000 More than Men to Own a Car and Home," Jerry, May 24, 2023, https://getjerry.com/studies/women-pay-up-to-usd37-000-more-than-men-to-own-a-car-and-home.

[65] Learn more at https://www.defynance.com/.

her application to qualify for student loan forgiveness through the federal government. May Allah ﷻ help her get through this. Ameen!

THE FUNDING GAP

When you have a great idea and are ready to launch your business, you need some initial money. Maybe you'll invest your own personal funds to get started. But what if you don't have any money? You turn to venture capital. Venture capital is a type of financing provided to startup companies that show high growth potential. Venture capital is usually provided by wealthy individuals, venture capital firms, or investors who are willing to invest money in exchange for ownership or equity in a new company. In 2018, female founders barely raised 2.2% of that year's venture capital total for their businesses. In a $130 billion market, all of the female founders put together accounted for $2.88 billion of venture capital raised. If women lack the funding to start their businesses, how can they dream of financial stability? No wonder so many women have side hustles and struggle to scale their businesses! If a woman has a great product, she must prove product viability, scalability, customer demand, and profitability margins before investors loosen their purse strings. If a man has a mere sketch of an idea, investors are willing to put millions into testing it out.

You know how we can change this? We need more female venture capitalists! Imagine if there were more Muslim women with money to invest and build up aspiring Muslim women startups? If we build up our financial acumen—which builds up our wealth—then we will have money to invest in new businesses.

WORKPLACE ENVIRONMENTS

Ever notice how hostile and toxic some places of work are for women? The United States is one of the few developed countries that provides no paid maternity leave for new mothers. Of the 193 countries that make up the United Nations, only 7 do not have a national paid parental leave law: New Guinea, Suriname, a few South Pacific island nations, and the United States.[66] As the only highly developed country on this list, the US is a notable outlier.

The US also does not offer childcare support for working parents. And if your child gets the flu, you will more than likely have to dip into your paid time off (PTO) to cover your absence. And this shortsighted lack of compassion is not just limited to motherhood. Those of us who are caretakers to parents, siblings, in-laws, or other loved ones are provided no grace or support for that unpaid labor, neither by the companies we work for nor the government we are supporting with our taxes and productivity.

Whether in an office setting or a warehouse, sexual harassment and assault against women also continue to be an issue.[67] Women who work for male supervisors can be at greater risk of experiencing sexual harassment or discrimination, as their supervisors may use their power to exert pressure on them or create a hostile work environment. A 2019 survey by the Society for Human Resource Management found that 60% of women reported experiencing unwanted sexual attention or sexual coercion in the workplace. And that number is likely an underestimate as many cases go unreported.[68] From foul language to crass jokes and suggestive gestures, from inappropriate interactions to denial of recognition and promotion, a woman's work environment can resemble a gauntlet. And to top it all off, she must continuously show up with

---

66   Jessica Deahl, "Countries Around the World Beat the U.S. on Paid Parental Leave," NPR, October 6, 2016, https://www.npr.org/2016/10/06/495839588/countries-around-the-world-beat-the-u-s-on-paid-parental-leave.

67   Chai R. Feldblum and Victoria A. Lipnic, "Select Task Force on the Study of Harassment in the Workplace: Report of the Co-Chairs of the EEOC," *Equal Employment Opportunity Commission,* June 2016, https://www.eeoc.gov/select-task-force-study-harassment-workplace.

68   Feldblum and Lipnic, "Select Task Force."

her whole self and pretend like nothing negative is happening. A woman has to put up with a colossal amount of difficulty just to earn a living. How can she be expected to focus on her finances, invest in herself, and plan for her future when she must show up in a toxic work environment every day?

OK, I know this chapter feels daunting and full of negativity, but we can't move forward until we highlight the problems and find solutions that work. Despite inequities and discrimination, there is still hope. When women stand together and build one another up through sisterhood, we hold a lot of power. We can create major waves and raise our collective voice against these inequities.

Intentional Change

When I founded RISE, I tried my best to address the gender pay gap and the hostile work environment. I raised money so I could hire women and pay them more than other Muslim-led nonprofits paid. I continued to raise more money so that they could get annual pay increases, personal development funds, and workplace benefits. We created a self-care stipend benefit and offered paid maternity leave. We offered health care insurance and covered the entire monthly premium. We incorporated flexibility into our schedules to manage our caretaking duties well before the pandemic made us work from home. Note the change from "I" to "we." This is the power of collective female strength.

When I was leaving RISE, we did not have a policy on severance packages or exit packages. Why? Because we weren't aware these existed. I was fortunate enough to have hired an operations and human resources manager during my time, and she not only had experience in her field, but she was also pursuing her master's degree in HR and organizational development. A month before my last day, Sumaya approached me. "Nausheena, have you thought about your severance package?" No, of course not. I wasn't being fired or let go. We don't give severance packages to people who choose to leave...or do we? Sumaya assured me that this was a common practice in the nonprofit sector. She even provided me with an example of someone receiving almost $20,000 in compensation as they left their job. I was shocked. I asked her to help me understand this better, and she set out to compile more information specific to our organization's size and sector to help me understand how this might apply in my situation.

Meanwhile, I tapped into my network. During the pandemic, there was a mass exodus of executive directors stepping down and moving on—including me! I had five friends who were on the same journey, and what a blessing they were! I connected with them over calls, texts, and dinners. Each had a different story and offered great personal insights on their exit package. Some called it severance, some called it an exit package, and some called it a parting gift.

I told them I wasn't getting anything beyond a PTO payout. "Well, have you asked for anything?" This question was affirming. But what exactly do I ask for? The current policy at RISE was that when you left you could cash out on five days of accumulated paid time off. One of my parting executive director friends was receiving a month's worth of severance pay and her COBRA[69] insurance payments paid for the rest of the year. One had a splendid board chair championing her exit package with the rest of the board. Another had a small nonprofit with a small budget, so the community hosted a fundraiser and provided her with a parting gift!

---

69   The Consolidated Omnibus Budget Reconciliation Act (COBRA) gives workers and their families who lose their health benefits the right to choose to continue group health benefits provided by their group health plan for limited periods of time under certain circumstances such as voluntary or involuntary job loss, reduction in the hours worked, transition between jobs, death, divorce, and other life events.

While I was gaining real-time knowledge on exit packages, Sumaya's research offered yet another option. As per her research, I could request one to two weeks of pay for every year I had worked at RISE. RISE was founded in 2015 and established in 2016. I didn't receive a paycheck until 2018, but I worked for seven years total as the executive director. I knew I deserved compensation for my years of service, but I couldn't work up the courage to ask for that much. I approached a board member and asked for her support in navigating this decision. Imposter syndrome was dimming my bright light. Since I was working for the betterment of society, being compensated for my services felt almost at odds with the spiritual rewards I might receive from Allah. I found myself at the crossroads of worth, value, and *ajr* and had to make a choice. Do I sacrifice one when I choose the other? Is it OK to ask for it all?

I needed to reframe my perspective. Yes, I should hope for my reward from Allah, but it should not be disconnected from fair compensation. I did some of my own research and found information on how to design a fair exit package[70] and see the exit package as a "happy ending" for my time.[71] I also learned that a global trend exists to provide exit packages in the nonprofit sector.[72]

I was looking forward to this exit package so I could take a radical sabbatical and not worry about money. I had moved from feeling undeserving of it to believing it was a gift from Allah!

Sumaya sent me an initial email full of great research and a contract template to complete. She had done all the legwork on the legal

---

[70] Tom Adams, Melanie Herman, and Tim Wolfred, "Exit Agreements for Nonprofit CEOs: A Guide for Boards and Executives," *Nonprofit Quarterly*, January 13, 2020, https://nonprofitquarterly.org/exit-agreements-nonprofit-ceo-guide-for-boards-and-executives/.

[71] Sonia J. Stamm and Ted LeBow, "The Ideal Exit of the Nonprofit Executive," *BoardEffect* (blog), February 25, 2016, https://www.boardeffect.com/blog/the-ideal-exit-of-the-nonprofit-executive/.

[72] The Human Capital Hub, "Exit Packages Global Trend," accessed September 4, 2023, https://thehumancapitalhub.com/articles/exit-packages-global-trend.

side and laid out the next steps, which included a conversation with the new executive director. And that's when I lost my confidence. Again. I didn't want to have this conversation.

Why was I feeling this uncomfortable and scared? I'd helped recruit the new executive director, who also was a good friend. I couldn't be happier that she was my successor. We had trust, but the power dynamic felt like it had shifted. I no longer oversaw the budget of the organization. It was her organization. And she now had the power to make decisions on how the organization should spend its funds. I had to respect that. I wanted to honor her decisions. But my brain began making a lot of assumptions before even having the conversation with her! What if she had never heard of exit packages or didn't think it was the right thing to do? I was scared that she would not approve it and that it would affect our friendship.

I shared my hesitations with Sumaya in an email. My imposter syndrome wrote that email.

Her response was incredible:

> I've taken a few HR classes and I only found out about severance pay from my friend who works in HR.
>
> I don't think you should even hesitate to ask for this. It's totally normal to feel insecure to ask, talking about money can be uncomfortable especially because as women we're socialized to not ask for $$. But no one is more deserving of severance pay at RISE than you. If it was a man he would ask for it. I don't want you to regret not asking for this in a month or two. Money is a big stressor, inflation is going to continue...for how long no one knows. Severance pay will help as you transition out of RISE. You deserve to get severance pay.
>
> Think of a severance package as a negotiation. The employee (you)

and the employer (RISE and its ED) will enter the conversation open-minded. You know the organization's budget better than anyone. I personally don't think you should shortchange yourself. Allah ﷻ has always blessed RISE mashallah and I believe the money will come. Just like negotiating a raise.

Since I've emailed you [and the new ED] and I [am in charge of] HR, how can I support you? What do you need for me to get things moving forward? I'm more than willing to help. I just want to make sure if severance is what you want that you meet with [ED] while you are still employed at RISE, that is when you have more leverage to negotiate vs. if you have this conversation in a week or two. When senior level staff leave an agency and negotiate severance there are a variety of reasons a board/ED are inclined to grant it. a.) wants to maintain a good work relationship with former ED, b.) it's a gesture of goodwill and c.) recognition of an employee's service etc.

Don't forget to pray istikhara about this and let me know if there's anything I can do to help you navigate this process.

I prayed *istikhāra*,[73] which is this beautiful gift from Allah ﷻ for when it's hard to make decisions and you need guidance. From the Sincere Seeker's blog, "The term *istikhāra* means 'to look for Allah's guidance, wisdom, support, supervision, consultation, goodness, and blessings.'"[74] I wanted Allah ﷻ by my side as I was navigating this conversation. I wanted His supervision, and I wanted His blessings.

In my last week with the organization, the new executive director wanted to meet one last time to ask a few questions and get some

---

73   *Istikhāra* is a special prayer in Islam where you ask Allah ﷻ to help guide you in the decision you need to make.

74   The Sincere Seeker, "What Is Istikhara Prayer and How to Pray Istikhara?," *Medium* (blog), April 2, 2023, https://thesincereseeker.medium.com/what-is-istikhara-prayer-how-to-pray-istikhara-e73d4e1e6cdc.

technical assistance on a list of topics. She sent me an email with an agenda, and the last thing on that list was the severance package. I felt a wave of relief seeing this. While I had been planning to bring up the topic myself, framing it as a policy change rather than a personal request, I had been anxious about how to initiate the conversation. Seeing the severance package on her list of topics boosted my confidence. It confirmed that this was a legitimate organizational matter and paved the way for a more comfortable discussion about implementing a fair severance policy.

With butterflies in my stomach and *dua* on my tongue, I shared with her what had transpired, only to learn that she, too, had approached Sumaya to do some research after having had a conversation with the board. She was almost offended on my behalf that, as a founder, I would exit the organization with only five days of PTO. She told Sumaya, "Oh no, no, no. We are not letting her go with just that." She brought up how hard I worked to establish RISE for Muslim women and mentioned RISE's local and national impact as a collective safe space and agency that affirmed the plight and struggles of the modern Muslim woman, as well as the growing Muslim sisterhood that RISE was establishing across the nation. She used her favorite basketball analogy to describe the importance of preserving "the house that Nausheena built for Muslim women." The basketball analogy about building a house illustrates the importance of establishing a strong foundation before focusing on more advanced or specialized skills. RISE is that strong foundation. I was beyond honored and humbled. Of course, there were tears. Emotions were high. I won't say who cried. OK, it was both of us.

Without skipping a beat, RISE's new executive director confirmed that my severance package would provide a full fourteen weeks of pay. She said this was about justice and *ḥaqq*[75]—and I felt affirmed

---

75   *Ḥaqq* is the Arabic word for "truth." It can also be interpreted as right or reality.

and grateful. I told her this shouldn't be just for me and asked her to consider creating a general staff severance policy to reward people for working at and growing our organization. While severance packages often reward bad behavior when we fire people, I wanted to instead create a culture where a parting gift said "Thank you! We couldn't have gotten this far without you on the team."

I also wanted to offer severance packages to more than just top leadership through an equitable policy that included every level of employment. I also requested that RISE incorporate a sabbatical policy that would give staff a period of time off to rejuvenate, rest, and recover.

I had come full circle. As the founder of an organization that advocated for women's rights in the workplace, it would have been hypocritical not to advocate for myself. I never imagined this money coming to me. This was the *rizq* that Allah ﷻ had ordained for me. I had to put in effort in order for it to find its way to me, and Allah ﷻ ensured that it did. I am so grateful, alhamdulillah.[76]

Do You See a Theme Here?

At each moment of my financial journey, a woman supported me. It began with my mom. She showed me how to hustle, how to save, and how to give. Her support put me through college. My sisters at RISE—including board and staff members—supported me, affirmed me, validated me, and pushed me. If there is one thing you take from my story, remember that we as women need to support each other, and by doing that, we lift each other up. A rising tide lifts all boats.

---

[76] Alhamdulillah is an Arabic phrase that means "praise be to God." It can also be translated as "thank God" or "thanks be to the Lord."

This chapter covered many different inequities, and I hope that you find a role in disrupting them. It starts with you. You can make a difference.

Reflection Exercise

1. Of all the different inequities women can experience, which one(s) have you faced and how did you handle it/them?

2. What are some ways you can stop the perpetuation of these inequities?

3. Think about a time when you had to negotiate your starting pay, a promotion, or a raise. How did you approach the conversation? Would you approach it differently now?

Chapter 6

How Do You Define Wealth?

I've been thinking about this a lot. What makes someone feel wealthy? At what point did I feel wealthy? How do I know if someone else is wealthy?

When I began pondering this, I asked my husband his thoughts about wealth and assets. He shared a story with me about his Nani Ami, his maternal grandmother, who owned water buffaloes in India. She had inherited or acquired some money and decided to purchase the buffaloes. She milked them and sold the milk. Whatever money she earned from selling that milk she placed into a tin box. Her tin box was the equivalent of a piggy bank. For safety reasons—the threat of bandits or burglars—she couldn't leave the money lying around the house. There was no concept of taking the money to the bank and putting it into a savings account, so that tin box was buried in the ground somewhere in the backyard. Using today's terminology, the investment was the purchase of the livestock. The profits came from the milk sales.

What's interesting is that Nani Ami's husband, Nana Ba, had no idea about this tin box, where it was buried, or how much money was in it. It was her money. She wasn't hiding it from him. She just didn't have any need to tell him. She had agency over her money and her investments. I wondered if women in the past had more independence and control over their finances. I wondered if this was different for women in other countries. I wondered if immigration to another country would have impacted her agency.

The more I thought about the impact of immigration on Muslim women's financial acumen and wealth, the more I realized how difficult it must be to move to a new land, with new financial practices, laws, and regulations. Had Nani Ami immigrated to the United States, what would she have done with those water buffaloes? What livestock would she have had the ability to purchase here? How would she have managed a tax system that makes it very difficult to separate incomes? So many systemic barriers in our economy have slowed down our ability to earn, invest, and build generational wealth.

I share the story of Nani Ami because it helped me understand that what we consider an investment or how we describe wealth has changed over time. Wealth has been measured in diverse ways across different cultures and environments. What is the modern-day American rubric of measuring a person's wealth?

Around fifteen hundred years ago, at the time of the Prophet Muhammad ﷺ, one of the metrics that defined wealth in the Arabian Peninsula was the ownership of camels.[77] The size of the herd indicated an individual's wealth. Why camels? Camels provided multitudinal benefits. They were an integral part of the economy in desert communities, considering their ability to conserve water and travel in an extremely hot and arid environment. Arabs employed camels for personal transportation and commercial trade, using them to transport goods between cities and markets. Camels were also a source of food and even medicine. Finally, camel hides were a source of clothing, rugs, blankets, and home goods. Given that camels furnished the goods people both consumed and traded, it logically followed that camels symbolized wealth.

| ***An aside:*** Have you ever had a camel burger or drunk camel

---

[77] Narrated Abū Saʿīd: Allah's Apostle ﷺ said, "No zakat is due on property amounting to less than five *uqiyyas* [of silver], and no zakat is due on less than five camels, and there is no zakat on less than five *wasqs*." [A *wasq* equals sixty *ṣāʿas*, and 1 *ṣāʿa* equals 3 kilograms.] *Ṣaḥīḥ al-Bukhārī*, no. 487.

milk? I had a camel burger at Safari Express in Global Midtown Market in Minneapolis, and wow! It was so delicious! I have yet to try camel milk. I wonder if Caribou Coffee can offer to make my white chocolate mocha with camel milk? I don't see that happening in the near future, but maybe coffee shops in Saudi Arabia have this option.

My friend Sarah (a different Sarah—I know, I have a lot of friends named Sarah!) shared that a local Middle Eastern shop sells camel milk. It's $11.99 for a sixteen-ounce bottle! Her advice: "You have to try camel milk at least once, so it's totally worth it!"

Did you know there's a camel milk farm in Colorado? Road trip anyone? Well, if not a road trip, I learned that Holy Land, a local Minnesota grocer and restaurant, sells camel milk too. I'm about to explore making camel milk lattes at home!

Another sign of wealth in the Arab peninsula was having many children, specifically sons, who were expected to grow up and be another source of income by working, earning, and contributing to the household's income. Sons were the equivalent of a modern pension plan or 401(k). They were expected to take care of aging parents, financially and physically. Having many children was also a sign of prestige because it meant one was able to afford feeding, clothing, housing, and raising them.

It's different today. Growing up in India, my mom and aunts highly valued owning gold. At every wedding, aunties would expertly appraise the gold sets and bangles of other aunties and nieces from across the room. "Oh, is this set new?" "Didn't you wear this at so-and-so's something?" "Did your in-laws give this to you?" Wearing artificial jewelry was taboo—a catastrophic mistake of epic proportions. Even a sliver of gold was better than artificial jewelry. Married women had to wear gold bangles, at least one on each wrist. Wearing multiple pieces of gold jewelry was, and still is, the ultimate stamp of wealth—a visible measure of prosperity. Gold represented status and accomplishment. But in addition to its decorative and declarative aspects, that gold was a form of investment, providing financial stability and building generational wealth. Most families, especially the women, invested their savings into gold, which was then passed down to their daughters or given to their son's brides. My mom gave me a substantial amount of gold she had been accumulating for me since I was born. I see my mom's hard work and care when I look at the gold bangles she gifted me at my wedding—a physical reminder of her efforts and love.

Jumping across the pond, owning a house is the ultimate American dream and one of this culture's most important signs of wealth. Owning the land your house sits on is more than just owning the house. It is another form of investing and wealth building. Investopedia defines an asset as "a resource with economic value that an individual, corporation, or country owns or controls with the expectation that it will provide a future benefit."[78] The larger the house, the more value it has.

Owning property does not come easy, but it is a fundamental step in establishing generational wealth. The first generation purchases land and builds a house, eventually paying off the mortgage. If you pay off your mortgage and pass down the house to your children, you are giving a fully paid-off asset to the next generation. This is what's called generational wealth.[79] Wealth that grows and

---

[78] Adam Barone, "What Is an Asset? Definition, Types, and Examples," Investopedia, accessed September 4, 2023, https://www.investopedia.com/terms/a/asset.asp.

[79] Twin Cities Habitat for Humanity, "How to Build Generational Wealth Through Homeownership," October 17, 2022, https://www.tchabitat.org/blog/how_to_build_generational_wealth_through_homeownership.

How Do You Define Wealth?

helps support future generations creates the generational wealth advantage whereby the second generation now has the freedom to build off this asset and grow their own wealth. In time, the third generation inherits and continues to grow and build wealth. For example, Grandpa and Grandma built a home and paid off their mortgage. They owned the home fully. Mom and Dad inherit the home with no mortgage payments. With one less major expense to cover, Mom and Dad have additional money to save or invest. When it's your time, you inherit the house, plus any other investments your parents may bequeath to you. Now you have even more financial freedom to invest and grow your wealth. Imagine the benefits your future generations could reap when you make wise financial choices.

One way wealth might be assessed by Muslims in the US is by the ability to go to *'umra*, the lesser pilgrimage, or Hajj, the major pilgrimage. Hajj is an obligation only if you are able to afford it and you are free from other obligations. You cannot borrow money, like get a loan from a bank, to fulfill this responsibility. So not everyone is in a position to afford Hajj.

I was blessed to be able to fulfill my Hajj duty in 2003. At that time, the travel packages cost $3,000 per person. I thought $3,000 packages were so expensive. Twenty years later, Hajj packages have gotten more lavish and more expensive, ranging anywhere from $13,000 to $25,000 per person! A couple—husband and wife, mother and son, brother and sister—would need $30,000 to $50,000 saved up in order to complete their fifth pillar of Islam. *'Umra* packages are now the same price as my Hajj package was, varying from $3,000–$5,000 per person.[80]

I have been to *'umra* twice. Once with my husband and his parents in 1998 and then a second time in 2017 with my husband and both

---

[80] "Umrah 2023," Dar El Salam, accessed September 4, 2023, https://dstworldtravel.com/umrah2023/.

my kids. I wanted to take my daughter especially because she was about to graduate high school and enter college. What better way to mark the end of one chapter and the start of another than to visit Allah's House? Our family had to budget close to $12,000 to cover the costs of air travel and accommodations. We had to plan, create a savings strategy, and request time off, which came from our vacation time. And we made *dua* for the invitation. We would love to be invited back when our son graduates college inshallah, so our cycle of planning and budgeting has begun again. We are making *dua*. We are exploring different packages with different travel agencies. We know that prices will increase, so we are planning for that increase in our budget. The fun part we added to our strategy is that we are accumulating miles on our loyalty program to offset the airline tickets!

The ability to pay zakat is also an indicator of wealth. Muslims are required to donate or give 2.5% of their wealth to the poor and needy. Not 2.5% of their income, but of their savings. If someone gives $25,000 in zakat, it means they have one million dollars in excess wealth. And when they donate that amount, they know that that $25,000 actually *belongs* to those in need. Zakat is such a beautiful concept! Make *dua* for the millionaires and make *dua* for yourself to be so financially stable with excess wealth that you can write zakat checks for six figures. May we all be able to return this wealth to those in need. *Ameen!*

There are many other signs of material wealth, including family vacations, traveling abroad, watches, red-bottomed shoes, and name-brand clothes. There are a lot of material signs that can signify you have money. But does it really mean you're wealthy? Perhaps you bought a nice house, but you have a thirty-year mortgage loan. Technically, the bank owns the house. Or maybe you have a Prada bag, Louboutin pumps, and a Rolex watch—but nothing in your savings account or your investment account. Sure, you might be living a fun life, but you might just be a big spender who is deep in debt.

All of these examples speak of material wealth. But what about nonmaterial wealth?

Nonmaterial wealth consists of the intangible assets that contribute to our well-being and happiness. For me, I feel grateful and happy when my health is good. Positive, healthy relationships with my family bring me joy. My circle of friends—my chosen family—provide me tremendous amounts of happiness. Here are some more examples of nonmaterial wealth.

KNOWLEDGE AND EDUCATION

Knowledge is a valuable asset that can enrich our lives and help us make better decisions. Education is a means to acquire knowledge and skills, which can lead to personal growth, career success, and a deeper understanding of the world around us. I will forever be a student. I have two master's degrees. As I am writing this book, I am a doctoral candidate hoping to graduate in May 2026. I love to read and watch documentaries, and I have a voracious appetite for learning new things. I also love sharing that knowledge and education with others. People describe me as having "a wealth of knowledge" in leadership, nonprofit management, and philanthropy. And it is being economically stable that allows me to continue building this nonmaterial wealth. Because guess what? This nonmaterial wealth costs money. Tuition, books, seminars, and conferences all have a price tag, so we must plan our finances to be able to afford our pursuit of knowledge and education.

RELATIONSHIPS AND SOCIAL CONNECTIONS

Having strong relationships with my family, friends, and community members has provided me with emotional support, a sense of belonging, and opportunities for personal growth.

I describe myself as a network weaver, someone who can comfortably strike up conversations with strangers that often lead to long-term relationships. Then I connect those people to others in my network. Often called "social capital," this form of nonmaterial wealth sometimes also costs money. I work hard to weave new relationships and maintain the meaningful ones I have already nurtured. Sometimes this means meeting for coffee or dinner, celebrating birthdays and anniversaries, and buying gifts. All of these things cost money. Having economic stability makes space in my budget for building this nonmaterial source of wealth.

HEALTH AND WELL-BEING

Good health is essential to our overall well-being, allowing us to pursue our goals and enjoy life to the fullest. Physical fitness, mental health, and spiritual growth are all important components of our well-being. When you hit your forties, you will soon feel the aches and pains of aging. Well, at least I did, and I was not having it! I joined the gym, changed my diet, and kept up with my annual physicals. My gym membership, healthy foods, and doctors' appointments all cost money. My budget and finances include these things.

TIME

Time is a precious resource that, once spent, we can never get back. Having the freedom to choose how we spend our time, whether it is pursuing our passions, spending time with loved ones, or simply enjoying leisure activities, is a form of nonmaterial wealth. You know when I felt the most time-rich? When I left social media! That's right. I slowly weaned myself off. (Don't cold turkey it!) Breaking habits needs to be a slow and steady process. So first I said goodbye to Facebook. That one was actually easy; I had thousands of followers on that platform and I didn't even know who most of them were. A year later, I left Instagram. I'll admit that one was a little harder; I kept up with a lot of family from all around the world there, so I might clean up my follower list and go back on. Thanks to Elon Musk, leaving Twitter behind was easy. I never really got into Snapchat, and I only use TikTok when I travel. LinkedIn is what I use for business purposes, so I do still post there. But wow, I feel like a gazillionaire with time now! Your time has value. When I left social media, it created time for me to reach my deadlines and achieve my goals.

PERSONAL VALUES AND BELIEFS

Our values and beliefs shape our worldview and guide our decisions. Having strong personal values and beliefs can provide a sense of purpose and direction in life. When I first figured out what my purpose in life was, it changed everything for me. I changed career paths, industries, life goals, spending habits, volunteer work, how I interacted with people, and the list goes on. My purpose is to serve Allah, and I do that by serving humanity. Incorporating my values into my career created more blessings in my earnings, and that is a form of nonmaterial wealth.

SPIRITUAL WEALTH

This is the most important form of nonmaterial wealth for me because it's about the inner resources that contribute to my spiritual growth and well-being. Here is my list of spiritual wealth:

Inner peace. A sense of inner calm and peace, which can be cultivated through practices such as salah,[81] *dua, dhikr,*[82] and *ṣadaqa*. I recognize that true inner peace is a gift from Allah, and I'm grateful for the moments when He grants me this tranquility.

Connection to Allah. I work on strengthening this connection

---

81   Salah is the Arabic term for the obligatory ritual prayer that Muslims perform five times a day. It is one of the five pillars of Islam.

82   *Dhikr* (literally, "remembrance") is a form of Islamic worship in which phrases or prayers are repeatedly recited for the purpose of remembering God.

daily through prayer, reflection, and studying the Quran. I'm deeply thankful when Allah ﷻ opens my heart to feel His presence, providing me with guidance, purpose, and meaning in life.

Gratitude. I consciously practice appreciation for the blessings Allah ﷻ has given me. This involves daily reflection and acknowledging His favors, which helps foster a positive outlook and a sense of abundance.

Compassion. I try to nurture empathy for others by volunteering and engaging with my community. I'm grateful when Allah ﷻ softens my heart, allowing me to develop deeper relationships and a sense of connection with others.

Forgiveness. A willingness to let go of grudges and resentments and to forgive ourselves and others for past mistakes creates a serenity that can lead to healing and a sense of emotional freedom. For me this also includes asking for forgiveness and saying I'm sorry when I've wronged someone and asking Allah ﷻ for forgiveness and His mercy.

Service. A willingness to help others and contribute to the greater good can provide a sense of purpose and fulfillment. This is why I love volunteering on boards, at my masjid, at local food shelves, and at different nonprofit events.

This is how I define spiritual wealth, and it has helped me find meaning and purpose in life. I've come to understand that spiritual wealth is not a constant state, but a continuous journey of growth and connection with Allah. When I was struggling with my spirituality, I saw it reflected in my spending habits; I indulged in unnecessary expenses and frivolous purchases. As my relationship with Allah ﷻ grew and deepened, I made better financial decisions. I became more purposeful with how I was earning and spending.

Ask yourself what it means to be rich. Are you trying to be money-rich or life-rich? Reflect on what life-rich means to you. Reflect on what afterlife-rich means to you. I remember somebody telling me that when you donate to a worthy cause, all you're doing is transferring money from your bank account in this world to your savings account in the next life.

My point is that wealth is not just measured in dollars. I want you to remember that you should be grateful for all of the blessings that Allah ﷻ has bestowed upon you. Cultivate a mindset of gratitude—you are wealthier than you think. You are wealthier than how others perceive you. Whatever you are blessed with, show gratitude for that.

Reflection Exercise: Do You Feel Wealthy?

1. What are some material things that make you feel financially stable?

2. What are some nonmaterial ways in which you feel rich?

3. What makes you feel wealthy in this life?

4. What do you think when you hear afterlife-rich? How are you building provisions for your *akhira*? [83]

---

83 *Akhira* is the Arabic word that refers to the afterlife.

Chapter 7

Shifting Mindsets: You Are Wealthier than You Think

THE *RIZQ* FACTOR

Yes, this is a play on *The Latte Factor* book title. Bach and Mann teach us that the small amounts of money we spend here and there on lattes and other things, if invested, can build wealth in the long term. They don't advocate giving up lattes or other small expenses but remind us that building wealth can happen with small amounts of money. In Arabic, the word *rizq* means provision or sustenance provided by Allah. Wealth is a form of *rizq*, but *rizq* is not limited to wealth. *Rizq* is all-encompassing and includes anything that brings goodness to us, like family ties, spirituality, and intellect.

Rizq is from Allah; one of the beautiful names of Allah ﷻ is al-Razzāq, the Provider, the Caretaker, the Supplier, the Bestower of sustenance. The One who creates all means of nourishment and subsistence. The One who provides everything that is needed. I listened to Dr. Jinan Yousef on the podcast DoubleTake, a Yaqeen Podcast,[84] and she elaborated on the meaning of this beautiful name of Allah, emphasizing that *rizq* should not be limited to wealth or food but "everything that a person can benefit from."

Dr. Yousef also shares the following hadith: It was narrated from Jābir ibn 'Abdullāh ﷺ that the Messenger of Allah ﷺ said:

---

84   Jinan Yousef and Mohamad Zaoud, "Trusting God, The Provider with Dr. Jinan Yousef," DoubleTake Podcast, February 8, 2023, https://yaqeeninstitute.org/jinan-yousef/trusting-god-the-provider-with-dr-jinan-yousef-doubletake-podcast.

> Oh people, fear Allah ﷻ and be moderate in seeking a living, for no soul will die until it has received all its provision, even if it is slow in coming. So fear Allah ﷻ and be moderate in seeking provision; take that which is permissible and leave that which is forbidden.[85]

Before you were born, the amount of *rizq* that you will receive in this lifetime was decreed. However, you must continue to strive and make an effort to receive these provisions from Allah. Work hard in permissible ways and make *dua* for Allah ﷻ to increase these blessings.

In the Quran, Sūrat al-Baqara verse 268, Allah ﷻ warns us that Shaytan[86] will promise us poverty if we are giving in charity:

الشَّيْطَانُ يَعِدُكُمُ الْفَقْرَ وَيَأْمُرُكُم بِالْفَحْشَاءِ وَاللَّهُ يَعِدُكُم مَّغْفِرَةً مِّنْهُ وَفَضْلاً وَاللَّهُ وَاسِعٌ عَلِيمٌ ۝

> The Devil threatens you with [the prospect of] poverty and bids you to the shameful deed [of stinginess], while Allah promises you forgiveness and [great] bounties from Him. And Allah is All-Bountiful, All-Knowing.
>
> **Quran 2:268**

I mention this verse now because increasing your wealth has implications for your charitable giving, including zakat and *ṣadaqa*. There is a very strong positive connection between charity and wealth. Don't let Shaytan scare you into believing that if you give in charity, you won't have money for yourself.

---

85 *Sunan Ibn Māja*, no. 2144.

86 In Islam, Shaytan is the devil. His name was Iblīs, and he was cast out of Heaven because he refused to obey Allah's command to bow down to Adam (*'alayhi al-salām*).

If your *rizq* is predetermined, then you're probably wondering, "How do I increase my *rizq*?" In her podcast, Dr. Yousef tells us that there are two types of *rizq*. The first is the kind that Allah ﷻ gives to us without us having to make any effort. I think about how lucky I am to have been born in a place where the sun shines, the grass is green, the air is clean to breathe, and I have access to fresh water. These provisions and blessings, provided by Allah, are given to me without me putting in any effort. However, there is a second category of *rizq* that is conditional. It is based on the effort we put into attaining that *rizq*. Dr. Yousef states, "My responsibilities are *sa'i*,[87] because Allah ﷻ is not going to ask me about the outcome. He's going to ask me about my effort, right?" Sure, wealth is the outcome. But the effort in striving for that wealth is what Allah ﷻ will look at. Did you work hard? Were your efforts within the bounds of what is permissible and halal? Did you make *dua* for Allah ﷻ to increase your *rizq* for you? These are the conditions needed. Allah ﷻ says this to us in the Quran.

وَلَوْ أَنَّ أَهْلَ ٱلْقُرَىٰٓ ءَامَنُوا۟ وَٱتَّقَوْا۟ لَفَتَحْنَا عَلَيْهِم بَرَكَٰتٍ مِّنَ ٱلسَّمَآءِ وَٱلْأَرْضِ ۝

> Had the people of those societies been faithful and mindful [of Allah], We would have overwhelmed them with blessings from heaven and earth.
>
> **Quran 7:96**

And you know what else was mind-blowing for me? Dr. Anse Tamara Gray, a.k.a. Anse Tamara, explained that you may be making *dua* for increasing your *rizq* in one area of your life, but Allah ﷻ expands your *rizq* in another area. I thought about this. One year, I was making so much *dua* for Allah ﷻ to increase my

---

87   Originally the word *sa'i* comes from the Arabic word *sa'ā*, which linguistically means "to pursue" or "to walk" or "to strive."

rizq in my consulting business. That year, I had a couple of health scares, which alhamdulillah, I have overcome and healed from. But I can see that the *rizq* I requested in the form of wealth manifested as *rizq* for my health, because Allah knew I needed that so greatly. Subhanallah![88]

I recently listened to a lecture by renowned scholar Mufti Menk,[89] who spoke about verses 10–14 of Sūrat Nūḥ in the Quran:

$$\text{فَقُلْتُ اسْتَغْفِرُوا رَبَّكُمْ إِنَّهُ كَانَ غَفَّارًا ۝ يُرْسِلِ السَّمَاءَ عَلَيْكُم مِّدْرَارًا ۝ وَيُمْدِدْكُم بِأَمْوَالٍ وَبَنِينَ وَيَجْعَل لَّكُمْ جَنَّاتٍ وَيَجْعَل لَّكُمْ أَنْهَارًا ۝ مَّا لَكُمْ لَا تَرْجُونَ لِلَّهِ وَقَارًا ۝ وَقَدْ خَلَقَكُمْ أَطْوَارًا ۝}$$

> Saying "Seek your Lord's forgiveness, [for] He is truly Most Forgiving. He will shower you with abundant rain, supply you with wealth and children, and give you gardens as well as rivers. What is the matter with you that you are not in awe of the Majesty of Allah, when He truly created you in stages [of development]?
>
> **Quran 71:10–14**

This *sūra* is about Prophet Nūḥ's (Noah's) efforts to convey the message of worshiping only Allah, of having a conscious awareness of Allah, and of following his own prophetic teachings. He tried everything to bring his nation to the right path. The people were instructed to repent, ask for forgiveness, and make *dua* in order to receive Allah's blessing. And these instructions are for us as well. For our *baraka*, or blessings, to increase in our wealth, we need to leave sins behind, ask for forgiveness, and perform good deeds. Have you ever noticed that when you do something good,

---

[88] Subhanallah is an Arabic phrase meaning "glory be to Allah"; it may be repeated as part of the Islamic practice of *dhikr*.

[89] Mufti Menk, "Sūra Nuh Part One," Muslim Central, May 8, 2016, https://muslimcentral.com/mufti-menk-sūra-nuh-part-one/.

something good happens to you later?

THE GARDENER

Sheikh Omar Suleiman in his Quran Weekly lessons[90] shared a hadith narrated by Abū Hurayra ﷺ[91] in *Ṣaḥīḥ Muslim*. The Prophet Muhammad ﷺ tells us a story about a man who sees a rain cloud that was commanded to rain on a certain person's garden. So he follows the cloud and sees that the owner of this garden is collecting rainwater while doing other gardening chores. The man wonders why this cloud was commanded to rain on this particular person's garden, so he asks the gardener, and the gardener responds by saying, "Well, what I do with my garden's harvest is distribute one-third of it to charity, feed my family with another third, and put the final third of it back into the garden."

Putting one-third back into the garden is another way of saying, "I reinvest my earnings back into the principal." Isn't it exciting and affirming to learn that Allah ﷻ reminds us to invest and reinvest in order for our wealth to grow? Of course nothing comes to us except by the decree of Allah. That cloud was commanded by Allah ﷻ to rain specifically on this person's garden. But it was the gardener's generous charitable giving (and his responsible reinvestment) that continued to grow his wealth. Remember, the purpose of having financial stability is not only to have all your needs fulfilled but also to create a pathway to giving charity and earning Allah's blessing. You are part of the Islamic economy, taking care of those who are less fortunate. So if you want to increase your wealth, give charity. Whenever something good happens to you, give charity. When something tragic is happening or you are being tested, give

---

90 Omar Suleiman, "Maximize Your Wealth – Omar Suleiman – Quran Weekly," Quran Weekly, posted August 8, 2014, YouTube, https://www.youtube.com/watch?v=yAPoLDfiRBs.

91 ﷺ *(raḍī Allāhu 'anhu)* is an Arabic phrase that means "May Allah be pleased with him." It is mentioned after the name of a companion of the Prophet ﷺ out of respect.

charity. Charity never diminishes your wealth. It purifies it, which multiplies it in unimaginable ways.

> مَّن ذَا ٱلَّذِى يُقْرِضُ ٱللَّهَ قَرْضًا حَسَنًا فَيُضَٰعِفَهُۥ لَهُۥٓ أَضْعَافًا كَثِيرَةً ۚ وَٱللَّهُ يَقْبِضُ وَيَبْصُۜطُ وَإِلَيْهِ تُرْجَعُونَ ﴿٢٤٥﴾

> Who will lend to Allah a good loan which Allah will multiply many times over? It is Allah [alone] who decreases and increases [wealth]. And to Him you will [all] be returned.
>
> Quran 2:245

During a Sunday *ḥalaqa*[92] at Rabata Cultural Center, Anse Tamara introduced us to *ḥaḍrat* Rabia al-Adawiyya and her experience with charitable giving. I think it's perfect to share the story here as it proves that giving charity never diminishes your wealth.

Rabia[93] was hosting a few pious people when someone approached her door requesting food. She had two loaves of bread, and instead of serving her guests, she fed the needy person. Soon after, a young girl came to her home with eighteen loaves of bread and stated, "The lady of my house has sent these." Rabia counted the loaves and refused acceptance, saying this must be a mistake. These are not for me. The girl returned to her mistress and conveyed what had occurred. Her mistress added two more loaves and sent them back to Rabia, who then accepted. Why did this happen? Rabia knew that Allah ﷻ rewards charitable giving tenfold. If she gave two loaves of bread, then Allah ﷻ would reward her with twenty. When only eighteen came to her, she knew that those eighteen

---

92 *Ḥalaqa*, which comes from the Arabic word for "circle" or "ring," is an Islamic tradition of religious gatherings or study circles for learning about Islam and the Quran.

93 Younus Y. Mirza, "The Deputy of Maryam – The Mystic Rābi'a al-'Adawiyya in Light of the Quranic Mary," *Maydan* (blog), August 15, 2023, https://themaydan.com/2023/08/the-deputy-of-maryam-the-mystic-rabia-al-adawiyya-in-light-of-the-quranic-mary/.

were not meant for her. When twenty came, she knew those were meant for her. She had amazing trust in Allah.

The Prophet ﷺ said, "Tie your camel and place your trust in Allah."[94] We still have to do the work, but the results come from Allah.

THE SCARCITY MINDSET

A scarcity mindset is a way of thinking that is characterized by a sense of lack or limitation. People with a scarcity mindset believe that resources such as money, time, and opportunities are limited and that there is not enough to go around. They often feel as if they are competing with others for these resources and that their success is dependent on their ability to outperform others. Dr. Tamara Gray's *Joy Jots: Exercises for a Happy Heart* has a chapter called, "There Is Enough." It's a beautiful story about hunger, a small bowl of milk, and sharing it with others. Read it and reflect upon it.

Sometimes, more money doesn't mean you're rich. When your income increases, so do your expenses. Think about it. When my husband and I both had full-time jobs, we paid off my student loans first. Then we moved out of our apartment and bought our first townhouse. A new house that needed new furniture and decor. We sold my car and bought a brand-new one! Then I went back to school for an MBA. As our income increased, so did our expenses, and consequently, our debt. We now had a mortgage and a car payment. As you grow your wealth, you may find that having more money doesn't necessarily translate into the financial surplus that you need to live a normal life. The more you make, the more you spend, the more you feel like you still don't have enough. So what is enough?

---

94   *Sunan al-Tirmidhi*, no. 2517.

Individuals with a scarcity mindset tend to focus on what they don't have rather than what they do have. They may be more likely to feel anxious or worried about the future, and they may struggle to take risks or pursue opportunities because of a fear of scarcity.

People with a scarcity mindset may worry about running out of money, time, or other resources. The scarcity mindset focuses on competition. Scarcity also evokes a sense of inadequacy. One may feel like they are not good enough or that they don't have the skills or resources to succeed. This may then make them unwilling to take risks or pursue opportunities because they fear failure or the possibility of not having enough resources to fall back on.

A scarcity mindset can be limiting and can prevent individuals from reaching their full potential. So how do we flip that? By adopting an abundance mindset. An abundance mindset shifts your focus to what you have and what you can create. It opens you up to new opportunities and possibilities.

In many societies, including the United States, consumerism and capitalism drive the economy. The economic system in these countries is structured around the idea of growth and expansion, with the goal of increasing profits and accumulating wealth. While this system can foster innovation and improve living standards, it can also lead to excessive materialism if not approached mindfully. There's a delicate balance between healthy financial progress—such as moving from renting to homeownership or acquiring necessary transportation—and falling into a cycle of endless consumption. The challenge lies in distinguishing between genuine needs and wants that improve our quality of life, and the pursuit of material possessions solely for the sake of having more. When we lose sight of this distinction, we risk getting trapped in a continuous cycle of desiring and acquiring, always seeking the next level of material wealth without finding true satisfaction. The key is to approach financial growth with intention, aligning our spending with our values and long-term well-being, rather than being driven by societal pressures or short-term desires.

The constant drive for more that capitalism often fosters can lead to a scarcity mindset, but the issue is even more complex. This mindset is rooted in the belief that there will never be enough—enough money, resources, or opportunities. Capitalism, while driving innovation and growth, can inadvertently reinforce this mentality by promoting constant competition for resources and wealth accumulation. This not only leads to a fear of scarcity but can also fuel excessive consumerism as we attempt to fill a perceived void with material possessions.

Consumerism, in turn, feeds back into the scarcity mindset. As we acquire more, we often find ourselves wanting even more, creating a cycle of perpetual dissatisfaction. This cycle can lead us to prioritize self-interest over communal well-being, as we fear there won't be enough to go around if we don't secure our own share first.

However, as Muslims, we have a powerful antidote to this mindset in the concept of divine *rizq*. When we truly embrace the belief that Allah ﷻ is the ultimate provider and that our sustenance is decreed, we can begin to break free from the grip of scarcity thinking. This doesn't mean we stop striving or working hard, but rather that we approach our efforts with a sense of trust and contentment.

By understanding that our true wealth lies not in material accumulation but in our relationship with Allah ﷻ and our community, we can resist the pull of excessive consumerism. This shift in perspective allows us to find a balance between meeting our needs, enjoying Allah's blessings, and contributing to the well-being of others. It encourages us to view resources as abundant rather than scarce, fostering generosity and cooperation instead of competition and hoarding.

It is common for immigrant parents to believe that their children can only achieve status and financial stability if they become doctors or engineers. Many of us who are children of immigrant parents object to that pressure and have started to move away from these careers, but there are still a lot of us choosing professions based on pay. Unfortunately, pursuing these higher earnings can cause people to gravitate toward materialism and consumerism and end up not doing enough for their communities. Set your intention that when you become a millionaire, you will increase your generosity and be responsible in your spending, just like the man whose garden was visited by Allah's special rain cloud.

To overcome the scarcity mindset, we need to reframe our approach to both earning and spending money. Our financial activities should not be about chasing the *dunyā*, but rather about aligning our actions with our values and serving a higher purpose. This involves a balanced approach to both earning and controlling our *nafs*.[95]

In Islam, the *nafs* is an important concept that deals with the innermost aspect of the human being and her relationship with God. In the Quran, we learn that the nafs is considered to have three levels or stages:

Nafs al-ammāra. The commanding self, which is inclined toward evil and desires.

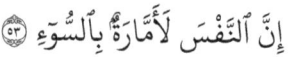

For indeed the soul is ever inclined to evil.
Quran 12:53

---

95 *Nafs* is an Arabic word literally meaning "self;" it has also been translated as "psyche" or "ego."

Nafs al-lawwāma. The self-accusing self, which is aware of its mistakes and seeks to correct them.

$$\text{وَلَآ أُقْسِمُ بِٱلنَّفْسِ ٱللَّوَّامَةِ ۝}$$

And I do swear by the self-reproaching soul!

Quran 75:2

Nafs al-muṭma'inna. The self at peace, which is content and satisfied with the will of God.

$$\text{يَـٰٓأَيَّتُهَا ٱلنَّفْسُ ٱلْمُطْمَئِنَّةُ ۝}$$

Allah will say to the righteous, "Oh tranquil soul!"

Quran 89:27

When faced with a purchasing decision, controlling our *nafs* becomes particularly crucial. We should ask ourselves whether we really need this item and how it aligns with our values and goals. It's important to remember our priorities, consult our budget, and think before we act. This mindful approach to spending is a form of striving against our impulses.

By being thoughtful in both our earning and spending, we can work toward increasing our *rizq* in its broadest sense—not only material wealth but also blessings, contentment, and spirituality. This balanced approach helps us appreciate what we have, use our resources wisely, and focus on our ultimate goal of pleasing Allah.

When we control our *nafs*, we can find a balance between *deen* and *dunyā*. Controlling the *nafs* can also have a positive impact on our finances, as it can help us to develop better financial habits and achieve financial balance. By controlling our *nafs*, we can avoid excessive spending and extravagance, which can lead to financial imbalances and debt. This can help us live within our means and avoid financial stress. This effort to align our financial behavior with our Islamic values can translate into an increase in all forms of *rizq*, fostering a sense of abundance rather than scarcity.

Controlling our *nafs* can also help us avoid excessive greed and materialism, which can lead to a constant desire for more money and possessions. By being content with what we have and avoiding excessive desires, we can achieve a more balanced and sustainable financial life.

A disciplined *nafs* gives freely. Be generous with your wealth, your time, and your talent. Help those in need—not just by your charitable giving, but also by volunteering your time and talents. This will also increase your sense of gratitude and contentment.

Finally, by controlling the *nafs*, we can avoid impulsive and risky investments that can lead to financial losses. Instead, we can make wise, calculated investments that are in line with our financial goals and values.

The ultimate goal of a Muslim is to purify her *nafs* and reach the stage of *nafs al-muṭma'inna*, which is the highest level of spiritual attainment. This can be achieved through aligning all our actions with our values in addition to various spiritual practices such as praying, fasting, giving charity, and following the teachings of the Quran and the Prophet Muhammad ﷺ.

WHAT IS THE ABUNDANCE MINDSET?

An abundance mindset is a way of thinking that focuses on the positive aspects of life and the belief that there is enough of everything to go around. It is a mindset that sees opportunities instead of obstacles and approaches life with a sense of gratitude

Shifting Mindsets: You Are Wealthier than You Think

and optimism.

People with an abundance mindset believe that there are always enough resources, such as wealth, love, and opportunities, to achieve their goals and desires. They see the world as a place of abundance, where there is always enough to share with others, and they believe that success and happiness are not limited to a select few, but are available to everyone.

One characteristic of an abundance mindset is gratitude. People with an abundance mindset appreciate the good things in life and focus on what they have rather than what they lack. I recently finished a book called *7 Daily Rituals for Gratitude* by Federica Avanzi. (If you haven't figured it out yet, I love reading. Find me on Goodreads, but don't ask me to join your book club.) This book is a very practical guide to appreciating every day to its fullest and being mindful in every action. It is a great starting point for a path to well-being and spiritual growth.

One of the ideas in the book is called Green Time. It begins with the idea that we live in a consumer society. When something breaks, we don't try to repair it anymore. We simply replace it. We are constantly buying new things.

In addition to consuming, we are also very wasteful. Did you know that we waste one-third of the food we buy? We order too much at the restaurant. We buy ingredients in bulk and then toss them when we don't use them before they expire. And we just don't need as much as we buy. Aren't we supposed to fill our bellies only one-third of the way with food anyway?[96] And we are constantly buying *things* as well—accumulating them in our houses and looking like hoarders. Green Time supports the idea of living a minimalist

---

96 Al-Miqdām ibn Ma'dīkarib said: "I heard the Messenger of Allah ﷺ say: A human being fills no worse vessel than his stomach. It is sufficient for a human being to eat a few mouthfuls to keep his spine straight. But if he must [fill it], then one-third for food, one-third for drink, and one-third for air." *Sunan Ibn Māja*, no. 3349.

lifestyle and controlling our *nafs*. It advocates living intentionally with just the things we need and being content with them.[97] Doesn't it sound liberating?

The abundance mindset reinforces a positive attitude. It creates a positive outlook on life and allows you to see challenges as opportunities for growth. You focus on finding solutions rather than dwelling on problems, and are not afraid to take risks. You are willing to share your resources with others and believe that helping others will benefit both you and them. It increases your generosity. The abundance mindset also guides you to open up to new ideas and not be limited by conventional thinking. Inhabiting this brain space helps you explore new avenues of creativity and ways of solving problems.

TIPS FOR DEVELOPING AN ABUNDANCE MINDSET

Developing an abundance mindset when it comes to money and material possessions can be challenging, especially if you have experienced scarcity or financial difficulties in the past. Here are some ways to get started.

Focus on abundance, not scarcity. Instead of thinking about what you lack, focus on what you have and what you can create.

Be grateful for what you have. When you focus on abundance, you can begin to practice gratitude and appreciation. Take time each day to express gratitude for the things Allah ﷻ has blessed you with, no matter how small they may seem. Appreciating what you have can help you feel more content and less focused on what you don't have.

---

97 Federica Avanzi and Simone Masserini, *7 Daily Rituals for Gratitude* (VMB Publishers, 2021).

$$\text{وَمَا كَانَ لِنَفْسٍ أَن تَمُوتَ إِلَّا بِإِذْنِ ٱللَّهِ كِتَٰبًا مُّؤَجَّلًا ۗ وَمَن يُرِدْ ثَوَابَ ٱلدُّنْيَا نُؤْتِهِۦ مِنْهَا وَمَن يُرِدْ ثَوَابَ ٱلْءَاخِرَةِ نُؤْتِهِۦ مِنْهَا ۚ وَسَنَجْزِى ٱلشَّٰكِرِينَ ۝}$$

> No soul can ever die without Allah's Will at the destined time. Those who desire worldly gain, We will let them have it, and those who desire heavenly reward, We will grant it to them. And We will reward those who are grateful.
>
> Quran 3:145

Practice mindfulness. Pay attention to your thoughts and feelings around money and material possessions. Notice any negative patterns or beliefs you may have and challenge them with positive affirmations. One of the best ways for me to practice mindfulness is through mindful actions, especially *dhikr*.

$$\text{ٱلَّذِينَ ءَامَنُوا۟ وَتَطْمَئِنُّ قُلُوبُهُم بِذِكْرِ ٱللَّهِ ۗ أَلَا بِذِكْرِ ٱللَّهِ تَطْمَئِنُّ ٱلْقُلُوبُ ۝}$$

> Those who believe and whose hearts find comfort in the remembrance of Allah. Surely in the remembrance of Allah do hearts find comfort.
>
> Quran 13:28

Mindful actions create positive change. During my sabbatical, I made a conscious decision to avoid purchasing new clothes because I had enough. My closet was abundant! I had clothes for every occasion: American clothes, Indian clothes, summer clothes, winter clothes, travel clothes, workout clothes, pajamas, t-shirts, hijabs, abayas, and prayer clothes! As I'm writing this book, it's been eight months since I purchased anything new (except for *wuḍū*[98] socks). Alhamdulillah, my credit card bill is lower, I have more money to spend on travel and experiences, and my closet is lean and organized. No one notices if I wear the same black hijab the next time they see me.

My next mindfulness change was in the book department. I love books, but I really have a problem with buying them and not reading them! My personal library, which is organized by the ROYGBIV color system,[99] has over five hundred books. I count forty-nine unread, meaning 10% of the books I spent money on have not been read. My annual Goodreads Challenge is only thirty books! So I have made a conscious, mindful decision not to purchase more books until I finish this stack of unread ones. After that, I plan to find alternate sources for obtaining books—book exchanges, free libraries, or requesting books as gifts. Once I achieve this goal, then I can purchase books again, because realistically...What? No, I didn't just add two books to my cart. OK, maybe I did. Baby steps, y'all. I promise I'll read them.

Be generous. Giving to others can help you feel more abundant and grateful for what you have. Consider donating money or volunteering your time to a cause you care about. In the Quran, we are reminded:

ٱلَّذِينَ يُنفِقُونَ أَمْوَٰلَهُمْ فِى سَبِيلِ ٱللَّهِ ثُمَّ لَا يُتْبِعُونَ مَآ أَنفَقُوا۟ مَنًّا وَلَآ أَذًى لَّهُمْ أَجْرُهُمْ عِندَ رَبِّهِمْ وَلَا خَوْفٌ عَلَيْهِمْ وَلَا هُمْ يَحْزَنُونَ ۝

Those who spend their wealth in the cause of Allah and do not follow their charity with reminders of their generosity or hurtful

---

98   *Wuḍū'* is an Islamic ritual of ablution, or cleansing the body, that is an important part of ritual purity before worship. It involves washing the hands, mouth, nose, face, hair, ears, and feet.

99   ROYGBIV is an acronym for the sequence of hues commonly described as making up a rainbow: red, orange, yellow, green, blue, indigo, and violet.

words—they will get their reward from their Lord, and there will be no fear for them, nor will they grieve.

Quran 2:262

Focus on creating value. Instead of focusing on how much money you can make, focus on creating value for others. When you create value, the money will follow. I spent twelve years in corporate roles and eleven years in nonprofit roles, doing my best to improve the lives of others. And I've learned that when you do that, opportunities create themselves. People come to me now for advice, for assistance, or to invite me to speak to their communities about my work. There is value in my journey and experience that I am able to share. And it has translated into monetary rewards. I am paid honoraria for my speaking engagements, am hired to consult on projects, and am compensated for my coaching services. My business, nonprofit, and philanthropic knowledge holds value and people recognize that.

Visualize *baraka* and seek Allah's blessings. Imagine yourself living a life filled with *baraka* and financial freedom, always remembering that true abundance comes from Allah. Make *dua* regularly, asking Allah ﷻ to grant you halal *rizq* and the wisdom to use it wisely. Set your *niyya* to use your wealth in ways that please Allah ﷻ and benefit the *ummah*. Incorporate sunna practices into your daily life, such as giving *ṣadaqa*, even if it's a small amount, as our beloved Prophet ﷺ said:

Save yourself from Hellfire even by giving half a date in charity.[100]

Create a vision board that reflects not just material goals, but also spiritual aspirations. Include images or quotes that remind you of acts of *ʿibāda*, such as Hajj or prayer. What *duas* are on that board? Add spiritual goals like memorizing Quran or teaching Islamic

---

100 *Ṣaḥīḥ al-Bukhārī*, no. 1417.

knowledge. What can you add to your board that represents using your wealth for the sake of Allah? Remember, true abundance in this life and the next comes from aligning your financial goals with your spiritual journey. Make *istikhāra* (the prayer for guidance) before making significant financial decisions and trust in Allah's plan for you.

Learn about personal finance. That's what this book is for! Educate yourself about personal finance and money management. When you feel confident and in control of your finances, you are more likely to feel abundant and secure. The first time I calculated my zakat, I used a spreadsheet to understand my wealth. Looking back at that first spreadsheet, there has been growth, and that helps me recognize my financial abundance and security. Alhamdulillah!

Remember that developing an abundance mindset takes time and practice. Be patient with yourself and celebrate small successes along the way. By adopting an abundance mindset, you can create a more positive relationship with money and material possessions and live a more fulfilling life.

THE MINIMALIST LIFESTYLE

A minimalist lifestyle means being very intentional about what you buy and own. You focus on things that you absolutely need, reducing what you have and simplifying your life. Although not perfect, there are some aspects of living a minimalist lifestyle that I find beneficial. What I took away from this philosophy that supports my abundance mindset was controlling my *nafs* regarding materialism.

A focus on what's important. Minimalism involves simplifying your life by removing excess possessions, activities, and commitments. This can help you focus on what's truly important to you, such as relationships, personal growth, spirituality, and

Shifting Mindsets: You Are Wealthier than You Think

experiences. By focusing on what brings you joy and fulfillment, you can cultivate a sense of abundance and contentment in your life. You don't need to have everything to be content, you just need enough of what's truly important to you.

Appreciation for what you choose to retain. When you live a minimalist lifestyle, you learn to appreciate and value the possessions you have. You become more mindful of your purchases and begin to prioritize quality over quantity. This can help you feel more grateful for what you have, rather than constantly striving for more. It might seem like I am being repetitive, but gratitude is so important to practice. Allah ﷻ says in the Quran:

وَإِذْ تَأَذَّنَ رَبُّكُمْ لَئِن شَكَرْتُمْ لَأَزِيدَنَّكُمْ ۖ وَلَئِن كَفَرْتُمْ إِنَّ عَذَابِي لَشَدِيدٌ ۝

And [remember] when your Lord proclaimed, "If you are grateful, I will certainly give you more. But if you are ungrateful, surely My punishment is severe."

Quran 14:7

Reduced financial stress. By living with less, you can reduce your expenses and financial obligations. This can lead to a sense of financial security and freedom, which can support an abundance mindset. When you're not constantly worried about money, you can focus on other areas of your life that bring you joy and fulfillment.

Environmental consciousness. Minimalism is often associated with a commitment to environmental sustainability. By reducing your consumption and living more simply, you can contribute to a healthier planet and a sense of interconnectedness with the natural world. Think about the amount of packaging involved in each purchase and how reducing this alone can lead to less waste and a smaller environmental footprint.

There are parts of the minimalist lifestyle that can support an abundance mindset by allowing you to focus on what's truly important, to appreciate what you have, to reduce financial stress, and to contribute to a greater sense of purpose and interconnectedness.

Living the minimalist lifestyle might seem like the latest trend, but it really reminded me of the things the Prophet Muhammad ﷺ taught us. He emphasized the importance of moderation, avoided excess, and encouraged his followers to do the same.

The Prophet Muhammad ﷺ wore simple clothing made from natural materials. He would wear a garment called a *thawb*, which was made from cotton or wool, and would often mend his own clothes. I recognize that during the beginning of Islam, the Muslim community didn't have much. Boycotts, persecution, oppression, and violence all limited what the Prophet Muhammad ﷺ owned. I'm not referring to that time. I'm referring to the time after the migration to Medina and the establishment of the community there. During this time of growth and abundance, the Prophet Muhammad ﷺ continued to live a simple life. His home was simple and modest, made from mud bricks and palm leaves. He did not accumulate unnecessary possessions and encouraged his followers to live with simplicity and humility.

While the Prophet ﷺ encouraged his followers to increase their wealth (to benefit the community at large), he also discouraged them from indulging in luxury. When the Prophet ﷺ sent Muʿādh ibn Jabal ؓ to Yemen in order to call the people to Islam, he warned him not to use his position of authority to live extravagantly. Muʿādh ibn Jabal reported: The Messenger of Allah ﷺ sent me to Yemen and he said:

> Beware of luxury. Verily, the servants of Allah do not live luxuriously.[101]

I want to live this sunna of simplicity and not feel overwhelmed by clutter. I looked at all the things in my home, and there was just too much stuff everywhere. I was constantly buying decor and trinkets for my home, tools, cutlery, dishware, bedding—so much stuff. And yet I hated to part with it. I didn't donate it; I hid stuff away in storage bins in the garage and basement. It actually became a distraction for me. When I needed to focus on my prayers, work on my book, or study, the junk called me, "Come organize me! Come look at all this nostalgia. Save me in new boxes."

So I began to declutter. Room by room, I kept what I needed to a minimum. When I decluttered my closet, it made picking out clothes for the day so much easier. I didn't have a hundred choices. I actually saved time!

In 2022, I helped my mom clean out her kitchen and linen closet. There was so much stuff. Expired food, old rags, plastic yogurt tubs, unmatched pillow cases, scratched-up pots and pans. She didn't want to get rid of any of it, even though she couldn't find anything she was looking for. I helped her reorganize, recycle, donate, and dispose of things.

Two months later, I found myself doing the same thing for my mother-in-law after she passed away. I wasn't upset that both moms had so much stuff. But after my mother-in-law's passing, I realized, like a slap in my face, that you don't take anything with you to the next life. All your possessions are left behind. Cleaning out a loved one's space is hard. All my mother-in-law's treasured belongings were donated, thrown away, or given to others. It was a huge undertaking, emotionally difficult and sad. So for your sake as well as your family's, try to work on clearing your space: Declutter

---

101   *Musnad Aḥmad*, no. 21600, grade: *ḥasan*.

and donate or discard things you don't need.

I think both moms had a scarcity mindset that resulted in them ending up with a lot of stuff in their homes. This can be seen very commonly in those who came from poverty or financial difficulty—especially those who came out of the Great Depression. The fear of not having enough often leads to accumulating and holding onto items, even when they're no longer needed or useful.

Consumerism and capitalism contribute to this mindset by constantly making us feel like we don't have enough. However, when we shift to an abundance mindset, we realize we have what we need. Minimalism is about being intentional in what we value and removing what distracts us. This aligns well with Islamic teachings. Consider the sunna: How many possessions did the Prophet Muhammad ﷺ have? How many pieces of clothing, furniture, bedding, or dishes? His example reminds us that a life of simplicity can be rich in meaning and spiritual fulfillment.

I found the most important aspect of a minimalist lifestyle was that it helped me control my *nafs*'s tendency to always want more. I cut my spending on clothing, home decor, trinkets, and other material things. Instead, I spend that money on travel, seeing my family, taking friends out to dinner, and eating healthier organic foods. These are the things I value. I value spending time with my mom. I value deepening my relationships with my friends while sharing a meal. I value eating healthy and not being distracted by sugar! The things I retain with intention align with my goals, and removing the distractions helps me achieve my goals in the realms of career, family, spirituality, and finances.

Buying less and decluttering are just two aspects of controlling my *nafs*. Buying things secondhand, fixing things that break, and buying things that will last longer are also forms of minimalism. Buying free trade, patching up torn clothes, and repurposing old things also counts. Buying used cars is a big part of this. My husband and I learned this the hard way. Brand-new cars are just too expensive. Buying a car a few years old with some miles is less expensive. Do your homework on cars. My Toyota Highlander is fourteen years old with over 230,000 miles on it. All it needs is an oil change and car wash from time to time. Yes, I've changed the brakes and tires on her. But that was more affordable than buying another car for $30,000! I value this car and I'm not distracted by purchasing another one. This minimalist action has multiple effects on my financial freedom.

Controlling the *nafs* and having an abundance mindset also means that you are happy when others have things. You believe there is plenty for everyone. And you also have strong *'aqīda*[102] and *tawakkul*[103] in Allah's plan of *rizq* for you.

---

102 *'Aqīda* is the Arabic word for "creed."
103 In Arabic, *tawakkul* means "to have reliance or trust in Allah's plan."

Reflection Exercise

1. What are some thoughts of scarcity you may have?

2. What are some thoughts of abundance you may have?

3. Do you think a minimalist lifestyle perpetuates a scarcity mindset or abundance mindset? How so?

4. What are some ways you can shift your lifestyle and control your *nafs* regarding materialism?

Chapter 8

Connecting the Economic Empowerment Dots

TikTok. Judge me all you want, but you can learn a lot on social media, especially TikTok. When the pandemic first began in 2020, I joined TikTok to better understand the new social media platform and how to use it for the nonprofit I was leading. This video platform was fun for me as I watched cat videos, viral dances, and other hilarious shorts. But it also taught me things like how to organize my linen closet, wash fruits in vinegar water, and find the best halal restaurants when I traveled. I once watched a TikTok reel where a woman narrated her mother's advice that she should settle down and find herself a rich man. It was one of those transition videos, where the person's outfit changes. With that change, she looked like a corporate tycoon. And she said, "But Mom, I *am* a rich man." This made me giggle and reminded me that women can financially take care of themselves. One of my coworkers at the time was struggling with her housing, finances, work performance, and personal health. During a team outing, she said, "I need to find a rich husband." My heart ached a little hearing her say that.

Financial literacy and economic empowerment are crucial for everyone, regardless of their circumstances. While some may rely on financial support from family members or partners for a variety of reasons—cultural expectations, caregiving responsibilities, or economic constraints—it's important to recognize that these situations can change unexpectedly. Understanding finances and being economically empowered provides a safety net and a sense of agency, even for those who may not currently manage their own finances. In this chapter, I want to share a few scenarios to illustrate why financial knowledge is valuable for all women, whether they're financially independent or part of an interdependent family structure.

DIVORCE

In the Quran, Allah ﷻ says,

$$وَمِن كُلِّ شَيْءٍ خَلَقْنَا زَوْجَيْنِ لَعَلَّكُمْ تَذَكَّرُونَ ۝$$

> And We created pairs of all things so perhaps you would be mindful.
>
> **Quran 51:49**

Ibn Kathīr *(raḥimahu Allāh)*[104] said this means that all things are created in pairs: heaven and earth, night and day, sun and moon, land and sea, light and darkness, faith and disbelief, death and life, misery and happiness, Paradise and Hell, and even animate beings—jinn and humans, male and female (even in plants).

When I reflect on this verse, I think about the male and female pair and how it relates to economic and financial stability. As spouses, we are supposed to take care of each other in many different ways, including spiritual, emotional, intellectual, and financial. We find in the Quran that the husband's responsibility is to support his wife. Allah ﷻ says:

$$ٱلرِّجَالُ قَوَّامُونَ عَلَى ٱلنِّسَاءِ بِمَا فَضَّلَ ٱللَّهُ بَعْضَهُمْ عَلَىٰ بَعْضٍ وَبِمَا أَنفَقُوا مِنْ أَمْوَٰلِهِمْ ۝$$

Men are the caretakers of women, as men have been provisioned

---

[104] This Arabic phrase means "May Allah have mercy on him."

by Allah over women and tasked with supporting them financially.
Quran 4:34

A husband is required to financially provide for his wife, his kids, and sometimes even his parents, sisters, aunts, and other needy family members. Men should pursue their careers and earn money to support their families—in the lifestyle their families are accustomed to. If a man cannot provide the basics and his wife chooses to contribute to the household finances—or even if his wife works simply because she wants to and spends some of her earnings on the family—this is considered an act of charity on her part and she will be rewarded for her contribution.[105] However, the reality in many modern families, including Muslim ones, often differs from this traditional model. Women frequently play dual roles: as unpaid caretakers (through motherhood and caring for elderly family members) and as financial contributors. The shift toward dual-income households has been significant. According to the US Census and the Pew Research Center, the number of dual-income families in the United States increased from 20.6 million in 1970 to approximately 41.0 million in 2019.[106]

As a Muslim woman, I, like many others, pursue a career and contribute to household expenses. This evolution reflects broader societal changes while also challenging us to balance traditional religious teachings with modern economic realities.

But even in dual-income households, what happens if the husband is no longer around? According to multiple research studies conducted by the Institute on Social Policy Understanding, divorce rates in the Muslim community are at around 30% and

---

105 Ṣaḥīḥ al-Bukhārī, no. 1466.
106 Jannik Lindner, "Struggles and Solutions: Two Income Families Statistics Unveiled," *Gitnux*, July 7, 2024, https://blog.gitnux.com/two-income-families-statistics/.

rising.[107] Understanding your money and having agency over it can mean the difference between being imprisoned by an abuser or being free from him. I know of two situations where women were in physically and emotionally abusive relationships. On top of that, their husbands were cheating on them. Both are still married to their abusers. They tried to leave but ended up coming back every time. Why? Neither woman had access to her money. Bank accounts were joint, and neither of these women wanted her husband to know she was withdrawing her money. They had no credit cards or lines of credit in their own names. They couldn't leave because they had no resources.

I also know of two women who were able to leave their abusive, cheating husbands. How? Because they had agency over their money. Even when they had joint accounts, both women created a separate account and had control over their own finances.

DEATH

Another reason to understand your finances and become economically empowered is the ever-present possibility of emergencies or sudden death. If the pandemic showed us anything, it was that death can come at any moment. What if your husband gets sick? I have a cousin whose husband contracted COVID-19 and ended up in the ICU fighting for his life. Meanwhile, she didn't have access to their money. She had to figure out how to pay her own bills *and* the staff at her husband's business. Imagine the stress! Not only are you begging Allah ﷻ to heal your husband, you're also worrying that your utilities will be shut off and you won't be able to buy groceries! Sisters, get a handle on your finances. Be proactive and educate yourselves. Know what is going on, how money is coming in and going out. Figure out monthly

---

107 Dalia Mogahed, "Five Surprising Facts about Divorce in American Muslim Communities," ISPU, January 7, 2021, https://www.ispu.org/five-facts-about-divorce/.

bills and banking details. Do you have access to mutual accounts, passwords, account managers, relevant contact information, or your own bank accounts?

Research studies show that, on average, women live longer than men. A report by the World Health Organization (WHO) in 2020 found that globally, the average life expectancy at birth for women is 75.6 years, compared to 70.8 years for men. In addition, there is often an age gap between spouses, with the husband being older. A study published by the United States Census Bureau in 2020 found that the average age gap between spouses in the United States is 2.3 years. This means that, on average, husbands are about 2.3 years older than their wives. My husband is eight years older than I am, so although there is of course a chance that I could die first, it is more likely that I will live anywhere from eight to twenty years longer than he will. Many women who have not prepared for this eventuality fall into poverty as widows during their golden years. This breaks my heart but also reminds me to take control of my finances. What is my mom going to do when my dad dies? My siblings and I will take care of her, but will she have agency and autonomy? Don't be left in the dark on money matters if and when your husband passes away. Make a plan. Understand your plan and update it as needed.

Muslim women! Allah ﷻ gave us agency over our money 1,400 years ago, so that we could serve as our own financial safety nets. We are guaranteed a portion of our parents' wealth when they pass, and what we inherit is ours. We are guaranteed a *mahr*, a bridal gift, from our husband at the time of our marriage, and we are not held responsible for the financial expenses of our household. Your money is your money. You should have separate bank accounts if you are married. It is your husband's job to provide for your basic needs like a roof over your head, clothes on your back, and food in your belly. He is accountable and responsible for these needs.

Some will argue that men only have to provide these at a basic level. Sure, he doesn't have to buy the million-dollar house or the Versace dress. But most scholars agree he must provide for you in at least the manner to which you were accustomed before the marriage. Abū Ḥanīfa says, "If the wife has a servant pre-marriage, then the husband must provide accommodation and expenses for the servant." Abū Yūsuf, Abū Ḥanīfa's student, comments, "If the wife has two servants, then the husband must cover accommodation and living expenses for both."[108]

So as your husband provides for your basic needs, you take control of your finances. I'm sure many of you have a joint account in your two-income households that covers the expenses of your lifestyle. And that's great! I love that for you. But remember—if you want to do something with your money like investing it, that is your business. That is your right.

Let's talk about Islamic prenuptial agreements real quick here. Many of us signed our *nikāḥ*[109] contract without clarifying our rights before entering into marriage. Prenuptial agreements can include many stipulations like ensuring you receive your *mahr*,[110] highlighting your right to earn money or stay out of the work market, reiterating the husband's responsibility of financial provision, providing for separate bank accounts, securing your right to manage your own wealth, and guaranteeing you alimony in the event of a divorce.

Especially in the context of living in the United States, sharia rules cannot be upheld in no-fault divorce states. So it is a very smart decision to talk through these things with your soon-to-

---

[108] Masʿūd Ibn Aḥmad al-Kāsānī, *Badāʾiʿ al-ṣanāʾiʿ fī tartīb al-sharāʾiʿ*, ed. ʿAlī Muḥammad Muʿauwaḍ (Dār al-Kutub al-ʿIlmīya, n.d.).

[109] *Nikāḥ* is the religious ceremony required by Islamic law to unite a Muslim man and woman in holy matrimony.

[110] A *mahr* is a wedding gift or contribution made by the groom to the bride for the purpose of financial security.

be husband before the wedding. Draft a mutually agreed upon marriage contract, get it notarized, and keep it in a safe place. Sometimes we fall into this belief that the sharia will protect us—after all, we have Islamic rules, laws, and Allah's commandments on our side. But the law of the land supersedes sharia in the US. If you get divorced, personal property will get divided up equally if your assets are in both your names.

I know plenty of women who don't have agency over their money. They have to ask permission from their husbands if they want to invest or give to a cause. Having a conversation with your husband about investing strategies is different from asking if you can invest your own money. My husband and I discuss new investing opportunities all the time. We share what we are learning, ideate, and give each other advice. He taught me about investing in properties. I showed him how to figure out if his stocks are sharia-compliant. But I don't ask him if I should invest in something because I'm seeking permission. I ask him because I value his guidance and advice.

SINGLE WOMEN

As for my single sisters, you are on a journey to financial independence. You are making financial decisions and investing, and your wealth is growing. US law may not protect you once these assets have grown, but Islam will.

Some women may not get married. But that doesn't mean they should not be on this journey of financial literacy and wealth building. Your role in the Muslim community will be very important. Your role as a daughter or sister will continue to grow. Your role as a community leader may also blossom. And you have life goals and *akhira* goals to achieve. Be financially stable and wealthy for yourself, your family, and the community.

Now, if you do consider marriage, look for a man who understands your rights—not only in life, but in death, as well. When you name him your benefactor or executor of your will, he should abide by Islamic principles and rules. You have worked really hard to acquire and grow your wealth for your own well-being, retirement, provisions for your children, and charitable giving. Don't let any man deprive you of that.

Also, please don't ask for $1, a cat, or the memorization of a sura as your *mahr*. The main purpose of a *mahr* is to give you respect, dignity, and financial independence and security in this life. This is a law that Allah ﷻ put in place for you for reasons He knows. How is a cat or the memorization of a chapter of the Quran going to provide you with financial security when you start your life out as a new bride or in the unfortunate event that you find yourself a widow or divorcée? Get the *mahr* and invest it. Get a cat later. Memorize suras together!

My friend Afshan posted on social media about a book called *I Will Teach You to Be Rich* by Ramit Sethi. I have a lot of respect for Afshan. She is an author, a fellow fundraiser, and the development director for Rabata, a nonprofit educational organization focusing on Muslim women and girls. So I immediately bought the book. I had just finished *The Latte Factor* and was surprised to find another book about finances coming into my line of sight at that moment. But in reality, this was Allah ﷻ helping me and guiding me on my journey.

What I like about this book is that it describes a six-week program with advice, stories, testimonials, and actual action steps that you can take. Some of the steps are easy and you can implement them right away. Some are harder, time-consuming, and FOMO-inducing.

The book is aimed at young adults in their twenties and thirties who want to learn how to manage their money, get out of debt, save for the future, and build wealth over time. In the book, Sethi shares a prenuptial conversation he had with his fiancée. It was uncomfortable for me to read; I can only imagine how uncomfortable it was for them to have. Their relationship was obviously in a good, healthy place when they had this conversation.

I think about my own husband and the decisions he makes for his finances. We have always separated our finances, but I'm his power of attorney and one of the beneficiaries should he pass away. As he is mine. He says that he trusts me to follow his will and its distribution according to sharia inheritance laws. (By the way, everyone needs a will. See Chapter 14: Wills—Do You Have One?)

I think about my daughter as she is building her investment portfolio and her wealth. I want to make sure she has full control over it so that when/if she gets married, her husband doesn't try to take it over. When the time comes and premarital discussions begin, she will need to discuss a lot and create a detailed Islamic marriage contract that will protect her in case our religion's rules are not upheld in court in case of a divorce or death. A marriage contract is more than the *nikāḥ* certificate!

WOMEN AND INHERITANCE

Finally, let's talk briefly about inheritance. Allah ﷻ has laid out rules of inheritance in the Quran, specifically in Sūrat al-Nisā':

يُوصِيكُمُ ٱللَّهُ فِىٓ أَوْلَٰدِكُمْ ۖ لِلذَّكَرِ مِثْلُ حَظِّ ٱلْأُنثَيَيْنِ ۚ فَإِن كُنَّ نِسَآءً فَوْقَ ٱثْنَتَيْنِ فَلَهُنَّ ثُلُثَا مَا تَرَكَ ۖ وَإِن كَانَتْ وَٰحِدَةً فَلَهَا ٱلنِّصْفُ ۚ وَلِأَبَوَيْهِ لِكُلِّ وَٰحِدٍ مِّنْهُمَا ٱلسُّدُسُ مِمَّا تَرَكَ إِن كَانَ لَهُۥ وَلَدٌ ۚ فَإِن لَّمْ يَكُن لَّهُۥ وَلَدٌ وَوَرِثَهُۥٓ أَبَوَاهُ فَلِأُمِّهِ ٱلثُّلُثُ ۚ فَإِن كَانَ لَهُۥٓ إِخْوَةٌ فَلِأُمِّهِ ٱلسُّدُسُ ۚ مِنۢ بَعْدِ وَصِيَّةٍ يُوصِى بِهَآ أَوْ دَيْنٍ ۗ ءَابَآؤُكُمْ وَأَبْنَآؤُكُمْ لَا تَدْرُونَ أَيُّهُمْ أَقْرَبُ لَكُمْ نَفْعًا ۚ فَرِيضَةً مِّنَ ٱللَّهِ ۗ إِنَّ ٱللَّهَ كَانَ عَلِيمًا حَكِيمًا ﴿١١﴾

> Allah commands you regarding your children: The share of the male will be twice that of the female. If you leave only two [or more] females, their share is two-thirds of the estate. But if there is only one female, her share will be one-half. Each parent is entitled to one-sixth if you leave offspring. But if you are childless and your parents are the only heirs, then your mother will receive one-third. But if you leave siblings, then your mother will receive one-sixth—after the fulfillment of bequests and debts. [Be fair to] your parents and children, as you do not [fully] know who is more beneficial to you. [This is] an obligation from Allah. Surely Allah ﷻ is All-Knowing, All-Wise.
>
> **Quran 4:11**

This verse lays out the rules for dividing an individual's estate after their death among their children, parents, and other family members. This verse is inspirational to me. It makes me want to leave something behind for my children. It encourages me to see that inheritance is a way to benefit my loved ones even after death, which is seen as a virtuous act in Islam. After reading this verse and reflecting on it, I am reminded that building generational wealth is something Allah ﷻ encourages. When I die, I hope to give some of my wealth to the causes I care about and to my children so they can continue my legacy. That's why it's important to me—and should be important to you—to understand money, build wealth, invest, and give.

BRINGING JOY TO OTHERS

Being financially stable also gives me the opportunity to bring others joy. Giving a thoughtful gift to someone I care about brings them joy. It doesn't have to be an expensive gift, but rather something that is meaningful and shows that I understand and appreciate them. Two hadiths come to mind that encourage giving gifts to others. The first is narrated by Abū Hurayra ﷺ, in which the Prophet Muhammad ﷺ said:

> Exchange gifts, as that will lead to increasing your love for one another.[111]

This hadith emphasizes the importance of giving gifts as a means of strengthening the bonds of love and affection between individuals. Another hadith, narrated by Jarīr ibn ʿAbdullāh *(raḥimahu Allāh)* stated that the Prophet Muhammad ﷺ said:

> He who is deprived of forbearance and gentleness is, in fact, deprived of all good.[112]

This hadith highlights the importance of showing kindness and generosity to others, which can include giving gifts.

Pay It Forward

I have to give credit to Christians, as this concept shows up often in December. I once pulled up at my local Caribou drive-through and the cashier told me I didn't have to pay because the driver in front of me had already paid for my drink. I was in shock. Someone who doesn't even know me showed me a random act of kindness. So I paid for the person behind me. What a beautiful chain reaction. Have you ever left an extra generous tip for a service provider who has done an exceptional job or just looked like they could use some kindness? If you haven't, try it out!

Support a Local Business

When I find a local business owned by a Muslim woman, I am ready to support her. This not only helps the business owner, but

---

111 *Al-Adab al-mufrad*, no. 594.
112 *Riyāḍ al-ṣāliḥīn*, no. 637.

also increases the Muslim contribution to the local economy. As these businesses grow, they create job opportunities, often for other Muslim women who might face barriers in the mainstream job market. The money spent at these businesses tends to circulate within the local Muslim community, creating a positive economic ripple effect. Moreover, successful Muslim women entrepreneurs become powerful role models, inspiring and mentoring others to start their own ventures. This leads to increased visibility and participation of Muslim women across various economic sectors, fostering more diverse and inclusive local economies. And these businesses often cater to specific needs within the Muslim community, driving innovation and filling important market gaps.

By supporting these enterprises, we're not just making a purchase—we're investing in the economic empowerment of Muslim women, challenging stereotypes, and contributing to long-term wealth creation within our community. It's a tangible way to strengthen the presence and influence of our local Muslim economy. Let me share an example!

Annie Qaiser, who is also my book's copyeditor, launched Silkroad Wellness in 2018. The company offers a variety of halal, natural health and wellness products, including herbal supplements, essential oils, and skincare products. The products are amazing, so I asked Annie to make me thirty gift sets for friends and family. I gave those out on Eid one year, benefitting both Annie and the recipients!

BUILDING GENERATIONAL WEALTH

Generational wealth is of course the accumulated assets, resources, and privileges that are passed down within a family from one generation to the next. This can include financial assets such as money, investments, and property, as well as social, intellectual, and cultural capital like education, skills, and connections. For example, I share with my children not only monetary wealth but also the things I have learned in college, workshops, and webinars. When I learn a skill like cooking a new rice dish, I teach it to my son. When I realize there is someone in my network my daughter could benefit from, I introduce her.

Generational wealth often creates a cycle of advantages and opportunities that can persist over time, allowing future generations to have access to more resources and opportunities than previous generations. This can create a significant advantage for families that have accumulated wealth over several generations, while also making it more difficult for families without generational wealth to achieve financial stability and upward mobility.

In the United States, the wealth gap continues to widen among racial minorities. The Survey of Consumer Finance (SCF) found that the median net worth of white households was $189,100. Hispanic households had a median net worth of $36,050, Black households' median net worth was $24,100, and the group categorized as "Other" maintained a median net worth of $74,500.[113] We need a multipronged approach to narrow this gap, including public policy changes and financial literacy education.

Another reason I want to invest and earn is so I can give our kids a chance at financial stability sooner than I had. I've observed how some families, particularly those who have benefited from generational wealth, are able to help their children succeed financially. While this isn't true for all families of any background, it's a privilege I'd like to work toward for our own family. I want that for my grandbabies and great-grandbabies.

Finally, the most important reason I want to build my wealth is so

---

113 Aditya Aladangady and Akila Forde, "Wealth Inequality and the Racial Wealth Gap," Federal Reserve System, October 22, 2021, https://www.federalreserve.gov/econres/notes/feds-notes/wealth-inequality-and-the-racial-wealth-gap-20211022.html.

I can give it back. Keep reading, because I'll explain why later in the book!

Reflection Exercise

1. You've read eight chapters of this book. What are some things it has helped you realize are important in building your wealth?

2. Are there things that you now see as less important than you did before?

3. What are some action steps you can take today to better understand your finances and become more financially knowledgeable?

Chapter 9

Assessing My Financial Situation

With the change from paper money to checking accounts to digital wallets, I became absent-minded regarding my own financial situation. I knew how much I earned and how much was deposited into my checking account. I paid my credit card bill on time every month, in full. I had auto payments set up. My car was paid off. I had paid off my student loans.

But I rarely looked at the 401(k) from my corporate days, my IRA, my savings account, or my stocks. In fact, the only time I looked at them was when I needed to calculate zakat every Ramadan. I didn't look at credit card statements, meaning I didn't fully understand what I was spending money on or if I was getting overcharged for anything. I never looked at my bank statements. I wasn't bothering to compare rates, monitor late fees, or budget for my goals.

This was lazy and irresponsible of me. However, that all changed when I started reading finance books and educating myself about personal finance. I realized the importance of being actively engaged with my finances and began to implement the strategies I was learning.

Remember the personal finance book I read called *I Will Teach You To Be Rich* by Ramit Sethi? I found a lot of benefit in this book because of the six-week program that Sethi laid out with advice, stories, testimonials, and action steps. Full transparency: I did not take every single step. But those I did take helped me create my plan "to become rich." And I'll be honest with you, I wasn't trying to become rich. I wasn't expecting to become a billionaire at the end of six weeks. But I did want to understand my financial situation. I took a notebook and sectioned off the six-week plan. Each week, I assessed my current situation based on what I had just read in the book. Then I created action steps that I could take next.

Pause now and assess your own situation. To help you with this, I created a worksheet. Some of its questions come from Sethi's book. Some of them come from my own ideas and reflections. It's a starting point. Complete the following worksheet, reflect, and you may come up with a couple of additional actionable steps of your own. Bismillah[114] and good luck!

---

114 The phrase "bismillah" translates to "in the name of Allah."

Worksheet: Assess Your Financial Situation

1. Do you have a source of revenue like a job, allowance, inheritance, assets, etc.? List them all below:

    a. How much money do you make monthly and annually from your job?

    b. How much money comes in from other sources?

2. Do you have a bank account? Savings or checking?

    a. How much is in your checking account?

    b. How much is in your savings account?

    c. Are your bank accounts interest bearing?

    d. If yes, can you switch to a non-interest-bearing account?

    e. If no, can you find non-interest-bearing accounts at another bank and switch?

3. Do you have debt?

    a. What is your student loan debt?

    b. What is your credit card debt?

c. If you own a home, what is your home loan debt?

d. What other debt do you have?

4. What are your monthly expenses? List them all out.

    a. Do you see any that can be lowered or cut?

5. Do you have a 401(k)/403(b)? (Learn about these in Chapter 12.)

    a. How long have you been investing?

    b. How much is in it right now?

    c. Does your company match?

    d. Are you contributing the maximum amount?

    e. Have you checked to make sure the investments are halal?

6. Do you have a Roth IRA, SIMPLE IRA, or SEP IRA? (Learn about these in Chapter 13.)

    a. Have you contributed the maximum amount?

Worksheet: Assess Your Financial Situation

    b. Is it fully invested?

    c. Have you checked to make sure the investments are halal?

7. Do you own stocks? If no, will you make a plan to begin investing in stocks?

    a. Are they sharia-compliant?

    b. How diverse are the stocks? Are they in several different sectors?

8. What are the costs associated with achieving your personal goals? See Chapter 3.

    a. Career Goals

    b. Family Goals

    c. Self Goals

    d. Health Goals

    e. Relationship Goals

    f. Financial Goals

g. Spiritual/Religious Goals

9. Married: Do you have separate finances from your husband?

   Single: Will you separate your finances if you should marry? Why or why not?

10. What is your credit score? See the next chapter on how to find it.

11. Do you have access to your Social Security benefits account? Have you set one up?

    a. If no, go to ssn.gov

    b. If yes, pull your report and understand what your monthly payout will be at different retirement ages.

12. Do you have a health care savings account (HSA) or a flexible spending account (FSA)?

    a. If yes, how much is in it?

13. Do you have a will?

    a. If yes, how old is it? Do you need to update it? Who has access to it?

    b. If not, see Chapter 14 on wills.

Worksheet: Assess Your Financial Situation

14. Do you have conversations with your family about finances?

    a. If yes, what do you talk about?

    b. If not, will you begin having them? When?

Reflection Exercise

1. What are some aha moments that you had during this assessment?

2. What are some action steps you came up with?

3. What are some changes you could make?

4. How are you feeling after completing this assessment?

Chapter 10

Just Start

I think the most important thing to realize right now is that you cannot continue talking about how difficult your financial situation is. You cannot continue wallowing in the misery of your debt or the fact that you don't have enough money. In his book, Sethi says, "Just start." Do something. If you have made it through this book to this point, you have started! Now, go at your own pace. Do one thing at a time. Take one step, one action, at a time. But it is very important that you do something. When I reread Sethi's book, I not only reviewed the steps I took last year, but I came up with new steps to take this year. Every year, I will continue to review and revise my action steps, inshallah.

Many financial advisers share that older people (like my age or older) often regret not starting earlier and feel that it's too late. Their advice is, "It's never too late!" It reminds me of the hadith of the Prophet Muhammad ﷺ that Anas ibn Mālik reported: The Messenger of Allah ﷺ said,

> Even if the Resurrection were established upon one of you while they have in their hand a sapling, let them plant it.[115]

Of course, starting younger is the best time for you to take control of your wealth and your investments. But if your youth was like mine, you were probably oblivious to the world of finances! And I had very limited resources for learning about it (there was no Google!).

---

115 *Musnad Aḥmad*, no. 12902.

There will be times when you will forget to do something or you will invest in the wrong stock or you will take out the wrong credit card. And it's OK. You're going to make mistakes. You will fix and learn from those mistakes. Continue to move forward and course correct. We make mistakes all the time in life. Recently, on my LinkedIn profile, a GIF was posted that showed how much you learn from theory (this book), from practice (doing), and from mistakes (oops!). The bar chart showed that the most learning comes from your mistakes.

There is no such thing as perfection. Only Allah ﷻ is perfect, so give yourself grace. When you do make mistakes and lose money, remember it wasn't part of your *rizq*. It was never meant to be with you. Maybe it was meant to be with you for that limited amount of time, and then it found its way to someone else. That is Allah's plan and His plan of *rizq* for you.

Sethi's book inspired me to spring into action. I want to quickly go through some of the things in it that I found useful, like optimizing your credit cards, banking with the right institution, investing, and resources. Fair warning, there are many things in his book that are not aligned with Islamic teachings, such as investment with interest. I will try my best to provide alternative solutions, and sometimes I'll just skip things he suggests. I'll share with you what I did, which doesn't necessarily mean it's the right thing for you. I'm trying to give you just a peek into what is possible. Hopefully, you can create a personalized financial action plan too!

OPTIMIZE YOUR CREDIT CARDS

I despise credit cards because when I was younger, I was not smart with them. As soon as I turned eighteen, the credit card offers poured in. I opened a card with Citibank, Disney, and another store. And I maxed them all out. I also let other family members use them, and they never paid me back. I couldn't pay off the cards because the interest rates never let my balance go down. Eventually, the cards were canceled and went to collections. My credit score tanked. It was such a horrible introduction to adulting. At this point, I felt credit cards were evil; they were haram because they dealt with interest and they ruined my life! It wasn't until after I got married and was able to clean up my credit that I was able to renew my relationship with credit cards.

Are credit cards permissible in Islam? Debatable. Some scholars believe they are not permissible because they deal with interest. But Ibrahim Khan of the Islamic Finance Guru shares four reasons why the use of credit cards is permissible based on a couple of scholarly opinions.[116] The first is that the act of borrowing on a credit card itself is not haram as long as we pay it back during the interest-free timeframe. The second is that we live in a society where interest charges for late payments are hardwired into our every contract. Buying a home, paying for utilities, buying cars, funding education, investing in business, and opening a savings account are all connected to interest. And if we are late on paying back any of these bills, we are charged interest plus a late fee. The third reason is that credit cards aren't just a short-term loan; they also come with additional benefits. I'll share more about this in a moment. Finally, credit card companies don't just make money from interest. They charge businesses that accept credit cards a processing fee. This is an additional revenue stream for them even if we pay off our credit cards on a monthly basis.

At the start of my financial assessment, I had three different credit cards with three different loyalty and rewards programs associated with them. I studied the benefits and perks to make sure they aligned with my spending habits and financial goals. Two important aspects of having credit cards are building your credit

---

116 Ibrahim Khan, "Are Credit Cards Haram or Halal?," *Islamic Finance Guru*, May 31, 2022, https://www.islamicfinanceguru.com/articles/are-credit-cards-haram-or-halal.

score and reaping the benefits they offer. Credit cards were created as a form of currency that was not cash or checks but have evolved into short-term loans with minimum payments and high interest rates. Learn this now: Do not use a credit card as a short-term loan. I repeat: Do not use credit cards to buy stuff you cannot afford. Making minimum payments with an interest rate of 25%–29% is a poor financial tactic. When you continue to carry the balance over to the next month, that balance accrues additional interest. You must pay off your full balance *every month* to avoid the interest! Don't even think about carrying a balance on your credit card! Pay it off in full every single month, no exceptions. Those interest charges are not your friend, so dodge them like your financial life and your *akhira* depend on it—because they do!

One of the credit cards I had was a store credit card. Although it had the Visa logo on it, the only benefit I was getting from this card was receiving points to shop back in that store. It was a waste for me, because it was a consumer electronics store and I was not purchasing electronics that often. It also carried restrictions when I traveled; I couldn't use it outside of the United States. I learned this the hard way when I was in transit with a layover in Amsterdam. I bought lunch for my kids and couldn't pay for it with this card. It was useless most of the time and offered no benefits when I traveled. So when I returned home, I quickly paid the last bill off and then called them up and closed the account. Having one less credit card to worry about helped me simplify my finances. Because I was not using this card very often, closing it had an added benefit: it minimized my exposure to common credit card risks such as fraud, identity theft, and unauthorized transactions. Also, why pay an annual fee to have a credit card that I'm not benefiting from?

My second credit card was for household purchases. I managed expenses like gas and groceries using this credit card. It also had a points program. If you accumulated enough points, you accessed a portal and used those points to purchase gift cards for other businesses. I would get gift cards for the movies, restaurants, and bookstores. There was an option of just getting cash back, but I chose the gift cards because I thought I was getting more value out of them. Except that I would order gift cards and then lose them or forget about them! Remember Blockbuster Video? I chose gift cards for Blockbuster, and then Blockbuster went out of business.

My third credit card came with an annual fee that felt quite significant to me at the time. I had to carefully weigh the benefits to ensure it was worth the cost. This was a travel rewards card that offered a much higher earning rate for points compared to my other cards. Specifically, it allowed me to earn 7 points for every dollar spent on eligible purchases, while my standard cards typically offered only 1 point per dollar. This sevenfold multiplier made accumulating travel rewards much faster, potentially offsetting the annual fee for frequent travelers. It also had other travel perks such as free checked bags, TSA PreCheck, and rental car insurance. I loved this card because I immediately saw that the points could be used to upgrade my airplane seat from one cabin to another. After having this card for some time, I received complimentary upgrades to fly first class to a few domestic locations. It felt so bougie!

Recently, I used points from this card for free round-trip tickets to Chicago. Did I mention that after a year, I also received a free domestic companion ticket? I love to travel. It's one of my goals every year to visit and experience a new part of the world. This card helps me travel in comfort. Look, at my age, I don't enjoy sitting in those tiny seats in economy class. I have varicose veins and they flare up during air travel. I appreciate more space to stretch out my long old legs. I kept this card, and this year, I upgraded it to a higher level (Platinum) so I can benefit from more perks. This is the card I use for my personal expenses. Each month, I use this card to pay for things like going out to restaurants with friends, birthday presents for my husband, donations, toiletries, subscription services, and vacations. When my monthly statement comes in the mail, I review my expenses just to make sure nothing looks wrong. And I pay it off in full, ensuring interest never accrues. That way, I earn travel points while maintaining Platinum status.

Though credit cards have become a true necessity, as most transactions today are carried out digitally, credit card companies are also predators. They charge exorbitantly high interest rates—ranging from 14%–29%—and if you miss a payment, they will charge you an additional $27–$40. So I say again: Do not use a credit card as a loan.

Let's say you have a credit card with an APR of 21%, and you max it out at $10,000. Your minimum monthly payment will be 3%–5% of the outstanding balance. Every month you pay $300, but your balance is actually increasing! That's because every month you are being charged $175 in interest on that $10,000. And a good chunk of your payment is going toward that interest rather than reducing your principal balance. You are not making any progress paying off your bill; you are simply giving the credit card company your money! Don't use credit cards as a loan. Think about a credit card like a thirty-day deferred payment plan that allows you to take advantage of the associated perks and points.

The best way to do this is to automate your credit card payments so that you pay off the full amount every single month. When you open a credit card and get access to its online portal, go in and set up automatic payments immediately. So many people forget to pay their bills on time; life happens. And credit card companies make billions of dollars off of those late fees and accruing interest fees that make that $100 purchase a gazillion dollars later on. (My math might be a little off on that, but not by much!)

Once you have your autopay turned on, remember to pay attention to what's in your bank account. Don't overdraft it and accrue even more fees and charges. Be a conscious spender and know what you have to work with before you spend.

Two quick reminders: First, opening and closing credit cards can have an impact on your credit score. Be careful how many you are opening or signing up for. Don't open three cards all at the same time and then close them right away because they weren't working out. Be diligent and thoughtful when you are reviewing your current cards and researching which one you want to open next. Having a credit card, paying it off, and not having late fees has a positive impact on your credit score. But if you are randomly opening and closing cards with very short account histories or too many late fees, this will lower your credit score.

Second, automation can seduce you into not paying attention to your expenses or spending. You should still be reviewing your bank statements, your credit card statements, and any other reports. Make sure you aren't being charged fees that you shouldn't be charged. Look for any fraudulent activity. But also, have an awareness of your monthly financials. Automating is a technique to help you manage your time and organize the process. Not set it and forget it like a Ronco rotisserie oven.

Reflection Exercise

1. Assess your credit cards. What credit cards do you have right now and what is the amount of money you owe? What benefits do they provide? Use this information to determine if you should keep or close them.

Name of Credit Card	Amount Owed	Benefits	Keep or Close?

2. What steps can you take to pay off those credit cards? Create a plan with action steps and a timeline. Here is a sample plan.

Tactic	Action	Due Date	Results & Next Steps
Pay more than the minimum	Pay $100/month instead of $25	Start in three months	
Automate payments	Go online and link bank account	Complete in two weeks	
Consolidate credit cards	Look for 0% transfer credit card and apply	Complete in three months	
Negotiate lower interest rate	Call up credit card companies and ask to lower rate	Call today!	

3. Do some research. Are there better credit cards out there that you could have instead?

CREDIT SCORES

Asia (AH-see-uh) Mohamed is the founder and CEO of Premier Starter, a financial growth company that is on a mission to close the financial literacy and racial equity gap in America for underestimated entrepreneurs and individuals. While I was at RISE, we invited Asia to come speak to our Muslim sisters about credit scores as part of our Economic Empowerment Series. She presented information on what credit is and how to understand it. What I appreciated about Asia's work was that she was able to use plain words to help me and others understand what a credit score is, how it's calculated, who calculates it, and why it is an important element of your financial stability.

What Is a Credit Score?

Credit scores involve math. And you know I love math! A credit score falls in the range between 300 and 850. The higher your score, the better. Credit bureaus like Equifax, Transunion, and Experian are independent reporting agencies that assess the likelihood that you will pay back any money a lendor lends you. A credit score determines whether or not you can get a loan to borrow money for a house, a car, or even a business.

Credit scores are approval metrics. It's one thing to get approved for the loan, but your credit score determines the interest level at which you can borrow that money. The lower your credit score, the higher the interest rate. The higher your credit score, the lower the interest rate. For example, if you have a credit score between 620 and 639 and are applying for a loan to buy a house, a lender may charge you an 8% interest rate. If you had a credit score of 760–850, the lender would be more likely to charge you an interest rate of 6.5%. This 1.5% difference may seem insignificant, but it's not. When you borrow $300,000 to pay for your new home, you will pay close to $500,000 in interest over a thirty-year mortgage at

8% versus $376,000 at 6.5%. Forcing people to pay that much more than the original loan amount is financial oppression, which is why it is forbidden in Islam.

So, how is a credit score calculated? Credit bureaus determine your credit score by looking at your payment history. Your payment history includes the number of on-time payments you have made on your other loans and credit card bills. One late payment can drop your score by 60–70 points.

Next, credit bureaus look at your capacity. How much of your credit card limit is available? It is a positive thing if you are using your credit cards, but the bureau is watching how you are utilizing each line of credit. Are you maxed out? Or do you have access to a healthy, available line of credit?

The bureaus also take into consideration the length of your credit history, which means how long have you had this loan or that credit card. A longer credit history positively affects your credit score. Younger people have shorter lengths of credit than older people. I've had one credit card for over seventeen years!

A credit score also reflects the types of credit used. Do you have installment loans or revolving credit? For example, an installment loan is when a bank gives you a lump sum of money to buy a new house. You then have fixed, scheduled payments you are required to make until the loan is paid off in full. An example of revolving credit is a credit card. It allows you to spend the money you borrowed, repay it, and borrow again as needed. Having "mixed credit," or both kinds of loans, is ideal.

One of the reasons you have to be so strategic about which credit cards to apply for is that *just applying* affects your credit score. When you apply for new credit, either through a new loan or a credit card, it results in a "hard inquiry" on your credit report. This can temporarily lower your score for two reasons:

1. It suggests you might be taking on new debt, which could be seen as a risk.

2. Multiple applications in a short time can make you appear desperate for credit.

Each hard inquiry typically drops your score by a few points—usually less than five.

I got a new card this year, so my score dropped slightly. As the year progressed, I used the card and paid off my monthly bills. My credit score then returned to the same number it was before I received the new card. It bounced back up based on my spending habits and consistent payments.

The time it takes for your score to rebound can vary, but generally:

- Hard inquiries remain on your credit report for two years but usually only impact your score for a few months.

- If you use the new credit responsibly, your score often recovers within three to six months.

- In some cases, a new credit card can actually improve your score in the long run by increasing your available credit and improving your credit mix.

Remember, the impact of applying for new credit is usually small and temporary, especially if you have a long credit history and good credit score.

How do I know that? I learned to check my credit score. One of my credit cards provides a free credit report. Check and see if yours does. If not, visit www.annualcreditreport.com and pull your free, once-a-year credit score and report. Reading your credit report regularly is crucial for maintaining your financial health. When reviewing your report, look for accuracy in your personal information, credit accounts, and payment history. My employer information was wrong. Check for any unauthorized accounts or hard inquiries, which could indicate identity theft. Review public records, credit utilization, and the length of your credit history. Pay close attention to negative items like late payments or collections. This review process can help you to catch and dispute errors that could unfairly lower your score, to detect potential identity theft early, and to understand the factors affecting your creditworthiness. By staying informed about your credit report, you're empowered to take control of your financial reputation and make smart decisions about your credit use. Remember, you're entitled to one free credit report from each of the three major credit bureaus annually—take advantage of this to stay on top of your credit health. If there are any errors, report it to the bureaus. Send a letter or email to the three big bureaus (Equifax, TransUnion, and Experian) stating what information is wrong and providing corrected information.

There is a common rumor that if you check your credit score it will lower it. This is partially false. When you personally check your own credit score, this is called a soft inquiry. It does not affect your score. However, if a lender or creditor checks your credit score, this is called a hard inquiry and does lower your score, because it is associated with an application for new credit.

Look for unfamiliar activity. Identity theft is real. If there is a loan or credit card that you can't remember having or taking out, investigate it. If it truly isn't yours and someone else opened it in your name—report it. Make a police report *and* contact the Federal Trade Commission (FTC) online at IdentityTheft.gov or call 1-877-438-4338. Protect yourself.

It takes time to build up your credit score. My score was below 600 when I graduated from college. It took me a few years to clean it up, but I knew I was playing the long game. After I pulled and reviewed my credit report, I closed accounts, paid off debt, and let life progress. One of my first goals was to never have a late payment. I had to make on-time payments. So I automated my credit card bill payments through my bank account.

Something I had never thought of that Asia shared with us was that if you are facing hardship and missing payments, communicate. Reach out to your lender (the credit card company or the bank your loan is through) and share your story. Tell them what is going on and why you are missing payments. Life happens. Ask for help. Ask if you can receive some additional assistance. Ask them what options are available. Set up a new payment plan before you skip any payments.

Missing payments affects your credit score significantly. Your lender reports the missed payment to the credit bureaus, which can negatively impact your credit score. If you continue to miss payments, the lender may eventually sell your debt to a collection agency. Before your credit score takes a serious hit, it's crucial to get ahead of the situation! If there are missed payments on your credit report, consider reaching out to your lender. If you've gotten back on track with your payments, you can ask them if they'd be willing to remove the negative mark. While they're not obligated to do so, some lenders might agree if you've resumed regular payments and have an otherwise good payment history. Don't be shy—it's worth making the call to your lender to discuss your options

Every January, I have made it a habit to pull my credit report and review my credit score. Through consistent effort and responsible financial habits, I've managed to maintain an excellent credit score. I encourage you to set a similar annual reminder for yourself—reviewing your credit report regularly is a crucial step in taking control of your financial health. What's your current credit score, and what steps can you take to improve or maintain it this year?

Activity

Let's run your credit score right now!

Go to your credit card's website and find out if they offer customers a free report. If yes, pull your credit score report. If not, visit www.annualcreditreport.com

Now, let's review your report.

1. What's your score?

    a. Is it fair, good, or excellent?

2. How many late payments are reported?

    a. Is there something you can do to avoid late payments in the future?

    b. Can you automate payments?

3. How many inquiries are on your report?

    a. What are they?

    b. Do they look familiar?

4. Determine how long your credit history has been reported.

    a. Note how many years of credit history your report shows.

    b. Determine how many years ago you opened your first credit account (credit card, loan, etc.).

    c. Now subtract a from b. The difference between these two numbers can help you understand if the report you're looking at is capturing your full credit history.

5. What's your available credit amount?

6. Is there any incorrect information?

7. How can you correct it?

8. Any weird things like credit cards that are not familiar? Beware of identity theft! Report it.

BANKS

Banks are self-benefiting institutions that ravage your financial situation without you even knowing it. Banks are for-profit entities that charge excessive overdraft fees, late fees, mailing-your-paper-statement fees, and many other hidden fees. It's ridiculous. I looked at my bank statement recently, and I was shocked to see that my bank charges me $6.95 a month for some maintenance fee on my checking account. It also has an interest rate, meaning that the bank uses my money and then gives me back a rate of return. I fought the maintenance fee and was able to get it waived. Check your bank statements. Do you see a maintenance fee on it? Call your bank and ask for this fee to be waived.

I feel so gross about the interest accumulating in my checking account. Even though it is only $0.21 a month, it taints my money. It's like a drop of pee in my glass of water. So I'm looking at closing that bank account. It will be a pain because I have tons of bill payments automated through it. But I'm making a plan. I am spending a day mapping out all the changes I need to make. Then I'll slowly move my automated bills over to the new account. First, though, I'll be figuring out where to transfer my checking account to. It will have to be a bank that offers interest-free checking accounts. Most likely, it will be a local bank or a credit union.

Local banks and credit unions have their advantages over larger banks. They offer lower transaction fees and better customer service. Credit unions are not-for-profit institutions. When we opened up our first bank account for RISE, we chose a local credit union. Here are a couple of things I noticed right away.

Let's start with lower fees. The overdraft fee at the credit union is $33 per item, whereas at the national bank it was $35. The monthly service fee for a business account is $0 at the credit union, but $10 at the national bank. The first 200 debits and credits in an account at the credit union are free. At the national bank, it's the first 150, and they charged $0.50 for each additional transaction above that. When you're running a business or nonprofit, or even just have a personal account, these things add up.

I had an issue with the credit union at one point because they sent me this poorly written communication on how they rejected a wire transfer from a funder. I sent a "Minnesota nice"[117] response back. Before you know it, the branch vice president called me. She was apologetic and agreed that the automated response lacked compassion and demonstrated a transactional relationship with us, and she was committed to changing the process. The fees were reversed and the wire transfer went through. I had a cordial conversation with this helpful woman. I wasn't yelling at her, just sharing my frustrations—and she listened. She listened, showed some humanity, and made things better.

Final point, credit unions are not-for-profits. In principle, they are here to serve the community. They are owned by the community members in a cooperative model. They strive to offer financial products with favorable terms for their members. I hope we can create a credit union for Muslims and offer Islamic financial products in Minnesota, inshallah. I found Maun Federal Credit Union in New Jersey and Jafari No-Interest Credit Union in Texas. They give me hope!

After I read the chapter on banks in Sethi's book (twice), I thought to myself, "If banks are so horrible and shady, ingraining *ribā* into

---

117 "Minnesota nice" is a cultural stereotype referring to the behavior of people from Minnesota, implying that residents are unusually courteous, reserved, and mild-mannered compared to people from other states.

us, then why do we keep our money there? Why don't we put our savings into our investment portfolio?" Isn't it more halal to own shares in a publicly traded company than to keep your money in an interest-bearing bank account? The interest earned on a savings or checking account is haram and taints the rest of our hard-earned money. So I decided to try it out. I took 50% of the savings in my bank account and moved it into my investment portfolio. I know right now the markets are really struggling, but my goal was to get away from the interest. I'll review this strategy next year to see if it was worth it. Stay tuned!

Did you know there are actually people who don't have bank accounts? The "unbanked." Obviously, some are not unbanked by choice, but I won't get into detail about that here. There are, however, others who choose not to turn to the banks for their savings accounts and checking transactions. They use services like check cashing to cash their paychecks and money orders or prepaid debit cards for paying bills. They don't trust banks. (Who remembers the Wells Fargo scam where employees created millions of fake accounts for their customers without their consent?[118])

The unbanked don't want to be penalized for not maintaining minimum balances or fined overdraft and other fees. And really, who does? But we live in a world where it is really hard to live without a bank account. Personally, I don't know how to be unbanked. But I do know that I want to be careful with what my bank does with my money, the fees they charge, and the types of financial services and products they provide. Look for an interest-free checking account and create a halal investment account. More on how to do that in Chapter 12!

---

118   Jack Kelly, "Former Wells Fargo Executives Could Face Serious Criminal Charges," *Forbes*, January 1, 2020, https://www.forbes.com/sites/jackkelly/2020/01/07/former-wells-fargo-executives-could-face-serious-criminal-charges/.

Reflection Exercise

1. What bank do you use now, and what do you like about your bank?

2. Are you struggling with interest accumulating on your checking or savings accounts? What steps are you considering to get away from this *ribā*?

3. Have you assessed your bank and the services they provide or the fees and interest they charge? What did you learn, and are there any actions you want to take?

Chapter 11

Interest, Taxes, Inflation, and Financial Advisers

One thing I have observed in my investment journey is the challenge that traditional capitalist investments pose to my own religious practices. In almost every single financial independence or financial empowerment book, workshop, webinar, or blog, there is a significant and constant emphasis on compound interest. Compound interest is what most financial advisers sell you in terms of growing your investments. However, in Islam, interest is haram.

يَـٰٓأَيُّهَا ٱلَّذِينَ ءَامَنُوا۟ ٱتَّقُوا۟ ٱللَّهَ وَذَرُوا۟ مَا بَقِىَ مِنَ ٱلرِّبَوٰٓا۟ إِن كُنتُم مُّؤْمِنِينَ

Oh believers! Fear Allah, and give up outstanding interest if you are [true] believers.

Quran 2:278

The prohibition of interest prevents the unjust imbalance of power and wealth between lenders and borrowers that leads to exploitation, oppression, and economic instability. Interest-bearing transactions are in violation of Islamic principles, and Muslims are encouraged to engage in ethical and socially responsible economic activities that promote the well-being of individuals and society as a whole.

ٱلَّذِينَ يَأْكُلُونَ ٱلرِّبَوٰا۟ لَا يَقُومُونَ إِلَّا كَمَا يَقُومُ ٱلَّذِى يَتَخَبَّطُهُ ٱلشَّيْطَٰنُ مِنَ ٱلْمَسِّ ۚ ذَٰلِكَ بِأَنَّهُمْ قَالُوٓا۟ إِنَّمَا ٱلْبَيْعُ مِثْلُ ٱلرِّبَوٰا۟ ۗ وَأَحَلَّ ٱللَّهُ ٱلْبَيْعَ وَحَرَّمَ ٱلرِّبَوٰا۟ ۚ فَمَن جَآءَهُۥ مَوْعِظَةٌ مِّن رَّبِّهِۦ فَٱنتَهَىٰ فَلَهُۥ مَا سَلَفَ وَأَمْرُهُۥٓ إِلَى ٱللَّهِ ۖ وَمَنْ عَادَ فَأُو۟لَٰٓئِكَ أَصْحَٰبُ ٱلنَّارِ ۖ هُمْ فِيهَا خَٰلِدُونَ ۝

> Those who consume interest will stand [on Judgment Day] like those driven to madness by Satan's touch. That is because they say, "Trade is no different than interest." But Allah has permitted trading and forbidden interest. Whoever refrains—after having received warning from their Lord—may keep their previous gains, and their case is left to Allah. As for those who persist, it is they who will be the residents of the Fire. They will be there forever.
>
> **Quran 2:275**

Islam emphasizes the importance of fairness, equality, and social justice, and views the charging of interest as a form of exploitation that benefits the lender at the expense of the borrower.

The Prophet Muhammad ﷺ also told us in numerous hadiths to avoid interest:

> Allah has cursed the one who consumes interest, the one who gives it, the one who records it, and the two witnesses to the transaction.[119]

> A dirham of *ribā* which a man receives knowingly is worse than committing adultery thirty-six times.[120]

These references emphasize the severity of the prohibition of interest in Islam and the negative consequences associated with it. Allah ﷻ says in the Quran:

---

119 *Ṣaḥīḥ Muslim*, no. 1598.
120 *Mishkāt al-Maṣābīḥ*, no. 2825.

Interest, Taxes, Inflation, and Financial Advisers

فَإِن لَّمْ تَفْعَلُوا فَأْذَنُوا بِحَرْبٍ مِّنَ ٱللَّهِ وَرَسُولِهِۦ ۖ وَإِن تُبْتُمْ فَلَكُمْ رُءُوسُ أَمْوَٰلِكُمْ لَا تَظْلِمُونَ وَلَا تُظْلَمُونَ ۝

If you do not [give up interest], then beware of a war with Allah and His Messenger! But if you repent, you may retain your principal—neither inflicting nor suffering harm.

Quran 2:279

This is why Halal Investing 101 is such an important topic for economic empowerment. *Interest* is haram, but *investing* is halal. We need to learn about halal investment alternatives that will keep us within the parameters of Islam. If people just have the vague notion that Islam imposes too many limitations on investing, they'll either ignore them and do whatever they want, or ignore them and do nothing with their money.

ALTERNATIVES

Islamic finance has developed alternative mechanisms for facilitating financial transactions without engaging in interest. When I first learned about this, all I could think of was how beautiful our religion is. Subhanallah, it has everything! It's an all-encompassing ecosystem. So what is Islamic finance and what is its goal?

Islamic finance is a financial system based on the principles of sharia, or Islamic law. It is designed to be consistent with Islamic ethical and moral values and to avoid practices that are exploitative or harmful to individuals and society.

Islamic finance operates under a different set of principles than conventional (read: Western) finance, which is based on the charging and paying of interest *(ribā)* and the use of financial instruments that are considered speculative, or similar to gambling.

Conventional finance treats money like a product that can be "rented out." Money is rented (loaned) out, and interest is charged on that renting (loan). Islamic finance treats money as a mode of exchange for goods and services. It also emphasizes the principles of fairness, social responsibility, and the sharing of risk and reward.

The main features of Islamic finance include the following:

Prohibition of *ribā*. Islamic finance prohibits the charging and paying of interest, as it is considered exploitative and unjust.[121]

Use of profit-sharing and equity-based contracts. Islamic finance relies on contracts that share risk and reward between the parties involved. These include:

- Profit-sharing contracts (*muḍāraba*). Where one party provides capital and the other provides expertise, with profits shared according to a predetermined ratio.

- Equity-based contracts (*mushāraka*). Similar to joint ventures, where multiple parties contribute capital and share both profits and losses.

- Sale-based contracts (*murābaḥa*). A form of cost-plus financing where the financial institution purchases an asset and sells it to the client at a marked-up price, with payment typically made in installments.[122]

Prohibition of speculative, unethical, or harmful activities. Islamic finance prohibits speculative activities such as gambling and speculation in uncertain outcomes, as these are considered harmful to individuals and society. Allah ﷻ says in the Quran:

---

121 Omar Suleiman, *40 on Justice: The Prophetic Voice on Social Reform* (Kube Publishing, 2021).
122 Fatemah A. Al Maddah, "Islamic Finance and the Concept of Profit and Risk Sharing," *Middle East Journal of Entrepreneurship, Leadership and Sustainable Development* 1, no. 1 (2017): 89–95.

Interest, Taxes, Inflation, and Financial Advisers

يَـٰٓأَيُّهَا ٱلَّذِينَ ءَامَنُوٓا۟ إِنَّمَا ٱلْخَمْرُ وَٱلْمَيْسِرُ وَٱلْأَنصَابُ وَٱلْأَزْلَـٰمُ رِجْسٌ مِّنْ عَمَلِ ٱلشَّيْطَـٰنِ فَٱجْتَنِبُوهُ لَعَلَّكُمْ تُفْلِحُونَ ۝

Oh believers! Intoxicants, gambling, idols, and drawing lots for decisions are all evil of Satan's handiwork. So shun them so you may be successful.

Quran 5:90

Prohibition of activities that harm people. Islamic finance prohibits investments in activities that are considered to be unethical or harmful to individuals and society, such as alcohol, pork, and pornography. They are haram—beyond just unethical and harmful.

Investment in real assets. Islamic finance encourages investment in real assets. Real assets are tangible assets, such as property, infrastructure, and businesses that have intrinsic value due to their physical properties. While investment in intangible assets (like intellectual property or digital assets) is not strictly prohibited, it is subject to careful scrutiny to ensure compliance with sharia principles.

Promotion of social welfare. Islamic finance aims to promote social welfare by encouraging investments in projects and businesses that have positive social and environmental impacts.[123]

After learning about the principles of Islamic finance, I was left wishing for such a system—one that aims to promote financial stability, social justice, and ethical business practices. I'm grateful that Islam provides a framework for such a system. But today's reality is frustratingly complex.

---

123 Anthony Clarke, "Islamic Finance: Unlocking Opportunities Beyond Religious Boundaries," Nasdaq, July 11, 2023, https://www.nasdaq.com/articles/islamic-finance-unlocking-opportunities-beyond-religious-boundaries.

While Islamic finance has made significant strides globally, a comprehensive, accessible, and universally trusted system of Islamic finance is still a work in progress in many parts of the world, including where I live. The implementation of these principles faces challenges such as varying interpretations, limited product offerings, and the need for greater standardization across different regions. Despite these hurdles, I remain committed to engaging with and supporting the development of Islamic financial practices to the best of my ability, recognizing that it's an evolving field with room for growth and improvement.

TAXES

There are a couple of things I've come to understand about taxes and retirement plans that I think are really important. When your company offers 401(k) plans or employee stock purchase plans, you have the opportunity to contribute money from your paycheck before taxes are taken out. These are known as pretax contributions. By contributing to these pretax accounts, you effectively lower your taxable income for the year.

Here's how it works: Let's say your annual salary is $50,000, and you contribute $5,000 to your 401(k). Instead of paying taxes on $50,000, you'll only pay taxes on $45,000. This means you're paying less in taxes now, while also saving for your future. Rather than giving more money to the government in taxes, you're investing it for your future retirement. This money can remain tax-deferred and grow until you withdraw it in retirement. By taking advantage of these investment opportunities, you're not only potentially reducing your current tax burden but also building your long-term financial security. It's a strategy that can benefit both your present and future financial situation.

You may argue that the government will provide Social Security benefits and Medicare for us when we retire. However, the long-

Interest, Taxes, Inflation, and Financial Advisers

term sustainability of these programs is a concern. According to the Social Security Administration's 2021 Trustees Report, "As a result of changes to Social Security enacted in 1983, benefits are now expected to be payable in full on a timely basis until 2037, when the trust fund reserves are projected to become exhausted." Similarly, the June 2022 Medicare Trustees Report announced that Medicare's Hospital Insurance Trust Fund will run out of money in 2028. These projections highlight the potential future limitations of these retirement support systems.

It's important to note that Medicaid, while not specifically a retirement program, can play a role for low-income seniors who need long-term care. During the COVID-19 pandemic, the federal government implemented measures to prevent people from losing Medicaid coverage. As the pandemic crisis abates, changes to these policies could affect many beneficiaries, including some elderly individuals who rely on Medicaid for long-term care services not covered by Medicare.

Given these uncertainties surrounding government programs, it becomes even more crucial to take personal responsibility for our retirement planning and not rely solely on these systems for our future financial security.

In other words, we need to think about our retirement and our future. "Tie your camel." Because the government may not be able to help you.

Another way I know to lower your income taxes is through charitable giving. When you donate money or goods to a qualified charitable organization, the value of your donation is subtracted from your taxable income. This can reduce your overall tax liability and result in a lower tax bill.

In the United States, charitable donations are tax-deductible. When you file your taxes, you will list out your charitable donations on your tax return form in a section called Schedule A. This is known as "itemizing deductions." By itemizing your deductions, you may be able to reduce your taxable income by the amount you've donated to qualified charitable organizations, potentially lowering your overall tax bill. If you have too many donations (mashallah!) and it's hard to track down all your giving, you can take a standard deduction. If you are single, the current standard deduction is $13,850, and if you are married filing jointly, it is $27,700. This amount reduces your income, which then reduces the amount of taxes you owe the government.[124]

The amount you can deduct for charitable donations is subject to certain limitations, such as a percentage of your adjusted gross income (AGI). It's important to keep accurate records of your donations, including receipts and documentation from the charity, to support your deduction list in case of an audit. Please consult your tax accountant about this if you haven't already done so.

INFLATION

What is inflation? Every year, a cost of living adjustment (COLA) metric is calculated by our government. Looking at recent history, from 2012 to 2021, the average annual inflation rate was about 1.9%. Many companies use this rate to determine annual salary increases. However, it's important to note that inflation can vary significantly from year to year. In 2022, the third year of the pandemic, we saw the cost of living increase by 9.1%. This number is important to understand for two reasons.

First, if your employer only provides you a cost of living raise each year, you need to make sure it reflects and stays up to date with the current inflation rate. In 2022, I hope your employer provided you

---

[124] Tina Orem and Ramona Paden, "Tax Deductible Donations: Rules for Charitable Giving," NerdWallet, July 11, 2023, https://www.nerdwallet.com/article/taxes/tax-deductible-donations-charity.

Interest, Taxes, Inflation, and Financial Advisers

with a 9.1% salary increase. If you only received 3%, you should interpret that as a salary decrease, not a raise. In the future, ask for it. Don't be scared or shy. Advocate for yourself, share with other employees, do your homework on inflation rates, and ask your boss for the right rate. Even your boss will benefit from this! When employees successfully advocate for inflation-matching raises, it often leads to company-wide adjustments, including increases for management. By fostering open discussions about fair, inflation-adjusted compensation, you contribute to a more financially healthy workplace for all, from entry-level employees all the way up to leadership.

Reason number two: If you save money in a non-interest-bearing bank account, every year your money loses value equivalent to the cost of living or inflation number. Would a math equation help here?

Let's consider a simple example to understand the impact of inflation on your savings. Imagine you have $100 in your savings account. In 2021, when many items at discount stores were priced at $1.00, your $100 could buy 100 items. However, due to high inflation in 2022, let's say the price of these items increased to $1.25 each. Now, your same $100 can only buy 80 items. This means the purchasing power of your $100 savings has decreased by 20%. In other words, even though you still have $100 in your account, its real value in terms of what it can buy has gone down significantly due to inflation. This 20% decrease in purchasing power aligns more closely with the high inflation rates experienced in 2022.

I have a friend named Sarah who shared something that her father said to her: Money in a savings account that does not earn anything is actually losing money. This includes the money you are saving under your mattress or in your piggy banks at home. In a typical year with about 3% inflation, the purchasing power of your savings diminishes by roughly 3%. In times of higher inflation, like we saw in 2022, the effect is even more dramatic. For instance, with inflation at 9.1%, the purchasing power of money in a savings account decreased by that 9.1% in just one year. Sarah's story made me reflect on how girls are often taught to save money, but her father went a step further. He was teaching her how to make money work for her. He encouraged her to invest so that her money could generate more money, potentially outpacing inflation.

Now consider the alternative of investing your money in accounts such as stocks or mutual funds. While the stock market can be volatile, with significant ups and downs, it has historically shown long-term growth that can potentially make an investor enough money to counter and even surpass the inflation rate, thus creating real wealth that can continue to grow. However, it's important to acknowledge the risks. Major market downturns like the 1929 crash or the 2008 recession can lead to substantial short-term losses. These events remind us that the market can be unpredictable and sometimes ruthless.

Despite these risks, many financial experts argue that for long-term savings, the potential benefits of investing often outweigh the near certainty of losing purchasing power to inflation. The key is to adopt a balanced approach. Once I learned about the impact of inflation on my savings, I decided to diversify. I moved 50% of my savings into an investment portfolio, focusing on different types of sharia-compliant stocks and funds. This approach allows me to potentially grow my wealth while still maintaining a safety net in more stable savings accounts.

It's crucial to understand that investing involves risks, and past performance doesn't guarantee future results. Before making any investment decisions, it's wise to research thoroughly, consider your risk tolerance, and possibly consult with a financial adviser to create a strategy that aligns with your goals and comfort level.

Interest, Taxes, Inflation, and Financial Advisers

INVESTMENT MANAGEMENT FIRM

Remember the woman from our very first community conversation with Muslim women in 2015? The one who voiced a common sentiment when she said, "I don't know where to go to meet Muslim women and make connections"? Her words continued to resonate as we developed our programs. One of the things I had imagined for our Muslim sisters was a safe community space just for us. A gathering space where we could come and connect or just hang out. Meet other Muslim women. Learn and grow. Have fun. And our feedback surveys reflected that goal in the women's answers—we want a space of our own.

I imagined a facility that not only housed the offices of our nonprofit organization but would also have space for workshops and conference rooms. I imagined a prayer space that would be branded in our brand colors, so it would be pink, gold, and gray. I imagined that we would have a social enterprise...maybe a coffee shop. It would be a gathering space where Muslim women could enjoy a cup of chai or a mocha along with some delicious *sambusa*s, all while visiting with other Muslim women from all walks of life, coming and going and enjoying themselves.

At the time of this writing, the only space in our area that is meeting those criteria is the Rabata Cultural Center (RCC), which I love. It is such a beautiful space. It's purple and pretty, and when I walk in there, I feel like I belong. I can host workshops there. I can meet people for a conversation. I can enjoy the free coffee they provide. I can buy a book from their bookstore and hang out with other Muslim sisters. I can pray in their prayer room. I can go there to have iftar during Ramadan. I wanted that same kind of space for the women RISE served.

The financial reality for most Muslim-led nonprofits is challenging. Many barely have enough budget to execute their programs and events. Numerous nonprofits led by Muslim women don't even have a paid-staff model yet. RISE, however, was in a unique position. Not only did we have a sustainable budget, but we were also generating a surplus from our operations. Our revenue consistently exceeded our expenses, allowing us to build up reserves. With this financial stability, we knew that creating a physical facility was a realistic goal for our future. This wasn't just a dream; it was a plan—a very tangible and achievable objective based on our financial performance.

Then I started to learn about endowment funds. An endowment is a donation of money or property to a nonprofit organization. That money is invested, and the income from that investment can be used for the operations of the nonprofit or for some other purpose.[125] Creating an endowment made me nervous, because the principal is invested and can never be touched. This was a huge risk to take, because we didn't have enough money to build an endowment that could generate returns right away.

Many of us are familiar with Harvard University's massive endowment fund, which stood at approximately $57 billion as of 2023. But what's less known is its humble beginning. Harvard's endowment traces back to 1638, just two years after the college's founding, when John Harvard bequeathed £779 (about half of his estate) and his four-hundred-volume library to the fledgling institution. This initial gift, worth approximately $129,000 in today's currency, was the seed that grew into the largest academic endowment in the world. Inspired by this example of starting small and growing over time, we at RISE wanted to begin our own endowment journey. We understood that even a modest start, managed wisely over time, could grow into a significant resource for our community.

---

125 Tim Smith, "Understanding Endowments: Types and Policies That Govern Them," Investopedia, July 9, 2022, https://www.investopedia.com/terms/e/endowment.asp.

We had net profits that were just sitting in our checking account. And like I said before, money just sitting in a bank account does not grow. It is losing value. So I met with a friend of mine who is in the financial sector and talked to her about our vision of owning a building. My friend Kate showed me that we didn't need an endowment fund. We needed a capital fund. A capital fund allows you to invest money and still have access to all of the initial principal.

While I was having this conversation with Kate, we had a potential donor asking if we accepted stock as a donation. No, we did not. I had no idea how people donated stock to nonprofits. So I asked another nonprofit leader, and he advised me to create a brokerage account and talk to his friend at Saturna Capital. A brokerage account is like a bank account for stocks. It is an investment account where you can buy and sell different types of investments like stocks, bonds, mutual funds, and exchange traded funds (ETFs). After speaking to someone at Saturna Capital, I realized that all we had to do was create a brokerage account and that would allow us to accept stock from donors. That stock would later be sold, and the money would be available for us to spend. A few days later, we accepted our first stock donation from a very generous community member.

We took it a step further and created an investment account with Saturna Capital as well. Saturna would sell any stocks donated to us and deposit the funds into our investment account. This investment account is basically our capital fund for the building we imagine owning one day. Everything I was learning about financial freedom and investing, I was applying to the nonprofit organization I was running. So we were not only relying on donations and grants but also on returns on investments.

Nonprofits can't sustain constant donor engagement and will eventually run out of grants to apply for. We need to diversify our fundraising portfolios. Capital funds are one way to do that.

Why am I sharing a capital fund story from a nonprofit organization? Well, creating a capital fund for a nonprofit and opening an investment account as an individual are two distinct financial actions, but they share some similarities in terms of investment principles and long-term financial planning. When the capital fund was created for RISE, the goal was to provide a stable and sustainable source of income to support the organization's mission and activities over the long term. The capital fund's investments are geared toward preserving and growing the principal amount while also generating income. It is very similar to when an individual opens an investment account. Some common goals when opening an investment account are to save for retirement, fund education, achieve specific financial milestones, or simply to grow wealth over time.

SHOULD YOU PAY FOR A FINANCIAL ADVISER?

Here's a friendly reminder that Muslim women are smart. I know right now this work of financial assessment, acumen, and literacy may seem overwhelming. However, I have complete confidence that you are capable of figuring most of it out. You are intelligent. You are educated. You are bright. You are a problem solver. If we have proven anything, it is that Muslim women get things done. Muslim women are change makers leading national protests for the right to wear hijab in non-Muslim countries. We are trailblazers; we have among our numbers the first Muslim woman member of Congress, Olympian, and federal judge. We are the ones who make the world a better place.

So why wouldn't we be able to figure this out? I know it seems easier to just find somebody to do the work for you. And you certainly can do that. But if you do, you will not get the satisfaction of understanding things yourself, being able to make informed

Interest, Taxes, Inflation, and Financial Advisers

decisions, and having control over your own finances. In the beginning, take small steps so that you are not overwhelmed. Talk to friends. You can do this. You got this. When your investments expand and your wealth expands along with them, you may want more help understanding additional investment vehicles. This would be the time for you to find a financial adviser.

I created my first investment portfolio at Fidelity Investments, which is a brokerage firm and financial investments company.[126] I bought some stocks and then I began learning about new companies. I watched growing trends in the market and observed how the world was changing in terms of technology, medicine, and travel. I compared companies and purchased stocks in the companies I was intrigued by. In 2021, I began to learn about all the different Islamic and sharia-compliant investment products and started to invest in them. The more I researched these products, the more I learned about Islamic finance and laws. It was fascinating, and the learner in me kept seeking out more information. It was at this point that I decided there was so much information I needed a guide. I contacted ShariaPortfolio and now have a financial adviser.

Early in 2023, I learned about halal stock screener tools, which are designed to help Muslim investors identify stocks and investment opportunities that comply with Islamic principles, particularly sharia law. The tools can be found on websites or as apps. I ran all of the stocks I owned through the Zoya Finance app to make sure they were sharia-compliant. Sadly, I found that half my portfolio was not! So I took my concerns to my financial adviser and sought her help. She suggested transfering the non-sharia-compliant stocks to ShariaPortfolio and letting the team help purify my money. Alhamdulillah I was able to do this. Are you ready to take your next step of opening an investment account? Read on!

---

126 Check out www.fidelity.com to learn more.

Reflection Exercise

1. What are you excited about after reading this chapter?

2. What are you nervous about?

3. What is something new you learned about taxes or inflation?

Chapter 12

Halal Investing 101

Remember Ishaq Uncle? Ishaq Uncle is my *khalu*. *Khalu* means uncle, but specifically it denotes that he is my mom's brother-in-law, married to my mom's sister. My mom lived with my uncle and aunt when she first moved to the United States. I was born in his house, and I consider him my first dad. He works at ShariaPortfolio as an investment adviser. According to their website, ShariaPortfolio is a boutique asset management firm specializing in socially responsible and halal investing and sharia-compliant wealth management. Shafaq Kazi is one of the female Muslim investment advisers at ShariaPorfolio. I invited Shafaq to come present Halal Investing 101 training at RISE. It was the second workshop in the Economic Empowerment Series. I was fascinated that Shafaq was a Muslim, hijabi, Desi, working mom. We shared the same intersecting identities. She was welcoming, savvy, and well-versed in halal investing, and I was enamored by her. Her presentation helped me understand not only the basics of investing but also how to invest within the parameters of Islam.

Shafaq defined common terms such as stocks, the stock market, bonds, *sukūk* (a sharia-compliant alternative to bonds), and portfolio. A stock is a share of ownership in a company. If you own a stock in a company, it means that you share ownership of that company; you are a shareholder. The stock market is where you purchase or sell stocks.

A bond is essentially a loan that investors make to a government or company. When a government or company needs to raise money, they issue bonds, which are purchased by investors like you and me. The issuer (whether government or company) promises to repay the loan amount (principal) plus interest over a specified period. This interest is seen as a return for the investors. However, from an Islamic perspective, because interest *(ribā)* is forbidden, traditional bonds are not considered halal. As a result, observant Muslims typically do not invest in conventional bonds. Instead, the Islamic financial market has developed an alternative called *sukūk*, which are structured to comply with Islamic financial principles.

Sukūk are a sharia-compliant alternative to bonds where the capital is backed by tangible assets. Instead of receiving interest, investors receive a return on those tangible assets. While these financial instruments were new to me and I was fascinated to learn about them, *sukūk* actually have a long history in Islamic finance. The concept dates back to the Umayyad Caliphate, demonstrating how Muslims have long used Islamic principles to create permissible forms of investing. My discovery of *sukūk* opened my eyes to the rich tradition of Islamic finance and its ability to provide alternatives to conventional Western financial instruments.[127]

A portfolio is the totality of all your investments. Your portfolio can include stock, real estate, precious metals, etc. It is highly recommended to keep your portfolio diverse by maintaining different types of investments. This mitigates your risk when the market is volatile. For example, when the stock market is not doing well, real estate values may remain stable or even increase. When real estate values decrease, precious metals might provide stability. However, it's important to note that these relationships are not guaranteed and can vary depending on economic conditions and other factors.

---

127 Hasan Zaman, "Historical Origins of Sukuk," *International Journal of Sukuk and Waqf Research* 1, no. 1 (2020): 27–29, http://cribfb.com/journal/index.php/IJSWR/article/view/1145.

As you begin creating your investment portfolio, you are going to look at short-term and long-term investing strategies. In the short term, you might be saving for something in the next three to five years. A great example of this is Hajj. I went on Hajj in 2003, and it cost me around $3,500. I thought that was so expensive. But Hajj packages offered by Dar El Salam and Qalam in 2020 cost around $14,600! So if an unsuspecting couple was hoping to complete their fifth pillar before the pandemic in 2020, they would have needed at least $30,000 in savings to make it happen. And remember, you cannot take out a loan or borrow money to perform Hajj. Enter: investing.

Imagine if at the start of the pandemic you purchased a share of Target at $92. That share in September 2022 would have been worth $162. That rate of return is amazing on a short-term investment strategy (ignoring capital gains taxes) compared to what it would have been if you had tucked away a few dollars every week into a savings account. (More about taxes in Chapter 11: Interest, Taxes, Inflation, and Financial Advisers.)

But if you are saving for retirement, then the long-term outlook is where it's at. And there you will see a generally increasing trajectory. In *The Latte Factor*, I read that there should be a 10% growth in the stock market every ten years during your lifetime until you retire. And when I look at my own individual stock portfolio, I have seen this growth in two particular stocks I've held for more than ten years. Yes, there have been dips and moments where the market is down or even crashing. In fact, the stock market has been quite volatile for the past few weeks. As of this writing, I'm watching a war in Ukraine, protests in Iran, hurricanes in Puerto Rico heading toward Florida, gas prices that are still too high, and inflation rates triple what they were last year. All of these events impact the stock market. For example, when the government increases interest rates in an effort to curb inflation, the stock market tends to come down. It's a vicious cyle! But we need to be patient and, over the long term, the stock market will gain and grow inshallah. "Focus on time in the market, not timing the market," says Shafaq.

WHAT IS HALAL INVESTING?

In Islam, the term halal means permissible. Many people hear the word halal and think it only pertains to food. Halal meat. But it actually applies to anything that is deemed permissible in Islam. How does this concept apply to investing?

Let's dive into how ShariaPortfolio, one Islamic brokerage firm, ensures your investments stay halal. They follow guidelines set by the Accounting and Auditing Organization for Islamic Financial Institutions (AAOIFI), which is basically the gold standard for Islamic finance.

But it's not always that straightforward. They also examine financial ratios, which might sound dull, but it's actually pretty interesting. These ratios help determine if a company might be indirectly profiting from interest or other activities that don't align with Islamic law.

Their screening process is thorough. They steer clear of investments in alcohol, gambling, weapons, tobacco, adult entertainment, pork products, and even highly leveraged businesses. They even avoid companies that make too much money from music, movies, or broadcasting. In fact, if a company earns more than 5% of its revenue from any of these sources, it's off the table.

ShariaPortfolio considers stocks and Islamic ETFs, but they won't touch preferred shares or interest-paying securities. It's all part of their commitment to keeping your investments halal.[128]

So when you invest with ShariaPortfolio or another firm that is

---

128   See https://shariaportfolio.com/.

committed to following AAOIFI standards, you can feel confident that they've done their due diligence. They're essentially your halal investing experts, making sure your money adheres to Islamic principles while still aiming for solid returns.

During Shafaq's presentation, I began to reflect on how I got started in investing. I worked for a corporation that offered a 401(k) plan as well as an employee stock purchase plan. At twenty-one years old, this was my first foray into the investing world. In my second job, at another Fortune 500 corporation, I continued investing, but at a higher rate. One, I was earning significantly more at this job than I had at my first. And two, I had learned that when you are young, you should max out on your contribution to your 401(k) and take full advantage of the company match. Not taking that match is leaving money on the table! I put 15% of my pretax salary into my 401(k) plan and my company matched every dollar with fifty cents. Win-win.

Now I was making four times as much as I had been in my first job out of college. So I also invested more dollars in the employee stock purchase plan (ESPP), which is a great opportunity to buy company stock at a 15% discount. Just buying it puts me at a 15% gain! Imagine that stock currently costs $100 per share. Through the ESPP, I was able to purchase those shares for $85 each. After almost five years investing into this plan, I had purchased almost 2,000 shares.

In 2011, I left the corporate world to join the nonprofit sector, which did not have any of these investment vehicles. I had to open another investment account and transfer the stock that I had purchased at my company to it. This was the beginning of the second stage of my investment journey. This stage was dormancy. I did nothing. I hate to admit it, but I literally just ignored it all. For at least ten years, I didn't bother looking at my portfolios except in Ramadan, and that was only to calculate my zakat. I didn't buy new stock. I didn't sell the stock I held. I couldn't grow my retirement account, and I didn't save much money. My salary was reduced by almost 80% in the first six years of my nonprofit career and I thought I had no options.

Like many novice investors, I behaved with a risk-averse mentality grounded in scarcity and didn't have patience with the market. Shafaq was kind and compassionate as she explained markets and displayed a human-centric approach in helping me move my money into the right investment vehicles.

Some really interesting advice Shafaq shared was to keep a small amount of money as cash in my investment account. Because when the market tanks, I shouldn't be fretting about my portfolio's value. Rather, I should be focusing on what stocks I could purchase at this lower price. The market really does level out and usually grows over time. Bach and Mann taught me this in *The Latte Factor* too. I've watched my first employer's stock, which I bought at $46 in 1999, grow to $502 as I type this sentence. Be patient, strategic, and dream long-term!

At the end of Shafaq's presentation, Muslim sisters had a chance to ask questions. I remember one sister asked, "After paying $1,000 to open an account with ShariaPortfolio, what's the bare minimum I would need to spend in order to continue investing?" Now, what I loved about Shafaq's answer was that before she addressed the question, she corrected the language of "paying $1,000." That $1,000 is not a form of payment; it is your money being invested into an account. You're not paying $1,000; you're investing $1,000. The only thing ShariaPortfolio does is manage that initial $1,000 by investing it into the stock market. As you speak about your financial journey and investing, think about how you frame your language. Use words that accurately define and describe your actions. Using clear and concise language is important because it helps prevent misunderstandings and ensures that both you and others truly understand what you are conveying.

The second part of the question dealt with the bare minimum investment needed to start an investment account. Shafaq responded that there was no requirement. You can start by investing $100 or $1,000. As Bach and Mann put it in *The Latte Factor*, "pay yourself first." What does that mean? Take one hour of pay per week and automatically transfer that into your investment account for the investment advisers to manage.

EXAMPLE:

Salary ÷ Number of hours = Hourly wage

If you make $25,000 per year, your math would look like this:

$25,000 ÷ 2080 (40 hours/per week x 52 weeks/year) = $12.02/ hour

Beware of opening your account and failing to continuously invest in it. Regularly contributing to your investment account is known as dollar-cost averaging (DCA). It is the practice of systematically investing equal amounts of money—in this case your hourly wage—at regular intervals, regardless of the price of a share. The benefit is that it removes the emotional aspect of investing and saves you time. Whatever amount you contribute, it will grow over time.

The final thing that I want to share about Shafaq's presentation is the sheer amount of questions these Muslim women asked around whether they should do A or whether they should do B? Should I invest in an IRA or in the stock market? Should I invest in a 401(k) or should I invest in the stock market? Shafaq's answer was always, "Both!" She said if you can put money away in either of those investment vehicles, you would always operate from a diversified portfolio perspective. Don't put all your eggs in one basket. Make sure that you spread out your investments so you reduce your chances of losing money in the market. If stocks are going down in one area, perhaps your IRA will be going up. A particular stock in a different sector may be volatile, but when you have stock diversity, you can look at the portfolio as a whole. That way, you will see a larger bird's-eye view of the group instead of each individual stock moving up and down.

DIVERSIFYING YOUR STOCK PORTFOLIO

Your investment portfolio should contain different types of assets. An asset is something you own that has monetary value, generates income, or increases in price. There are different types of assets you can own besides stock. I will tell you, I didn't know this when I first opened up an account. Now, though, I've learned a couple of things and I want to share them with you. And keep in mind, I'm still learning. So if you have additional ideas on how to diversify a portfolio, email me.

There are five ways you can diversify your portfolio: company stock, mutual funds, *sukūk*, ETFs, and REITs. Let's begin with company stock.

Company Stock

My first brokerage account only had stock from the two companies I had worked at. When one company wasn't doing well, it dragged the entire account down. When one company was doing phenomenal, it made my account look stellar! But guess what happened when we hit a recession and I only had these two stocks? It looked really red and I was scared. Remember what Shafaq said about what to do when the market is down? Buy. So I started to buy shares in companies from different sectors.

How did I pick these shares? I Googled "halal stocks" and began researching how a stock gets that halal stamp of approval. Warning:

There is math involved. First off, stay away from companies that sell haram products or that are unethical in their business practices. Let's not buy shares in a company that sells alcohol, OK? Is the company's service or product itself engaged in interest? I have steered clear of banks and credit card companies. If you really like doing research, check out the company's annual reports and see if they received any revenue from non-sharia-compliant investments. And if you love financial ratios, what is the nonliquid to total assets ratio? Because in order for it to be considered a halal stock, that ratio needs to be more than 20%. Mustafa Khan wrote a blog post on Islamic Finance Guru on May 31, 2021, outlining a few other metrics to look at:[129]

- The 5% rule states that income generated from haram investments in a company should not be greater than 5% of their gross revenue.

- The percentage of total interest-bearing debt of a company should not exceed 33% compared to their total assets.

- The percentage of accounts receivable compared to the company's total assets should not be greater than 45%.

I don't know about you, but this stuff started to make my head spin. I didn't have the patience or attention span to do all that. Luckily, Muslims have created halal stock screener apps like Zoya, Islamicly, Musaffa, Wahed, and Finispia![130] What caught my eye with these apps was that their screener tool uses the same methodology the AAOIFI uses to create reports on stocks you're interested in.

I bought some shares, little by little, and diversified my portfolio. Today, I have a dozen different types of stock. As I'm writing this, I

---

129 Mustafa Khan, "How to Buy Halal Stocks – Stock Screening Method," IFG, May 31, 2022, https://www.islamicfinanceguru.com/articles/investment/how-to-screen-for-halal-sharia-compliant-shares.
130 Links to these screeners are at the end of the book under Resources.

googled "halal stocks" again. Quite a few new ones came up, and I want to research them all! As I research these companies, I'm also going to run them through one of the halal stock screener apps.

Screening your stocks at the time of the initial purchase isn't enough, though. I learned the hard way that companies change. Their investment strategies, their product lines, their objectives—all that can change. At one point they may be sharia-compliant, and then a few years later they might not be. When you come across a stock that turns noncompliant, you'll need to purify your portfolio—meaning sell that stock and donate the appreciated value to charity. Work with your financial adviser on how to purify your portfolio.

Mutual Funds

Investopedia defines mutual funds as "an investment vehicle consisting of a portfolio of stocks, bonds, or other securities, overseen by a professional money manager." So instead of you having to diversify your portfolio, you could invest in mutual funds because they would already be diversified. This is great, except that most mutual funds contain bonds, which are interest-bearing. Not very sharia-compliant, right? But never fear! There are sharia-compliant mutual funds. The most well-known is the Amana Mutual Fund.

Amana has four different types of mutual funds. If you want to learn more, I would recommend checking out Saturna Capital's Amana Fund Selector. You'll learn about the history of the fund, its past performance, and get to use the Fund Selector, which has a good set of questions to answer that will help you understand your own risk tolerance and goals. You'll learn which fund matches or most closely aligns with your values and objectives. Once you figure this out, you can purchase shares in Amana Mutual Funds and add them to your growing stock portfolio to diversify. (Note:

Amana Mutual Funds are one example. Other halal mutual funds include Azzad Wise Capital Fund, Azzad Ethical Fund, and Iman Fund.)

Sukūk

I explained this a little in the beginning of this chapter, but here's a quick refresher. Bonds are haram because they earn interest. Muslims have an alternative to bonds, known as *sukūk*. These are sharia-compliant Islamic financial certificates. Bonds raise money in the form of debt, but *sukūk* give you a share of ownership in an asset. Check out Azzad Asset Management, Saturna Capital, or ShariaPorfolio's websites and read their blogs or white papers on *sukūk*. Links are in the Resources section at the end of this book. They go into much greater detail.

Do your research before you invest in *sukūk*. My research found seven different types of *sukūk* in the market. They come with different credit ratings and minimum requirements, and they vary in sharia compliance. The non-Islamic financial gurus rate these very low, with below average returns. But they don't have the same values to consider that we do. You should look at the long term.

Fatima Iqbal is a Senior Investment Strategist and Financial Planner at Azzad Asset Management. I met her early in 2023, as we were both invited to participate in a webinar about Muslim donors. I was pleasantly surprised and excited to meet yet another hijabi Muslim woman in the field of investing and financial planning, and I learned a lot from her in that limited time. Azzad has a fixed-income fund called the Azzad Wise Capital Fund. It was the first halal, fixed-income fund, and was launched in 2010. The goal of a halal fixed-income fund is to provide the investor with a steady and predictable stream of income while adhering to Islamic financial principles. The Azzad Wise Capital Fund invests in *sukūk*s, Islamic bank deposits, and trade finance contracts in order to provide capital preservation. But what does capital preservation mean? It's a strategy aimed at protecting the initial investment from loss, even if it means achieving lower returns. In practical terms for Muslim investors, this fund offers a way to potentially maintain the value of their money while earning some return, all without dealing in interest. It's designed to be a relatively low-risk option, similar to how a savings account might function in conventional banking, but structured to comply with Islamic financial principles.

Exchange-Traded Fund (ETF)

An ETF is a type of investment that combines features of a stock and a mutual fund. It is like a basket of different assets, including stocks, *sukūk*, and other assets. When you buy shares of an ETF, you are effectively buying a piece of that basket. ETFs are traded on the stock market exchange, just like individual stocks, making it easier for us to buy and sell them. I found ten different types of sharia-compliant ETFs in the market. I've only invested in one so far, and I'm watching its performance and considering a couple more to diversify my portfolio.

As a fairly novice investor, I'm learning that I have to also look beyond returns. This is where the real work lies. It's one thing to use the internet to learn about a company or a fund. But it's another thing entirely to read the prospectus of each fund or ETF in order to understand all the risks involved. Most of us can't put in that much legwork, but I do know a few steps to take to avoid investing in high-risk or potentially risky assets: diversify your portfolio, consider ETFs and mutual funds, and start small.

Real Estate Investment Trust (REIT)

Thank you, Investopedia, for explaining this in the simplest way possible for me. "A real estate investment trust (REIT) is a company that owns, operates, or finances income-generating real estate. Modeled after mutual funds, REITs pool the capital of numerous investors. This makes it possible for individual investors to earn dividends from real estate investments—without having to buy, manage, or finance any properties themselves."[131] REITs also need to be sharia-compliant. What if its real estate purchases were made with interest or haram money? What if it's a hotel REIT where alcohol is served or sold? Recently, I learned about REITs in Malaysia, Dubai, and Singapore. ShariaPortfolio created an ETF REIT. Its ticker symbol[132] is SPRE. This is something to study and watch closely because it is the first of its kind on this side of the world.

REITs also provide natural protection against inflation. Real estate values and rents tend to increase when prices do. According to Statista, inflation rates at the start of the pandemic in 2020 were 2.3%. By June of 2022, rates hit 9.1%. Meanwhile, the real estate market was booming. CNN reported that home sales were going to reach their highest level in the past fifteen years, with six million homes sold in 2021. The Federal Housing Finance Agency reported that homeowners, on average, saw a 20% increase in the value of their homes that year. And as property values increase, landlords can increase rents. Leases are impacted by inflation. When you invest in a REIT during a time of inflation, you will see dividend growth that provides a reliable stream of income.

Fatima Iqbal is an investment adviser and senior financial planner at Azzad Asset Management. She taught me that aside from diversifying your portfolio across types of investments, it is important to diversify across sectors and asset classes. Why? Let's

---

[131] Peter Gratton, "Real Estate Investment Trust (REIT): How They Work and How to Invest," Investopedia, July 19, 2024, https://www.investopedia.com/terms/r/reit.asp.

[132] A ticker symbol or stock symbol is an abbreviation used to uniquely identify publicly traded shares of a particular stock on a particular stock market.

say all my stocks, mutual funds, and ETFs are in technology, and some catastrophic event occurs in that sector. The value of all the assets in the technology sector will fall, so my portfolio will decline. But if I had diversified and included stocks in health care, real estate, energy, and utilities, I wouldn't have felt the negative decline as intensely.

One last thing Fatima reminded me of was how incredibly powerful Islamic finance and halal investing options are. During a down market, these Islamic investing tools fared much better than their counterparts. So much so that some of them received major industry awards. Informa Financial Intelligence's PSN manager database, North America's longest-running database of investment managers, designated five investment strategies of Azzad Asset Management as "Top Guns." CNBC FA 100 ranked Azzad on their list of wealth management firms that offer the most comprehensive planning and financial services to help clients navigate their financial lives. Azzad Wise Capital Fund won the 2023 Lipper Fund Award, which is based on the Lipper Leader for Consistent Return rating. I felt great pride in learning that sharia-compliant investment strategies and products perform better by following Allah's rules. High-quality halal investments can compete alongside others and even outperform them!

Now you're probably wondering, "Nausheena, why don't you just tell me which companies to buy stock in, which mutual fund to invest in, which ETF or REIT to buy?" Because I'm not your financial adviser and I don't know your goals or, quite frankly, your values. I want you to learn, do the research, and make your own informed decisions.

OWNING COMPANY STOCK IS NOT THE SAME AS GAMBLING

This question comes up often: "Isn't buying and selling stocks the same as gambling?" No. And let me count the ways.

Halal Investing 101

Gambling is haram—period. Haram means it is forbidden. Allah ﷻ has forbidden Muslims to gamble, which means that engaging in it is punishable.

> يَـٰٓأَيُّهَا ٱلَّذِينَ ءَامَنُوٓا۟ إِنَّمَا ٱلْخَمْرُ وَٱلْمَيْسِرُ وَٱلْأَنصَابُ وَٱلْأَزْلَـٰمُ رِجْسٌ مِّنْ عَمَلِ ٱلشَّيْطَـٰنِ فَٱجْتَنِبُوهُ لَعَلَّكُمْ تُفْلِحُونَ ۝ إِنَّمَا يُرِيدُ ٱلشَّيْطَـٰنُ أَن يُوقِعَ بَيْنَكُمُ ٱلْعَدَٰوَةَ وَٱلْبَغْضَآءَ فِى ٱلْخَمْرِ وَٱلْمَيْسِرِ وَيَصُدَّكُمْ عَن ذِكْرِ ٱللَّهِ وَعَنِ ٱلصَّلَوٰةِ ۖ فَهَلْ أَنتُم مُّنتَهُونَ ۝

> Oh believers! Intoxicants, gambling, idols, and drawing lots for decisions are all evil of Satan's handiwork. So shun them so you may be successful. Satan's plan is to stir up hostility and hatred between you with intoxicants and gambling and to prevent you from remembering Allah and praying. Will you not then abstain?
>
> **Quran 5:90–91**

To understand why Islam forbids gambling, it's important first to define what gambling is: It's the act of risking money or valuables on an event with an uncertain outcome, which is primarily determined by chance.

Ustadha Kaltun Karani of Hikmah Academy helped me better understand the Islamic perspective on this. She explained that all Islamic laws exist to serve five higher objectives: the protection of life, lineage, intellect, wealth, and religion. Gambling, she pointed out, directly contradicts the protection of wealth. "Taking chances when you are betting and gambling is not a way to protect your wealth," she said. "It doesn't have proper planning, it's not strategic, and it does not include Allah ﷻ in the equation."

Ustadha Kaltun then elaborated on how gambling conflicts with Islamic principles of faith and action. "As Muslims, we don't believe in mere chance," she explained. "We believe in Allah's power and His plan. This belief requires us to use our intellect and make thoughtful decisions." She emphasized that Muslims are called to put their faith into action through careful consideration and planning, not through reckless risk-taking.

"Gambling is contradictory to our principles," Ustadha Kaltun concluded. "Investing, on the other hand, requires a calculated risk. Not a risk of chance, but a thoughtful assessment of potential outcomes, always keeping our trust in Allah ﷻ at the forefront."

Gambling is considered detrimental and prohibited in Islam for numerous compelling reasons. Financially, it's destructive, often leading to significant losses and potential ruin for individuals and families. Psychologically, gambling can be profoundly harmful, fostering addiction and compulsive behavior that's difficult to overcome. Socially, its corrosive nature can damage family relationships and community ties, tearing at the fabric of society. Spiritually, gambling is compromising, as it relies on chance rather than trust in Allah's provision and plan. From an ethical standpoint, it's questionable because it inherently involves profiting from others' losses, creating a zero-sum game that contradicts the Islamic principles of mutual benefit and cooperation. Finally, gambling is intellectually unproductive, failing to utilize God-given faculties for constructive purposes as Islam encourages. Not to mention that the gambling environment is surrounded by alcohol, smoking, and many other haram things. It makes you forget Allah, your family, and your responsibilities. These multifaceted negative impacts clearly illustrate why Islam takes such a strong stance against gambling

I have seen many families ruined because of a gambling addiction. I know people who continuously took risks with their *rizq*, lost their weekly wages, got behind on bills, were not able to afford their daily living, and lost their house, their lifestyle, and their dignity. I watched someone lose their job and constantly ask to borrow money from others (while never paying them back) to feed their frenzied addiction. On the Day of Judgment, Allah ﷻ will ask us about our money—how we earned it and how we spent it. I would never want to say that I spent my hard-earned money on something He prohibited.

Investing in a company, on the other hand, is completely halal. Look at it from an economic perspective. Investing in companies advances our society in technology, health care, education, and many other sectors. You are investing in the creativity of a company's products or services that you support but can't invent yourself. Why am I investing in different health care companies? Because we have diseases and illnesses that are killing off our loved ones. I can't create heart stents, vaccines, or therapeutics, but certain companies can, and are carrying out that research and development.

Investing in productive and sharia-compliant companies ensures the expansion of different investing vehicles for Muslims. A healthy economy needs thriving businesses for job creation, the advancement of society, and to sustain a thriving community. As I was writing this book, some of the sharia-compliant companies I invested in were not making large returns, but I saw investing in them as a strategic move toward the success of healthy and moral financial vehicles.

When you buy stock, you're essentially purchasing a small ownership stake in a company. Your investment is based on the anticipation that the company will perform well and grow over time. The goal is for the value of your shares to increase as the company becomes more valuable. This appreciation of your investment is one way to potentially gain returns. Additionally, if the company is profitable and chooses to distribute some of those profits to shareholders, you may receive dividends.

As a stockholder, the company has a responsibility to report to you what they have done or are doing with your money. It's a system of checks and balances designed to ensure they maintain principled and upstanding business practices and are not involved in shady things like unethical or fraudulent activities, corporate malfeasance, or deceptive or exploitative practices.

Investing in a company is a long-term strategy, not a short-term bet. When you buy stock, you are not selling it a day later. You are hoping this company will perform really well going forward. Your financial returns accrue over a long period of time. That is not the case with gambling. Gambling is all about taking a chance on something meaningless in the short term—seconds or hours, not months or years.

Investing in company stocks can create a cash flow strategy, particularly through dividend-paying stocks. When you invest in companies that perform well and pay dividends, you receive regular payments, typically on a quarterly or annual basis. These dividends are essentially a share of the company's profits paid out to stockholders. Companies that consistently pay dividends are often viewed as financially stable, which can make their stocks attractive to other investors. This increased demand can potentially lead to an appreciation in the stock's value over time, though it's important to note that dividend payments themselves don't directly increase the stock price. The combination of regular dividend income and potential long-term stock price appreciation can create a favorable situation for investors. This approach offers a stark contrast to gambling, where you might make some quick cash right away, but you could just as easily lose it all immediately, with no potential for ongoing returns or long-term growth.

There are a ton of other reasons that investing is not the same as gambling. Talk to Islamic scholars, read the academic literature as well as Islamic finance books, and email me what you learn!

SAVING FOR COLLEGE

As we know, a degree increases your chances of earning a higher salary. But college is expensive. Tuition rates have climbed significantly faster than income. Many cannot afford it, so they don't attend college. Those who do go to college end up taking out loans which, as the student debt crisis shows us, the average student is unable to pay off because they simply aren't earning enough. Look at the fight for increasing the minimum wage!

I was fortunate to begin my college journey at a community college, where I spent two years on a full academic scholarship. This covered everything except books and lab fees, giving me a solid start without accumulating debt.

For my last two years, I transferred to a private university. This is where my wonderful mother's sacrifice truly shines. Like many families, we didn't qualify for financial aid, so my mom stepped up in an incredible way. She had just started working full-time as a cashier at Target, which was new to our small town in the mid-1990s. Every week, she diligently saved $125 from her paycheck, allowing her to contribute $500 monthly toward my tuition. I tear up every time I think about how hard she worked for me. Her efforts, combined with a partial scholarship, meant I only needed to take out about $13,000 in student loans. I can never repay her, and I don't think I'm even capable of working as hard as she did. May Allah ﷻ preserve my mom and all our mothers. *Ameen.*

Thanks to my mom's help and my scholarship, my student loan debt was manageable. Paying it off became one of my top priorities when I started working after college. I was able to manage that quickly, which allowed my husband and me to go on Hajj in 2003. Alhamdulillah.

Looking back, I realize how fortunate I was. Many others, including my younger siblings, are still paying off their student loans. This is why we are working toward financial empowerment. So that our kids will have some generational wealth to give them a leg up as they step out into the world.

When I was pregnant with my first child, my husband and I were advised to start a 529 plan—an investment account for college. A 529 plan is like a traditional IRA—you invest after-tax contributions into mutual funds and watch it grow. So along with that baby shower, ladies, open a college savings plan. Because in eighteen years, when it's time for her to go to college, your child can use that money for tuition. Sounds great, right?

Except that the traditional 529 plan is not halal. Why? First off, the mutual fund may have shares in companies that are not sharia-compliant. Second, it includes bonds, which are always interest-based. So then what's the alternative?

One, you could simply start a savings account in a bank once they are born and add to it. I wouldn't recommend this, though. Mainly because savings accounts accrue interest, but also, as we've discussed, money in a savings account decreases in value over time. Instead, you could open a Coverdell Education Savings Account (ESA). A Coverdell Education Savings Account (formerly Education IRA) is a tax-advantaged education savings account that you can establish for any child under age eighteen. It has an investment limitation of $2,000 annually. Withdrawals can be used to pay for qualified college, secondary, or even elementary school expenses. Contributors must meet certain income eligibility requirements. Azzad Asset Management offers a Coverdell ESA.

Two, you could open a brokerage account and invest in a halal mutual fund like Amana. Every month, add to this account. Buy more shares and let it grow over the next eighteen years. You would be managing this yourself.

Three, you could open a Uniform Gift to Minors Act (UGMA)

and Uniform Transfers to Minors Act (UTMA) custodial account. These can be used to save for college by allowing the custodial parent to hold assets for their child.

An ESA, a UGMA account, and a UTMA account each have their own benefits and disadvantages. I would recommend that before you open any of these, you speak to a financial adviser at ShariaPortfolio or Azzad Asset Management to understand your options.

Bottom line: Use the investing route to save for your child(ren)'s education. Help them be able to afford a college education that will help them start a career and earn more than a livable wage. Let's help our children begin life financially stable and debt-free, so they, too, can give back to their communities.

Reflections and Actions

1. Do you have an investment account?

2. If no, what is holding you back from opening one? What steps could you take today to explore opening one?

3. If yes, what are some steps you can take to ensure it is sharia-compliant and growing?

Chapter 13

Retirement Plans, 401(k)s, and IRAs

When you're a young graduate, fresh out of college at your first job, you're just starting your life. You're excited about buying a new car and getting your own place. Adulting! If you're lucky, that first job will have benefits like medical, dental, vision, life insurance, and a matching 401(k) plan. As you pass through the days of your youth, your adulting phase will need to include planning for your elder phase. This chapter is all about envisioning and planning for the future, when you are ready to enter retirement.

As part of your financial stability plan and security for when you retire, make this your mantra: I want to be FIRE—financially independent and retire early. That way you get to decide at what age you want to retire. It doesn't have to be at sixty-five. It can be earlier or later. You decide if you want to be semiretired or fully. But when you do, you want to be financially secure.

Earlier in this book, I shared that my first job offered a 401(k) plan. At twenty-one years old, I enrolled and invested about 5% of my pretax dollars into the plan. Luckily, my employer matched it. I only made $12 an hour at that job, but I'm telling you, I felt rich. It felt like so much money at the time. I was an employee at that company for about three years. When I left, I honestly didn't know what I was supposed to do with my 401(k) plan—so I left it behind.

My second job also offered a 401(k) plan and I immediately enrolled. My starting salary was almost double my previous job. By now, I had become smarter—like, I-have-an-MBA-now smarter. I knew I needed to max out on my contribution to my 401(k) plan to take full advantage of the company match. I invested 15% of my pretax salary into my 401(k) plan, and my company matched every dollar with fifty cents. I was an employee there for about six years. As you know, I had an epiphany and needed to find more purpose in life. So I left corporate America and leaped into the nonprofit sector—and again I left my 401(k) behind.

Before I continue with my story, I want to share that when I was investing in my 401(k), I had no idea that it also needed to be sharia-compliant. I didn't know where my money was being invested. At my first job, I didn't know I could direct that money. It was at my second job that I learned I could pick different investment options. I did my best to make informed choices, like investing in the stock of the company I worked for, as well as selecting various index funds. But when I reflect, I realize I didn't know how to screen those options for sharia compliance. I'm not advising you not to invest in the 401(k) program your company offers you, but here are some options for you to explore on your financial journey.

The first option is to check with your human resources or benefits department and see if your company offers a self-directed brokerage account (SDBA). An SDBA gives you the agency to choose your own investments, but you have to put in the effort. Don't just let your money sit there. Be active in selecting halal investment options.

If an SDBA is not available, it's time to do some advocacy work. I'm sure there are other Muslims in your company who need a retirement benefit that doesn't conflict with their religious beliefs. Ask for one. Remember, these are companies that started out with probably only white, Christian men. The employee base is diversifying, and so should the benefits. We've asked for prayer spaces, Eid holidays, halal meals, and hijab uniform accommodations. Ask for an SDBA to accommodate your religious requirements for a retirement fund.

For Muslims concerned about ensuring that their 401(k) investments comply with Islamic finance principles, there are several strategies to consider. Malak Kudaimi's blog on Zoya Financial's website offers valuable resources, including a sample letter template you can use to communicate your needs to your HR department. This letter can help you request sharia-compliant investment options in your company's 401(k) plan.[133]

Kudaimi's blog also suggests an alternative approach: minimizing the non-sharia-compliant holdings in your existing 401(k) account. However, this strategy comes with challenges, as it's often difficult to determine with certainty which holdings are in various investment options. To assist in this process, you can utilize fund screeners (such as those mentioned in the previous section) to identify which investments may not be sharia-compliant.

It's important to note that if your company's own stock is determined to be non-sharia-compliant, you may need to reconsider your overall approach to 401(k) participation. This situation raises broader questions about aligning your employment and financial decisions with your religious principles.

Ultimately, navigating 401(k) investments while adhering to Islamic finance principles requires careful consideration and may involve discussions with both financial and religious advisers to determine the best course of action for your individual circumstances.

Back to my own journey in retirement accounts. About ten years had gone by, and I had transitioned from working in the corporate sector to working in the nonprofit sector. Nonprofits, especially Muslim-led nonprofits, rarely provide any sort of benefits to their employees. It took four years before RISE could offer fully paid maternity leave, five years before we were able to provide health

---

133 Sample HR template can be found at https://blog.zoya.finance/is-my-401k-plan-halal/.

care insurance, and we still had no retirement savings plan when I left. Many of you are probably in the same boat. Maybe your employer doesn't offer a 401(k) plan, so you can't take advantage of some of these great investing vehicles. When you hear all this advice about putting deferred-tax or pretax dollars into retirement accounts, you get frustrated. Or like me, you feel hopeless. But guess what! There actually is something for you. It's called an individual retirement account (IRA).

It took me a long time to understand IRAs. First of all, there are so many different types: traditional, Roth, rollover, SIMPLE, and SEP. I spent time learning about some of them, and let me tell you, it was confusing! I'm going to share, in chronological order, which IRAs I opened up. This isn't the right way or the wrong way. It's just a personal historical sequence of events.

SEP IRA

Earlier I mentioned pension plans. I was referring to the SEP IRA, a simplified employee pension individual retirement account. The SEP IRA is an account adopted by business owners to provide retirement benefits for themselves and their employees. After I had quit my first corporate job, I was doing contract work under a small consulting company my husband had established. Because our firm was unable to provide a retirement benefit, we opted to open a SEP IRA with a mutual funds and investment company. The SEP IRA account offered many benefits, including tax-deferred compounding, higher contribution limits, a reduction in our taxable income, and a practical way to save for retirement.

If you are self-employed, a contractor, a consultant, or someone who receives a 1099, I believe this is the retirement account you should open up. You can currently contribute the lesser of 25% of your income or $69,000 a year. The contribution limits for SEP IRAs are typically quite generous, allowing you to contribute a significant percentage of your income, up to a high annual limit that's adjusted yearly for inflation. Because the contributions are made with pretax dollars, they lower your overall taxable income for the year. The benefit is that you take an income deduction when your income is high, and in retirement, if your income is lower, you'll pay lower taxes on withdrawals at that time.

ROLLOVER IRA AND SEP IRA

After attending Shafaq's presentation on Halal Investing 101, I realized the importance of aligning my retirement savings with Islamic principles. I had two 401(k) retirement plans from previous corporate employers that were likely not sharia-compliant. To address this, I initiated a rollover process, transferring both of these accounts to ShariaPortfolio. This move allowed me to purify my *rizq* and ensure my retirement savings adhered to Islamic guidelines.

In addition to the 401(k)s, I had a SEP IRA at another investment company. To maintain sharia compliance and simplify my financial management, I transferred this account to ShariaPortfolio as well. This consolidation made it much easier to track my investments and manage my retirement accounts, eliminating the need to juggle multiple logins, passwords, and financial reports.

The funds from my previous 401(k)s and SEP IRA are now in a rollover IRA at ShariaPortfolio. I've entrusted them with the management of this account. While I can no longer contribute to this rollover IRA, I expect ShariaPortfolio to make sound financial decisions that will grow this account until I'm ready to withdraw from it in retirement.

Since I can't make new contributions to the rollover IRA, I opened a new SEP IRA at ShariaPortfolio in 2021. This account allows me to continue building my retirement savings as a self-employed individual. For the past few years, I've received income from speaking engagements, and in 2023 I became fully self-employed again. Each year, my accountant calculates how much I can contribute to my SEP IRA based on my 1099 income. The maximum contribution is up to 25% of my net self-employment income, subject to annual IRS limits. Once I know this amount, I transfer the corresponding funds from my bank account to the SEP IRA. These contributions are made with pretax dollars, which reduces my taxable income for the year by the amount contributed.

This comprehensive approach allows me to maintain sharia-compliant retirement savings while also benefiting from tax advantages. By consolidating my accounts and establishing a clear contribution strategy, I've simplified my financial life while staying true to my Islamic values.

ROTH IRA

Because I worked for a nonprofit and then became self-employed, it was recommended that I also open a Roth IRA. So what is a Roth IRA? It is an individual retirement account that lets you set aside after-tax income, up to a specified amount, each year. That amount was $6,000 when I first opened the account. I still have about fifteen years before I can withdraw money from it, which means I'll have fifteen more years of earnings from it when I retire. And you know the fun part? After contributing to my Roth IRA for five years and turning 59½ years old, both the earnings on the account and the withdrawals are tax-free!

Hindsight being twenty-twenty, I realized that during the eleven years I was working for nonprofits, I hadn't been investing in any of my retirement plans. I wish I had opened a SEP IRA eleven years ago. Because for eleven years, I would have been able to contribute 20%–25% of my contracted work and honorariums. I wish I had had a Roth IRA and contributed the maximum amount, which would have been about $6,000 a year. Imagine $66,000 over those eleven years going into a Roth IRA, being invested and growing at an annual rate of 8%! I would have over $107,000 in that account today.

But that *rizq* was not meant for me.

After that realization, I thought about my own daughter, who was turning twenty-two years old the next Saturday. I texted the family WhatsApp thread and asked "Does Arshia have an IRA set up?" And immediately I got a text back that said "Yes." Fantastic! At the age of twenty-one, she already had a Roth IRA set up. We also set one up for my eighteen-year-old son. This is what young people need to be guided to. Because in forty to forty-five years, their IRA accounts will have grown significantly, enabling them to live a financially independent and stable life during their golden years.

Reflections and Actions

1. Do you have a retirement plan currently? If yes, how involved are you with it? Could you do more?

2. If not, what retirement plan option do you want to pursue (401[k] or one of the IRAs)? Why?

3. Imagine your golden years of retirement. At what age do you plan to retire? What do you plan on doing? Where will you live? What will your health be like? Will you have enough money to keep you financially stable and enjoying life?

Chapter 14

Wills–Do You Have One?

At the start of the pandemic, the chaos of doom and the inevitability of death were in our faces and at our doors. We were shaken and needed to plan. No one knew who was going to survive this. Subhanallah, we all thought the end was near. As a parent, I had to ask myself what would happen to my kids if I contracted COVID-19. My husband was a frontline worker in the ER in rural Minnesota. Our challenges were daunting. We had to tie our camel again.

My husband and I had written our wills for the first time in 2003, right before we left for Hajj, when we only had Arshia. Seventeen years later, we had another child, more assets, and an outdated will.

The Prophet Muhammad ﷺ said:

> It is not permissible for any Muslim who has something to bequeath to remain for two nights without having their Last Will and Testament written and kept ready with them.[134]

And Allah ﷻ says in the Quran:

كُتِبَ عَلَيْكُمْ إِذَا حَضَرَ أَحَدَكُمُ ٱلْمَوْتُ إِن تَرَكَ خَيْرًا ٱلْوَصِيَّةُ لِلْوَٰلِدَيْنِ وَٱلْأَقْرَبِينَ بِٱلْمَعْرُوفِ ۖ حَقًّا عَلَى ٱلْمُتَّقِينَ ﴿١٨٠﴾

It has been ordained upon you that when death is near one of you, leaving wealth behind, to make a will in favor of parents and close

---

134 *Ṣaḥīḥ al-Bukhārī*, no. 2738.

relatives, impartially. This is incumbent upon the pious.

Quran 2:180

If you don't have a will, guess who gets your money? The government. Your kids, and your parents if they are living, will have a difficult time fighting the courts for power over your estate. The court will assume control over the division of your assets, and it will not divide them according to Islamic law. Even more alarming, if your children are young, it will be a court that decides who takes care of them and manages their finances. By creating a will, you maintain autonomy over these crucial decisions. A will allows you to exercise your right to determine how your assets are distributed and, most importantly, to ensure your children's future care aligns with your values and wishes.

Quick sidebar. Something new and exciting I am learning about is trusts. Trusts are an important tool in financial and estate planning that can offer many benefits, including asset protection, tax advantages, and control over the distribution of your wealth. However, trusts can be complex legal instruments with significant implications. As I'm currently in the process of exploring trusts with my attorney and financial adviser, I encourage readers to seek professional guidance to understand how trusts might fit into their own financial plans. The right trust structure can be tailored to your specific situation and goals, potentially providing peace of mind for both you and your beneficiaries.

One last thing to note: Have an attorney review your will and trust, especially if you have different types of wealth assets. Print it out and have it notarized with two witnesses present. Some states don't require it to be notarized, but go to a notary and do it anyway. Finally, I would print it out and share copies with your spouse, your children, and any person you might assign as the executor of the will and trust. Keep a copy with your attorney.

Wills—Do You Have One?

There are many resources out there to create a will that is sharia-compliant. Check out the resources section at the end of the book.

My mom was diagnosed with dementia in the summer of 2022. As she began slowly losing her memory, I realized the urgent need to have a conversation with her about her wealth distribution. I was concerned when I discovered that she didn't have a written will. Recognizing the importance of documenting her wishes while she's still able to express them, I've taken on the responsibility of helping her create one. This process has led us to compile a comprehensive list of her assets. My sister and I are working diligently to gain access to her bank accounts, locate the key to her safe deposit box, and create an inventory of her jewelry. And who knows what other surprises we will find. We also want to ask her what she wants to give and to whom, especially if she wants to give to her local masjid or another Islamic institution. We are also exploring ways to create a *ṣadaqa jāriya* (a continuous charity) in her name.

In my extended family, I have seen it get really ugly when someone passes away without leaving a will. If you have family members who are non-Muslims or Muslims who aren't practicing or don't understand inheritance laws—get ready to fight. Your rights will not be preserved. And everyone comes out of the woodwork wanting a piece of the inheritance, even people who have no right to it.

Wills are an important aspect of your economic empowerment and the preservation of your wealth. Ensure the sanctity of yours by making it official. If you don't know enough about Islamic inheritance laws, find your local scholar and start your learning journey. Especially if you are a convert, a single mother, or have young children. Learn about who has rights over your wealth after you pass and ensure that it is distributed properly.

To ensure your wishes are carried out, your will must be tailored to comply with the laws of your state, be legally recognized by all fifty states, and be fully in line with the sharia. Safeguard your family's future by preparing your will.

Reflection Exercise

1. Do your parents have a will? Have you reviewed it? If they don't, will you have a conversation about this, and what will you talk about?

2. What is your plan for moving forward with your will creation?

3. Have you reviewed your current will and what do you need to revise?

Chapter 15

Secrets to Financial Freedom

In *The Latte Factor*, Bach and Mann introduce readers to three secrets of financial freedom: Pay yourself first, don't budget, and live rich now. If you don't know where to start, this might be a simple way to take action. It actually did help me, so I would recommend you try it out also.

SECRET #1: PAY YOURSELF FIRST—PUT YOURSELF FIRST

We all want to make money to cover our current living expenses. But what about earning money to build our lives? What about putting aside money to invest in ourselves? Bach and Mann explain that the first 20%–35% of your paycheck goes to the government before your money even hits your bank account. So with what you have left of the 65%–80%, you're paying your living expenses, your social expenses, and maybe have some left over to put into savings. But instead of saving what is left over, Bach and Mann advocate taking the equivalent of one hour's wages for every day you work and investing it.

Let's do this exercise together to help you see why this secret is so important to your future financial well-being.

What do you earn by the hour?	$25
Pay yourself one hour a day (assuming you work four days a week)	$100/week
	$400/month

	$4,800/year
Invest that into your brokerage account or move into IRA	10% growth rate over 10 years
I haven't invested in my 401(k) for 10 years	$48,000 not invested
Using a conservative 5% growth rate	**$60,373 missed by 2020** **$280,000 missed by 2038 when I retire**

First, I would like to clarify that I did not make $25 an hour when I moved into the nonprofit sector. I made less. So these calculations are simply an example to help you understand the opportunity you miss if you don't invest in yourself. At $25 an hour, if I worked four days a week, I should have invested $400 a month into my SEP IRA. For the past ten years, I have done nothing, though. Yes, I saved some money in my bank account, but due to inflation and the use of a non-interest-bearing account, my money did not grow. Had I transferred that money into my SEP IRA, I would have grown my investment by at least $12,000 in the last ten years. And if I kept investing every year until I retired, I would have approximately $280,000 when I turn sixty-two!

Now let's say you land your first job right after you graduate college, and your salary is $70,000 per year. (Mashallah! *Mabrūk!*) That is approximately $33.65 an hour.

$33.65/hour

$168.27/week

$673.08/month

$8,076.96/year

Transfer this amount into an investment account and buy stocks. If you transfer this amount every year for ten years (assuming you don't receive any pay raises), your principal amount would be $80,769.60. And using a conservative 5% growth rate, your investment will be worth $114,734.00.[135]

My first job out of college was at United Healthcare, which wasn't quite yet UnitedHealth Group but was definitely well on its way. When I started working as a marketing coordinator at a Fortune 500 company, I was twenty-two years old and making $12 an hour. I loved my job. I couldn't get over how much money I was making, and the fact that when I got home, I didn't have to study, write papers, or do any assignments. I was free from school! At twenty-three, I got promoted to sales administration manager, and my hourly wage jumped to $18. I felt like a millionaire! I worked until my daughter was born, when I decided I really wanted to be home with her during those precious growth years. (The irony is, I then went back to school and finished my MBA).

In those three years that I was working, I was able to purchase ninety shares of UHG stock through the employee stock purchase plan. The plan gave employees a 15% discount on the stock price, so I knew I was getting at least a 15% rate of return. I had ninety shares when I left UHG, but then the stock split and I had 180 shares! A stock split occurs when a company divides its existing shares into multiple shares, increasing the number of shares outstanding while proportionally decreasing the price per share. Companies typically implement stock splits to make their shares more affordable and accessible to a broader range of investors, potentially increasing liquidity and trading volume.

A few years later, the stock split again—giving me 360 shares. While earning $12 an hour, I had invested the equivalent of one hour's wage every paycheck into a stock purchase plan. I was only investing for three years, but look at the growth! Imagine if I had kept investing.

---

135   I used Smart Asset's investment and growth calculator: https://smartasset.com/investing/investment-calculator#123ll2rXqv.

Action	Value of one stock	Total value
Over 2.5 years, 90 shares purchased	$50/share	$4,500
Stock split --> 180 shares	$50/share	$9,000
Stock split --> 360 shares	$50/share	$18,000
360 shares 20 years later	$500/share	**$180,000**

SECRET #2: DON'T BUDGET—SPEND CONSCIOUSLY

Traditional budgeting doesn't work for everyone, and that's okay. While I've used budgets in my professional life, particularly in the nonprofit sector, I've found a different approach more effective for personal finances. Instead of rigid budgeting, I advocate for conscious spending—being mindful of where your money goes and aligning it with your values and goals.

This isn't to say that budgeting is wrong or unnecessary. For many, especially those managing tight finances or working toward specific financial goals, budgeting can be an essential tool. However, the key is finding a method that works for you and your circumstances.

Whether you use a detailed spreadsheet or a more flexible approach, the goal is the same: to gain control over your finances and make intentional choices about your spending. It's about understanding your cash flow and making informed decisions, regardless of your income level or financial situation.

Many financial gurus, from Bach to Sethi to Krawcheck, tell you not to budget. Why? Because financial success is not about budgeting; it's about understanding your spending habits.

We all know what we make either on an hourly basis or as a yearly salary, but after taxes and any pretax contributions, what is going into your bank account? And then what are we actually spending that money on? Sethi tells you to be a conscious spender. Instead of creating a personal budget, first create a conscious spending spreadsheet (I'll give you a template later in the reflection exercise).

In working toward conscious spending, I would recommend journaling your daily spending for about a week. Simply grab a notebook or open a notes app on your phone and start writing out what you are spending money on. Make it fun. Don't just make a list. Write out why you made that purchase, how it made you feel, was it planned or spontaneous? Be a conscious spending storyteller! After a week, go back and review what you wrote.

Now create a list of all the things you are spending money on monthly by using Sethi's Conscious Spending Plan.[136] This would be your regular monthly bills, expenses like rent, car payment, utilities, phone, etc. If you don't use much cash, your credit card company most likely has a tool on their website to show you these expenses. They categorize your expenses to show you what areas you are spending in and how much. Some even have those colorful pie charts we love! Again, after a month or a few months, look back and monitor your spending habits. Is your money going to the things you truly value? Flip to the end of this chapter for a simple template I created. Customize it for yourself.

I'm a Gen Xer. I grew up at a time when we would get actual paychecks at our place of employment. We would take that paycheck, physically drive it to the bank, then go in, complete a deposit slip, sign the back of the check, and wait for a teller to put it into our accounts. If we needed any cash, we would take it out right then and there. Later, if we needed more cash, we had to return to the bank to get it. With the passage of time, we were awed by the magic of new technology. At an ATM we could get our own cash out—even on the weekend!

---

136   Ramit Sethi, *I Will Teach You to Be Rich: No Guilt. No Excuses. No BS. Just a 6-Week Program That Works*, 2nd ed. (Workman Publishing, 2019).

How did we keep track of our money? We had to do math! Who remembers those little check registers you got with your box of checks? We used these to track our money. (If you don't even remember checks, well…aren't you just adorably young? Pat yourself on the back and let us oldies have our moment.)

Then life changed again with the invention of direct deposit and online access to your bank account. All of a sudden, tracking our spending got both easier and more hidden.

Automation Simplified Our Lives

The government really piloted the art of automation decades ago when they took their cut before our paycheck was even written out to us. Then capitalism followed by automatically deducting our monthly Netflix subscription, Spotify membership, and Mister Car Wash membership right out of our bank accounts.

These developments can make spending mindless, so how can we leverage the tools that automation provides us in our conscious spending efforts and investing goals? We can automate our payments for bills, credit cards, and loans. This means we pay on time, every time—avoiding late fees and interest charges and protecting our credit score! As you consciously track your spending, automation becomes your friend.

That's how we can pay others, but what about the "paying ourselves first" part? We can automate that as well!

Here are some quick steps to automate your investments:

1. **Open an investment brokerage account or an IRA.** Three companies that offer sharia-compliant options are ShariaPortfolio, Saturna Capital, and Azzad Asset Management. Their websites are listed in the Resources section at the end of the book. If you aren't going to open

an account with an Islamic company, you can create one with a traditional company like TD Ameritrade, Fidelity, or Charles Schwab. You can create a sharia-compliant portfolio at these firms, but know that the rest of the company may not have sharia-compliant practices. Do your research.

2. **Transfer that one hour's wage into the account.** For example, if you earn $15 an hour currently, set up an automatic transfer of $15 to your investment account once a week.

3. **Start with one hour and then gradually increase it.** If you already have an investment brokerage account, log in and buy one stock or several stocks. Become an investor. Build your halal portfolio one stock at a time.

Automating both your payments and your investments simplifies your life. It also saves money on late fees and additional charges. But again—friendly reminder—automation does not imply ignoring or becoming complacent about your spending. You must still review the monthly statements of all your accounts.

SECRET #3: LIVE RICH NOW

Here's the thing about conscious spending versus living rich now. You need to figure out what's important to you in terms of what is worth spending money on. Conscious spending isn't about being cheap or depriving yourself of joy and happiness. It's about stepping back and assessing what you are spending money on. Bach and Mann never said give up the latte. If lattes and mochas bring you joy, keep buying them and drinking them. But maybe you join the rewards program so you get points and can get free size upgrades. If your joy is in binging a favorite TV show, that's great! But perhaps reconsider whether you need Prime Video,

Hulu, Netflix, and Disney+ subscriptions all at the same time.

In fact, some of us may not have any clue as to what we are spending on, let alone if we are spending money on the things that actually make us happy. This lack of awareness can lead to mindless spending and missed opportunities for both enjoyment and financial growth.

However, it's equally important not to fall into the trap of constant guilt over spending. Look, I don't want to feel guilty about spending money. I don't want to feel like I'm wasting money every time I order dessert, pay for valet parking, or indulge in a personal vice. Moreover, we shouldn't feel guilty about splurging on something just because we think, "Oh, what a waste of money. Had I donated it to a needy cause, I would have earned more *ajr*." This kind of thinking creates a false binary between personal enjoyment and charitable giving. The reality is that we can (and should) do both! It's possible to enjoy life's pleasures responsibly while also being generous in our charitable giving.

The goal is not to be money-rich, but to be life-rich. Money just happens to be the tool that enables living a rich life. I want to experience joy and I want to bring joy to others. For me, living rich now means living a blessed life with gratitude for all the *rizq* Allah ﷻ has provided me.

How do you figure out what's worth spending money on? One morning I wrote in my gratitude journal about some of the best moments of my life. Let me share one particular moment that made me feel life-rich.

I love to travel. I love going to unique places and experiencing all of Allah's magnificent creations. I've been to Spain, Türkiye, Jerusalem, India, Malaysia, Iceland, Canada, Mexico, Colombia, Puerto Rico, The Bahamas, Costa Rica, Ireland, Portugal, England, and Dubai. Travel gives me so much joy! And travel costs money. Travel is part of my conscious spending tracker.

During the week of Thanksgiving in 2021, we booked a trip to Costa Rica for ourselves and the kids. It was one of the most phenomenal, amazing vacations that I have ever taken. The microclimates in Costa Rica are unbelievable. The flora and fauna are incredibly unique on the Caribbean side and oceanside. This country has so many different natural sites, including volcanoes, cloud forests, waterfalls, geothermal hot springs, and some of the best coffee farms in the world! Costa Ricans are very joyous people. We learned the phrase *"pura vida,"* which was both their greeting for seeing one another and for saying goodbye. *Pura vida* didn't just mean "live a beautiful life," but a free one, full of purity. The greeting embodied gratitude and living a joyful life. It complemented the "live rich now" mantra by which I was living.

We had a wonderful time picking guava from random trees on the side of the road and zip-lining in the forest high above the ground. We went white water rafting for the very first time. We stayed in hotels that were eco-friendly and found that the country respects its climate, its land, and its water. We ate fresh fruit like papaya and watermelon that were luscious and delicious. I can't describe to you the comparison between what we eat here in the United States and what we tasted there. Their fruits are grown in their natural habitats. And you didn't have to request organic foods; all their food is organic! And simple: meals of rice, beans, and fish. Juices were made with fresh fruit and not with a bunch of additives and preservatives. We shared everything we ate. We ordered four different plates of food and four different juices. Then we would just rotate the plates and glasses so we could try everything. This sharing made me feel rich in love and care.

The weather was everything. Some days we got sun, and other days we saw rain or fog. The very air we breathed—fresh and free of pollutants—felt like it was cleansing our lungs. The four of us were happy; vitamin D puts you in a good mood! We enjoyed long conversations, choreographed a dance for a TikTok, were in tears from laughing so hard, and even ran into a celebrity during one of our lunch outings—Bella Thorne!

But why was this vacation memorable for me? It wasn't the extravagance and luxury that made me feel rich. It was because it was the first vacation my family was able to take together in a long time (remember the pandemic?) and our first one with grown-up young adults. Believe me, a family vacation with grown adult children is a whole different experience from a family vacation with little kids.

My son was seventeen years old during that trip and my daughter was twenty-one. At one point, I remember my son saying, "When I was little, I liked all the vacations we went on, but I don't think I appreciated them." He actually enjoyed our company and all the crazy, different activities we tried together. I felt rich with happiness and joy.

After that trip, my son was off to college and my daughter was about to graduate from graduate school. I didn't know how many more opportunities we would have for family vacations with just the four of us. So this trip felt like ending one chapter in my life with memories and connections and anticipating the next chapter with the feeling that new riches were coming my way.

We would not have been able to afford our family trip to Costa Rica had we not assessed our finances. We managed our credit scores, expenses, and debt, and created conscious spending habits. All of this helped change our savings and investment strategies. People say, "Well, money doesn't buy happiness." And I say that the things that bring me happiness cost money. I don't know if the four of us will be able to spend time together like that again because in the future, my son will be away at college and my daughter may have a full-time job in another city. Or maybe they'll both be married and going on vacations with their spouses and families. So prioritizing spending on that trip as part of our conscious spending commitment made us all happy, and I'm so glad we did it.

What Does Living a Rich Life Now Mean to You?

I had been working for eighteen years with no gaps on my resume when I took my four-month sabbatical after serving as executive director at RISE. Those four months gave me time to rest. I had no plans other than to read, write, and travel. Living each day mindfully rather than constantly looking at a plan—a short-term plan and a long-term plan—was healing. I lived in the moment. I lived for the day. As I came to the end of my sabbatical, I didn't want to go back to a job. I didn't want to have a boss. I didn't want to be anyone's boss. I wanted to go from sabbatical to retirement at forty-six years old. "FIRE" me, please!

For me, living rich means working, but without the hustle and stress. I keep hearing that people want to retire early. I saw an article recently that said Gen Z plans to retire by fifty! (Remember, Sethi's acronym FIRE stands for financial independence, retire early.) As much as I love financial independence, I am a little torn about retiring. I watched both my father and my father-in-law come into retirement and have nothing to do. The lack of activities, a job, and hobbies combined with not having retirement savings or a retirement fund caused their mental and physical health to deteriorate quickly. That is not my goal. My husband and I have agreed that we are probably going to retire in terms of not having the intense careers and the associated hustle that we have right now. We want to have ease in the jobs that we do. But we will probably do some sort of work as long as we can.

Living rich now means taking care of my health. Eating healthy is about good nutrition. According to the WHO, it involves eating adequate, well-balanced meals to support your body's needs. It means eating fresh vegetables and fruits. It means eating fish. Sadly, healthy eating in the United States is an expensive lifestyle. I don't want to worry about how much a wild-caught salmon costs or if I can afford avocados this week. The price of a dozen cage-free eggs is $4.99 as I write this. I could buy five rice and bean burritos for that price at Taco Bell! Living rich now means enjoying healthy, nutritious meals and not having to worry about sacrificing my health to cut costs.

Living rich now also includes taking care of my body. Working out and exercising means I bought a FitBit to track my steps, only to learn that a dozen of my friends, including my anse, also have a FitBit and participate in a walking challenge every week—the Workweek Hustle. For the love of the All-Mighty, these ladies are competitive. When I first joined, no one was hitting ten thousand steps a day. I was winning that competition every week for a month—and then the summer hit. The group found the outdoors and were decimating my winning streak. I mean they even found a hiking hijabis group! I had to level up. I needed new walking shoes, a gym membership, proper workout clothes, and to upgrade my FitBit app in order to beat these women—I mean, ahem, to track my progress and reach my health goals. I don't want to worry about how much these things cost if it means it will cost me my health. Living rich now afforded me the ability to take care of my body.

I have to prepare myself for the possibility that I may get dementia. I will do as much as I can to slow it down. And that means living my life to the fullest now, becoming economically stable, and having an abundance mindset. I make *dua* that Allah ﷻ protects me from this disease. My Lord, I seek refuge in You from laziness and helpless old age. *Ameen!*

Living rich now means giving rich now. It means not limiting ourselves to thinking about only our lives here and now, but also our next life. Living rich now means living rich later as well. Being asked to give to a nonprofit and being on their list of top donors is a goal of mine. This is an important part of living rich now: living blessed and living rich later. I feel honored when someone asks me to give to an organization that is making the world a better place, especially if it's for Muslim women, by Muslim women. It's an honor because they are inviting me to *khayr*, goodness. Living rich now is living with *khayr*. It means I'm helping nonprofits realize their missions and goals! When someone invites me to that blessing, I don't want to think twice about whether or not I can give. I don't want to think twice about how much to give. I want to live rich now, give rich now, and live rich later! So as you can see, if we want to achieve our life goals, we're going to need money. And if we want to achieve our *akhira* goals, like giving *ṣadaqa*, renovating the masjid, or helping someone in need, we'll need money for that too.

Living rich now includes my friends and family. I want the ability to give gifts and to feed people. This isn't about bragging about having money. This is about bringing others joy. Abū Hurayra reported: The Prophet, peace and blessings be upon him, said,

> Give each other gifts and you will love each other.[137]

I love my friends and family and I want them to love me!

Living rich now includes shared meals and hosting. I love going out to eat and hosting gatherings at home. It brings me so much joy to meet a friend for coffee or lunch. It brings me joy to cook Indian food and have my friends over for dinner. When family or friends are sick, I feel blessed that I can send over a meal. Food is a great human connector. Breaking bread and sharing a meal have always strengthened the bonds of sisterhood and friendship.

---

137 *Al-Adab al-mufrad,* no. 594, grade: *ḥasan* (fair).

When my kids tell me, "Mom this food is *bussin'!*" I assume they mean it's delicious and they love me. In fact, when I made butter chicken, dal, and chana and invited friends over, my friend Sara kept saying, "You love us."

Define *your* rich life. What makes you feel life-rich? This isn't limited to money-rich, but remember, money is tied to living your life richly today and in the hereafter. Embrace the fullness of life in the present moment, savoring its richness and abundance. And start planning your finances to live a rich life now.

Reflection Exercise

1. What brings you joy? Close your eyes, and think back to a time in your life when you experienced flat-out, unbridled joy. Describe the sounds, smells, feelings, colors, and who was there.

2. What are some things you are anticipating in your life that you will need money for?

3. What are some things that make you feel like you can live rich now?

Pay Yourself First Exercise

What do you earn by the hour?	
Pay yourself one hour a day	$_____ /week
	$_____ /month
	$_____ /year
Invest that into your brokerage account or move into IRA	10% growth rate over 10 years
How many years until you retire?	_____
Using a conservative 5% growth rate	$_____

Conscious Spending Storytelling

Take a week to journal about all the things you are spending money on. Write down what you buy, how much it costs, and how that purchase made you feel. Was it planned or spontaneous? After a week, come back and review what you wrote. Did anything surprise you?

Monthly Conscious *Rizq* Spending Tracker

List out the expenses you're committed to paying each month			What is the dollar amount you are currently spending on this expense?
Housing (rent or mortgage)			
Installment payments			
		Childcare	
		Tuition	
Insurance			
		Home/renters	
		Auto	
		Health care	
		Dental	
Utilities			
		Water	
		Gas	
		Electric	
		Trash	
Communications			
		Phone	
		Internet	
		Cable	
Memberships			

Monthly Conscious Rizq Spending Tracker

	Gym	

Subscriptions

	Netflix/Disney+/etc.	
	Music streaming	
	Meal delivery	

Credit Card Payments

	Credit card #1	
	Credit card #2	
	Credit card #3	

Transportation

	Uber/Lyft	
	Bus	
	Gas	

Loans

	Student	
	Car	

Car

	Gas	
	Oil changes	
	Car washes	
	Maintenance	

Add other bills not mentioned above		

Part II: Philanthropy

Throughout this book, we've explored the why behind financial stability and the practical how of achieving it. For me, these exercises in understanding my purpose for attaining financial stability, achieving economic empowerment, and building wealth have been transformative. They've not only helped me become more intentional in writing this book but also in crafting my goals for what I want to accomplish by sharing this knowledge with you. As we've discussed, true richness isn't just about accumulating wealth—it's about living a life of purpose, security, and above all, generosity. Philanthropy isn't an afterthought to wealth; it's a central pillar of what it means to live rich. The ability to give freely, to support causes you believe in, and to make a positive impact in your community and the world at large—this is the ultimate expression of financial empowerment.

The next section of the book focuses on how being economically secure and stable can lead you to become a philanthropist. It's the natural progression of our journey: from understanding our why, to learning how to build wealth, and finally, to exploring ways we can use that wealth to enrich our lives and the lives of others. This is what it means to truly live rich—to have not just the means but also the heart and the wisdom to share your blessings generously.

Like me, you probably think of Mackenzie Scott, John D. Rockefeller, or Andrew Carnegie when you hear the word philanthropist. I always thought you had to be a billionaire before you could be considered a philanthropist. But after spending time in the nonprofit sector, the foundation world, and the world of philanthropy, I have learned that everyone has the potential and opportunity to be a philanthropist.

We all want to make the world a better place; we all want to help people in need. We all heed the rally cry to stand up against injustice and fight for equality and equity. Well, guess what? You need money for that too. As you become a conscious spender and take control of your finances, you will become more and more economically empowered to live rich now—and to help your community.

Philanthropy isn't a new concept. In fact, many philanthropic strategies and tools are rooted in our Islamic traditions of zakat, *ṣadaqa*, and gratitude. It isn't love of humankind that motivates us to do good. It's love for Allah ﷻ that drives us to help and care for all His creations—and because of this, we are all philanthropists.

Philanthropy is also not limited to just money or wealth. It includes so much more. And remember what Allah ﷻ told us:

لَّا يَسْتَوِى ٱلْقَـٰعِدُونَ مِنَ ٱلْمُؤْمِنِينَ غَيْرُ أُو۟لِى ٱلضَّرَرِ وَٱلْمُجَـٰهِدُونَ فِى سَبِيلِ ٱللَّهِ بِأَمْوَٰلِهِمْ وَأَنفُسِهِمْ ۚ فَضَّلَ ٱللَّهُ ٱلْمُجَـٰهِدِينَ بِأَمْوَٰلِهِمْ وَأَنفُسِهِمْ عَلَى ٱلْقَـٰعِدِينَ دَرَجَةً ۚ وَكُلًّا وَعَدَ ٱللَّهُ ٱلْحُسْنَىٰ ۚ وَفَضَّلَ ٱللَّهُ ٱلْمُجَـٰهِدِينَ عَلَى ٱلْقَـٰعِدِينَ أَجْرًا عَظِيمًا ۝

Those who stay at home—except those with valid excuses—are
not equal to those who strive in the cause of Allah with their
wealth and their lives. Allah has elevated in rank those who strive
with their wealth and their lives above those who stay behind
[with valid excuses]. Allah has promised each a fine reward, but
those who
strive will receive a far better reward than others.

Quran 4:95

Philanthropy is often thought of as consisting of financial support for charitable causes, but it can also encompass other forms of giving, including time, talent, testimony, ties to social initiatives and humanitarian causes, public policy advocacy, and so many other movement-building works. Here's what each of these terms means:

> **Time.** This refers to volunteering or donating one's time to a social initiative, such as helping out at a soup kitchen or mentoring a young person.
>
> **Talent.** This refers to donating one's skills, expertise, or knowledge, such as providing legal advice or teaching a class.
>
> **Treasure.** This refers to donating money or financial resources.
>
> **Testimony.** This refers to using one's voice or platform to advocate for a cause, such as speaking out about social justice issues or sharing one's personal story to raise awareness.
>
> **Ties.** This refers to using one's personal and professional networks to support a cause, such as organizing a fundraiser or rallying support for a cause on social media.

By encompassing a range of forms of giving, philanthropy can be inclusive and accessible to people with different backgrounds and resources, and can have a broader impact on the causes and communities that are supported. The five T's are a reflection of everyday philanthropists, including you and me.

Chapter 16

Philanthropy and Gratitude

As my wealth grew, I realized that gratitude was its companion. One thing I'd like you to take away as you are reading this book is the understanding of how to practice gratitude. Practice gratitude with the many blessings you already have, and soon you'll have created a habit. As you become more financially literate and stable and economically empowered, your habit of gratitude will help you focus on positive emotions, appreciate the good experiences, build deeper relationships, and remind you of your blessings. If you're blessed with a well-paying job with a salary that acknowledges your worth, your investments are growing, and you have disposable income, I want you to make sure you practice gratitude toward Allah ﷻ for blessing you with this *rizq*. And, if you are not quite there yet financially, trust in Allah's plan and continue to work diligently toward your goals. Know that your efforts and intentions are valuable, and continue to strive with patience and faith.

Dr. Tamer Desouky wrote a very meaningful paper about the art of gratitude and *shukr*[138] for Yaqeen Institute.[139] I was moved by his idea that practicing gratitude is a form of worship—it brings you closer to Allah. In the Quran, Allah ﷻ says:

---

138   *Shukr* is an Arabic term denoting thankfulness, gratitude, or acknowledgment by humans; it is a highly esteemed virtue in Islam.
139   Tamer Desouky, "The Art of Gratitude: Quranic Themes on Shukr," Yaqeen Institute for Islamic Research, April 20, 2022, https://yaqeeninstitute.org/read/paper/the-art-of-gratitude-quranic-themes-on-shukr.

> إِنَّا هَدَيْنَـٰهُ ٱلسَّبِيلَ إِمَّا شَاكِرًا وَإِمَّا كَفُورًا ۝
>
> We already showed them the Way, whether they [choose to] be grateful or ungrateful.
>
> **Quran 76:3**

Dr. Desouky points out that if practicing *shukr* brings you closer to Allah, then the exact opposite of *shukr* is *kufr*.[140] "In this context, *kufr* means to refuse to appreciate these benefits, thus hiding one's appreciation and not openly showing gratitude. Those who are ungrateful are ultimately labeled with disbelief, illustrating the magnitude of being ungrateful to Allah." Yikes! Count your blessings!

How do you practice gratitude and *shukr*? I practice gratitude by first acknowledging Allah's power and wisdom. By striving to constantly and consistently praise Allah. By waking up for *tahajjud* and making *dua* right before the Fajr *adhān*.[141] By praising Allah, and thanking Him for all of the things He blessed me with the day before. When a profound blessing comes my way, I pray an additional two *raka'as*[142] of gratitude, and I give a small *ṣadaqa* to the first organization that happens to come my way at that time.

Another way to express gratitude is toward Allah's creations—toward people. Show people you appreciate them, and tell them by thanking them. I was in a meeting over Zoom the other day, and it is so hard for me to speak up in online meetings, but another female colleague interrupted and invited me into the conversation. I felt so grateful. Just as she spoke up, I had been writing in my notes,

---

140 A significant concept in Islamic thought, the word *kufr* and its derivatives appear in the Quran 482 times. It means "ingratitude," or the willful refusal to appreciate the benefits that God has bestowed.

141 The *adhān* is the Islamic call to prayer, usually recited by a muezzin five times a day in a mosque, traditionally from a minaret.

142 A *raka'a* is the name used for the series of movements performed during salah.

"People talk too much and listen very little. They don't acknowledge how much space they are taking up. Nor do they look around to see who has not participated in the conversation. But a true leader with high emotional intelligence does." I sent a private message to my colleague thanking her and appreciating her invitation into the conversation.

Expressing gratitude doesn't always have to be verbal—it can also take tangible forms. One powerful way to show appreciation and strengthen relationships is through the act of giving gifts. This practice not only demonstrates thoughtfulness but also has deep roots in Islamic tradition.

Giving gifts is rooted in our sunna. Remember the hadith I mentioned earlier about gift giving? Well, it's worth repeating! Abū Hurayra reported: The Prophet, peace and blessings be upon him, said,

> Give each other gifts and you will love each other.[143]

The gifts don't need to be extravagant. I have a friend who loves coffee. I just bring her favorite drink once in a while. Some friends need flowers. When a friend is sick, I try to visit and bring a home-cooked meal. Everyone gives gifts when they are invited to a person's birthday, wedding, baby shower, and all, but giving a random gift is so much sweeter.

Gratitude isn't something we practice only when something big happens in our lives. Be thankful for those big things, but be thankful for the little things, too, and be thankful even (especially) during the hard times.

I am thankful Arshia spends time with her grandfathers. I never

---

143   *Al-Adab al-mufrad,* no. 594, grade: *ḥasan.*

had that. My paternal grandfather passed away well before I was born. My maternal grandfather lived in India, and I only met him three times that I can remember. He passed away when I was in sixth grade. My kids had both sets of grandparents for a great part of their lives. So when I see the time and effort my daughter puts into her relationship with her grandparents, my heart swells. My mother-in-law passed away in November of 2022. My father-in-law looks so lonely, it's heartbreaking. But every Friday, Arshia calls her grandfather at 12:00 p.m. to remind him she's coming to take him to the masjid for Friday prayers. One Friday, he thought it was Thursday. It's not easy interacting with elders who have dementia or memory loss. It's not easy driving completely out of the way to bring someone to a place that is down the street from you. And it's not easy doing all this during our harsh, polar-vortex winters in Minnesota.

I told Arshia I was really proud of her for spending time with her grandfather. I told her how much I appreciate her taking time to serve him with this act of kindness. I reminded her that her other grandfather, my dad, is so grateful that of all the grandkids, she's the one that calls once a week to check in on him and my mom. Her big heart and active love is something we all want to emulate, and I'm grateful she's a good kid. Mashallah.

I have a ton of books on gratitude and quite a few gratitude journals. A very important lesson to be learned about practicing gratitude is its impact on your mental health and well-being. Many studies, including "The Grateful Heart," have found that practicing gratitude reduces stress.[144] Researchers have found again and again that gratitude reanchors you to inner peace, which in turn makes you feel less stressed. The National Alliance on Mental Illness (NAMI) found that people who count their blessings are happier

---

144   Rollin McCraty and Doc Childre, "The Grateful Heart: The Psychophysiology of Appreciation," pp. 230–55 in *The Psychology of Gratitude*, ed. R. A. Emmons and M. E. McCullough (Oxford University Press, 2004).

and less depressed.[145]

I read an article on NPR about gratitude journaling, and the author wrote, "Giving thanks and counting blessings can help people sleep better, lower stress, and improve interpersonal relationships."[146] Think about this when you write in your gratitude journal. Do you notice these benefits? I know that after reflecting, I feel genuinely optimistic and know I have a blessed life.

Practicing gratitude during the pandemic helped center and ground me. During a time when it felt like the world was burning down all around me, this habit reminded me of the good that was still in abundance. I wrote my moments of gratitude in my journal. There is something about writing that is therapeutic. And going back through those pages—seeing the lists of things I was grateful for—gives me hope for the future.

The other thing that helped me practice gratitude during the difficult times of stay-at-home orders, the murder of George Floyd,[147] and the spike in anti-Asian hate was to tell others I appreciated them. I told my coworkers I appreciated them for showing grace and helping each other out. I told community members I appreciated them for stepping up and organizing mutual aid. I told my husband I appreciated his work as a frontline health care worker in the ER. Tell people you appreciate them.

And finally, one last thing: I did my best to pay it forward. I was

---

145 Joshua Brown and Joel Wong, "How Gratitude Changes You and Your Brain," Greater Good, June 6, 2017, https://greatergood.berkeley.edu/article/item/how_gratitude_changes_you_and_your_brain.

146 Andee Tagle and Malaka Gharib, "Want to Get Better at Being Thankful? Here Are Some Tips," NPR, November 23, 2022, https://www.npr.org/2022/11/18/1137822057/get-better-at-being-grateful.

147 George Floyd was an unarmed Black man who was killed while in police custody in Minneapolis, MN. Evan Hill, Ainara Tiefenthäler, Christiaan Triebert, Drew Jordan, Haley Willis, and Robin Stein, "How George Floyd Was Killed in Police Custody," New York Times, June 1, 2020, https://www.nytimes.com/2020/05/31/us/george-floyd-investigation.html.

grateful for all the blessings I had during this challenging time—blessings I knew others didn't have. So I did my best to collect essentials for mutual aid, sponsor iftars,[148] and volunteer at food drives. And of course, to give.

Allah ﷻ rewards you with more if you thank Him and thank others:

$$\text{وَمَا كَانَ لِنَفْسٍ أَن تَمُوتَ إِلَّا بِإِذْنِ ٱللَّهِ كِتَٰبًا مُّؤَجَّلًا ۗ وَمَن يُرِدْ ثَوَابَ ٱلدُّنْيَا نُؤْتِهِۦ مِنْهَا وَمَن يُرِدْ ثَوَابَ ٱلْءَاخِرَةِ نُؤْتِهِۦ مِنْهَا ۚ وَسَنَجْزِى ٱلشَّٰكِرِينَ}$$

> No soul can ever die without Allah's Will at the destined time. Those who desire worldly gain, We will let them have it, and those who desire heavenly reward, We will grant it to them. And We will reward those who are grateful.
>
> **Quran 3:145**

Now doesn't practicing gratitude seem like a great investment opportunity? It pays great dividends. And it makes you feel like a philanthropist. Practicing gratitude is part of our economic empowerment journey and philanthropic goals.

---

148   Iftar is the meal that breaks the fast. Ramadan, the month of fasting, occurred two months after the stay-at-home orders were announced in 2020.

Gratitude Exercise

1. Think about the last time you received a random gift or someone performed a random act of kindness for you. How did you feel?

2. When was the last time you told or showed someone you were grateful for them?

3. Mindfulness activity: What are you feeling in your body when you are grateful?

4. How do you practice gratitude? Look at the last few days and write down what you have been grateful for.

5. How will you practice gratitude as you see your money and wealth increase?

6. What are some ways to practice gratitude during difficulties, hardships, or financial loss?

Chapter 17

Muslim Philanthropy

OK, so now you have figured out your finances, you're investing some, and you're seeing returns. You're living your rich life, full of blessings and joy. What's next?

During my financial assessment, one of my goals was to grow my charitable giving beyond my required zakat and current ṣadaqa. I wanted to help people in need, especially those who may need some financial aid temporarily to get through the week or month. So many people struggle to make ends meet, and then life hands them a car repair, a health crisis, or a rent increase that completely throws off their monthly budget. I yearned to help the people of my masjid especially—the people I prayed Jumu'a with, ate iftar with, or prayed *tarāwīḥ*[149] with.

In addition to helping my Muslim sisters and brothers, I also wanted to help establish a new local masjid. From acquiring an actual building and completing the renovations to paying off the loan, we had dreams of building a spiritual community center for many generations to come.

And of course I wanted to give to all the amazing nonprofit organizations in Minnesota, organizations that focus on women and girls, protect our civil rights, house the homeless, keep our children on the straight path, and care for our most vulnerable.

I wanted to be a philanthropist.

---

149 *Tarāwīḥ* are special sunna prayers that are performed only in the month of Ramadan.

I completed a master's in philanthropic studies during the pandemic, with an emphasis on Muslim philanthropy. I know—that's a thing?

During my studies I learned some really cool concepts that flipped my mindset on what philanthropy means and who can be a philanthropist. At the heart of these revelations was Indiana University's Muslim Philanthropy Initiative (MPI). This groundbreaking program aims to expand and improve the Muslim philanthropic sector through various means: organizing symposiums and seminars, convening philanthropic leaders, conducting research, and recruiting Muslim Americans into the field. Their work is instrumental in training and empowering a new generation of philanthropic and nonprofit leaders, and the scope of their efforts fills me with excitement.

In their book *Understanding Philanthropy*, Robert Payton and Michael Moody provide a compelling metaphor for philanthropy as a "circus tent." Under this expansive canopy, they define a philanthropist as anyone who gives their time, talent, treasure, or testimony. This inclusive definition encompasses a wide range of activities: gifts and grants, volunteering and trusteeship, foundations and endowments, fundraising events, advocacy and reform, service learning, scholarships, nonprofits, and social enterprises. Importantly, Payton and Moody emphasize that "both the intentions and the actions of philanthropy are important."[150] This perspective aligns with Indiana University's Lilly School of Philanthropy's interpretation of philanthropy as a "voluntary action for the public good."[151]

As I continued my research on Muslim women's philanthropy, I found the literature to be limited. Much of it is Western-centric

---

150 Robert L. Payton and Michael P. Moody, *Understanding Philanthropy: Its Meaning and Mission* (Indiana University Press, 2008).
151 Payton and Moody, *Understanding Philanthropy*.

and viewed through a WEIRD—Western, educated, industrialized, rich, and democratic—lens.[152] But the concepts of philanthropy prevalent in the West often take different forms or go by different names in other parts of the world, where various expressions of generosity are practiced.

To truly capture the essence of philanthropy, we need an inclusive definition that acknowledges the diverse tapestry of voluntary actions aimed at bettering society. This definition should encompass acts driven by compassion, collective care, and a deep commitment to social justice. Payton and Moody's definition of a circus tent full of varied "voluntary action(s) for the public good" resonates with me, as it illustrates a broad, inclusive understanding of philanthropic activities.

The roots of Muslim philanthropy lie in both intention and action. This concept of "voluntary action for the public good" aligns closely with what many Muslims understand as "faith in action." As discussed in Chapter 3, Muslims are encouraged to begin every action with an intention. In Islamic belief, God rewards the intention even if the intended outcome isn't achieved. This principle is tied to the concept of *imān* (faith), which is not merely a feeling or verbal expression but manifests in actions and lived experiences.

So, when Muslims fulfill their obligations for zakat or give *ṣadaqa*, are they philanthropists? Absolutely! These acts embody the essence of philanthropy—voluntary actions driven by faith and compassion, aimed at achieving the greater good.

---

152 Pamala Wiepking, "The Global Study of Philanthropic Behavior," *VOLUNTAS: International Journal of Voluntary and Nonprofit Organizations* 32, no. 2 (2021): 194–203.

ZAKAT

In Islamic tradition, giving is primarily classified into two categories: zakat and *ṣadaqa*. Both of these encompass the concept of charity, which can be understood as the short-term (and ideally extended) relieving of suffering.

Commanded in the early years after the hijra (migration to Medina), zakat was required of Muslims to purify their wealth and souls by taking a 2.5% share of their wealth and returning it to those in need. Zakat is *farḍ*, an obligation, which means that if you fulfill it, you will be rewarded for it. And if you withhold it, you will be committing a major sin, and you would be liable for punishment in the hereafter. Not paying your zakat is a crime against humanity. Zakat doesn't benefit Allah; it benefits the community and, most importantly, it benefits the person giving it.

The third workshop in RISE's economic series was about zakat and donor-advised funds (DAFs). We invited Dr. Haifaa Younus from the Jannah Institute to provide us with a better understanding of zakat. She reminded us that in order for a person to owe zakat, she must meet three qualifications:

1. She must be Muslim. People of other faiths or those with no faith aren't obligated to pay zakat.

2. She must be an adult, having reached puberty. Children aren't obligated to pay zakat. You're probably wondering how a kid would even have wealth. But this rule takes into consideration orphans as well as children whose parents have passed and left them inheritances. This can vary depending on what school of thought you follow. In the Shafi'i and Maliki schools of thought, if children have any sort of savings, gold, or wealth, their guardians are responsible for paying zakat on that wealth.[153]

---

[153] There are four major schools of thought within Islamic jurisprudence: Hanafi, Maliki, Shafi'i, and Hanbali.

3. You must be in a state of mind where you possess intellect and rational faculty.

There is also a minimum amount, or threshold, of wealth you must possess before zakat is obligatory for you. That threshold is called *niṣāb*. The Prophet Muhammad ﷺ set the threshold based on gold and silver. If you own more than 87.48 grams of gold or 612.36 grams of silver, and you have maintained it in your possession for a year or more, then you have to pay zakat. Of course many of us do not keep our wealth in gold and silver these days. Instead, we take what the current market rate of gold and silver is and use that to determine the *niṣāb* threshold.

Who is eligible to receive zakat? In all honesty, I was never taught anything about this in Sunday school. Did you know there is a difference between the "poor" and the "needy"? I didn't. It wasn't until I started working in the Muslim nonprofit sector that I learned there are eight categories of people who can receive zakat. They are listed in the Quran.

إِنَّمَا ٱلصَّدَقَٰتُ لِلْفُقَرَآءِ وَٱلْمَسَٰكِينِ وَٱلْعَٰمِلِينَ عَلَيْهَا وَٱلْمُؤَلَّفَةِ قُلُوبُهُمْ وَفِي ٱلرِّقَابِ وَٱلْغَٰرِمِينَ وَفِي سَبِيلِ ٱللَّهِ وَٱبْنِ ٱلسَّبِيلِ ۖ فَرِيضَةً مِّنَ ٱللَّهِ ۗ وَٱللَّهُ عَلِيمٌ حَكِيمٌ ۝

Alms-tax is only for the poor and the needy, for those employed to administer it, for those whose hearts are attracted [to the faith], for [freeing] slaves, for those in debt, for Allah's cause, and for [needy] travelers. [This is] an obligation from Allah. And Allah is All-Knowing, All-Wise.

Quran 9:60

1. The poor (*al-fuqarāʾ*). Those in the low-income category, the indigent, or those in extreme poverty.

2. **The needy (*al-masākīn*).** Those facing a difficulty.[154]

3. **Zakat collectors.** In the times of the Prophet Muhammad ﷺ, zakat was collected by a zakat collector, who collected the zakat from his assigned neighborhood or community and immediately distributed it in that same community. The collector was paid for his work through zakat funds. At our masjid, we do not have a designated zakat collector. We have black donation boxes labeled "zakat," and the imam and masjid board distribute it.

4. **Those whose hearts are to be reconciled.** New Muslims fall into this category, as well as those who are on their journey to Islam but need assistance. I never realized the hardships that some converts go through when they accept Islam. Their families abandon them. Friends turn away from them. If the Muslim community doesn't step up and help them, how will they stay committed to the straight path? Even if they are not facing these hardships, our zakat can soften their hearts toward Islam and help them feel secure in their new community.

5. **Those in debt.** Debt Debt is a real oppressor. Help people get out of debt with your zakat.

6. **Those in bondage (slaves and captives).** This category has been expanded to include people who are being trafficked.

7. **Travelers.** This is for people who have faced hardship during their travels. If you ever have your passport and luggage stolen while on a trip, find Muslims to help you get back home. Homesick and feeling isolated or alone? Find Muslims to help you handle the difficulties of being away from home for a long time.

---

154 Depending on the school of thought, "poor" and "needy" have different definitions. Talk to your local scholar to understand these two categories better.

8. **For those struggling *fī sabīlillāh*.**[155] Historically, this included those fighting for a religious cause or a cause of God,[156] or for jihad in the way of Allah by means of pen, word, or sword,[157] or for Islamic warriors who fought against the aggressive disbelievers but were not salaried soldiers.

I want to recognize recent theological debates in contemporary America about zakat. People have varying opinions about different aspects of zakat. For example, can zakat be given to non-Muslims or should it be reserved solely for Muslims? Can it be given to institutions or must it be given directly to people? Should Muslim-serving nonprofits receive zakat or should they only receive *ṣadaqa*? Some Muslim-serving nonprofits will not accept zakat funds. If zakat funds are collected, they give them directly to people in need, who then assume complete ownership of the funds.

Almost twenty years ago, I cofounded an organization to help make college tuition more affordable for Muslim students through scholarships. Many argued it was not zakat eligible, and our ask offered *ṣadaqa* as a reason to give. I believe that by educating our future leaders and lessening the burden of student debt, we allow the next generation of leaders a chance to continue building the infrastructure of the Muslim community. Could this organization receive zakat to help less fortunate students?

I am not a learned scholar and can't answer all these questions for you. However, I would encourage you to learn more about it from your local scholars.

Payton and Moody would not consider zakat philanthropy. They

---

155 The phrase *fī sabīlillāh* is an Arabic expression meaning "in the way of God," or "for the sake of God."
156 Alexander De Waal, ed., *Islamism and Its Enemies in the Horn of Africa* (Indiana University Press, 2004).
157 David Jonsson, *Islamic Economics and the Final Jihad* (Salem Publishing, 2006).

categorized it as a wealth tax—and they aren't alone. Many Muslim scholars also consider zakat a wealth tax. It is not seen as voluntary because it's one of the five obligatory pillars of Islam. Zakat's obligatory nature disqualifies it from being a voluntary act of good. But your accountability for paying it is solely between you and Allah, Who will ask you about it on the Day of Judgment. So some Muslims and academics in philanthropy argue that it *is* voluntary when no one is forcing its collection. Furthermore, if there is no compulsion in religion, and I am voluntarily choosing to be Muslim, then, by extension, I am choosing to give zakat. So that makes zakat an act of philanthropy.

But it's also more than that! Zakat is a social justice obligation on Muslims with wealth. It involves the redistribution of wealth that cycles through families and communities and sometimes back to the original wealth distributor. Zakat is a *farḍ* upon you if you have accumulated wealth. In the Quran, Allah ﷻ mentions that zakat is a right due its recipients:

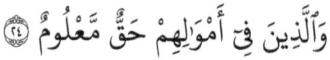

And who give the rightful share of their wealth.

Quran 70:24

Allah ﷻ designed zakat as an institution built on economic empowerment and equity. It not only addresses the short-term needs of the most vulnerable in the community but also has the long-term impact of breaking the cycle of poverty. Zakat addresses the root causes of poverty, while simultaneously trimming its branches. Although poverty has existed since the beginning of time and we can find charitable giving in every religion, zakat is a unique system that incorporates social justice, social insurance, and social solidarity. It is a system of equity that provides the vulnerable with what they need, creating human connectedness and a sense of belonging. Instead of cultivating individualism or dependence, it promotes a true sense of collective community care. Zakat has the potential to be a transformative force to eradicate the numerous disparities seen in housing, incarceration, health, and education.

The Muslim Philanthropy Initiative at IUPUI released the *Muslim American Zakat Report 2022*.[158] Their findings showed the incredible power of Muslim giving in Ramadan 2021. "Muslim Americans gave $1.8 billion in zakat funding to domestic and international causes in 2021." This averages out to $2,070 donated by each American Muslim household—and that's just zakat! The report goes on to include other types of charitable giving and generosity, which added up to $4.3 billion given just in Ramadan. Imagine if the report looked at the entire year? Mashallah!

What's interesting is the diversity in the giving. American Muslims give to organizations, the needy, extended family members, etc. The study also found that men gave significantly more than women to causes: $2,572 compared to $698 for faith-based causes and $1,984 compared to $523 for non-faith-based causes. You know I don't like comparing to or competing with men. So my takeaway from this is that I am happy to see that women are giving and that the study was able to slice the data to show women's giving. It also tells me that more data and research is needed to tell the story of Muslim American women's generosity behaviors. Guess what my next project will be?

My father-in-law came from humble means and identified education as a pathway out of generational poverty. He went to college and got his engineering degree. He moved from his hometown to another city in India for a new job. He tried to

---

158 Shariq Siddiqui, Raheel Wasif, Micah Hughes, Afshan Paarlberg, and Zeeshan Noor, *Muslim American Zakat Report 2022*, Muslim Philanthropy Initiative at Indiana University Lilly Family School of Philanthropy, 2022.

educate his brothers by sending them to college also, but from what I understand, they didn't have that same desire. This means that every year, he ends up having to distribute zakat from his wealth to his siblings. It's hard for him to provide this temporary relief once a year without seeing any improvement in their overall condition, so he now aims to disrupt the cycle of poverty by giving his nephews an opportunity to get an education and, inshallah, a career. If any one of them approaches him for college expenses, he gives generously.

In the context of investing, remember that zakat is actually an investment strategy for your next life. Just think about this: If zakat not only purifies your wealth but also multiplies it, wouldn't you want to give more? Your generous contributions to the community and to those in need not only please Allah, but they also increase your blessings, and your investment grows. Of course we know it could increase in this life. But the thought of receiving dividends on the Day of Judgment sounds like an excellent investment strategy to me! A win-win! You get something here and you get something there. Inshallah *khayr*.

Another observation in the giving or receiving of zakat is the gendered power dynamic in our society. There is a clear wage and wealth gap between men and women. Men are often the keepers of the wealth, and the majority of those in need are women. According to the Center on American Progress, thirty-eight million Americans are below the poverty line—and 56% of them are women.[159] There are many factors that cause this, including lower wages, lack of childcare support, and limited access to career advancement. And this statistic is even more dire when you break it down by race, marital status, and age. The same study showed

---

159 Center for American Progress, "The Basic Facts About Women in Poverty," August 3, 2020, https://www.americanprogress.org/article/basic-facts-women-poverty/.

that "thirteen percent of women over seventy-five years old are poor compared to six percent of men."[160]

Muslims are powerful agents of social change. If zakat collection and distribution were handled by a unified institution, it would have the potential to solve some of the most pressing issues in our communities.

I have to admit that initially I was quite offended by Payton's take on zakat being simply a tax, because the motivations for giving zakat are belief in and obedience to Allah.

ṢADAQA

Ṣadaqa is a broader concept of philanthropy, which is inclusive of everything from the *waqf*[161] to small acts of kindness. Ṣadaqa aligns closely with Payton and Moody's definition of philanthropy as a "circus tent" of voluntary actions for the public good.

Ṣadaqa is voluntary charity in its most traditional definition. It is a charity of time, talent, treasure, and testimony. It is not limited to a monetary form but includes random acts of kindness, skill-based volunteering, and invitations to others to join you in doing good. Even a smile is charity.

Jābir ibn ʿAbdullāh reported: The Messenger of Allah, peace and blessings be upon him, said,

> Every good deed is charity. Verily, it is a good deed to meet your brother with a cheerful face and to pour what is left from your bucket into the vessel of your brother.[162]

---

160 Center for American Progress, "Basic Facts."
161 A *waqf* is an inalienable charitable endowment under Islamic law. It typically involves donating a building, plot of land, or other assets for Muslim religious or charitable purposes with no intention of reclaiming the assets.
162 *Jāmiʿ at-Tirmidhī*, no. 1970.

Ṣadaqa is also faith in action. Amy Singer, in her research on charity in Islamic societies, states that "the goal of *ṣadaqa* is to demonstrate faith, to enhance the standing of the believer on the Day of Judgment, to benefit the Muslim community, and to serve the public good."[163]

Zakat is a *farḍ*, meaning when a Muslim gives zakat, she will be rewarded. If she doesn't pay her zakat, she will be punished by God. But *ṣadaqa* is not *farḍ*. *Ṣadaqa* falls in the sunna category. If you give *ṣadaqa*, you are rewarded for it, but there is no punishment for not giving it—it's completely voluntary.

The motivations for giving *ṣadaqa* are numerous and varied. Many look forward to a reward from Allah, some give to expiate sins, others give to ward off evil, and many give out of gratitude for their blessings. Those who are experiencing hardship or suffering from an illness also give *ṣadaqa* to heal.

One example that has stuck with me is that in their *ṣadaqa*, some people intend the preservation of their identity and heritage. In my Muslim philanthropy class, I learned how Muslim Africans, abducted and enslaved by colonizers, practiced *ṣadaqa*. Descendants of enslaved Muslims recall their grandmothers making rice ball cakes, called *saraka*, and handing them out to children on the holy day of Friday.[164] *Saraka* as *ṣadaqa*.

Because *ṣadaqa* encompasses a broad definition of charitable acts, the diversity of its practice is vast. While zakat's goal is to alleviate poverty, *ṣadaqa* has often helped build and reinforce the infrastructure of Muslim communities, both locally and globally. From the *awqāf* established during the Ottomon Empire to the Süleymaniye Mosque in Istanbul to Hürrem Sultan's community

---

[163] Amy Singer, *Charity in Islamic Societies* (Cambridge University Press, 2008).
[164] Kambiz GhaneaBassiri, "U.S. Muslim Philanthropy After 9/11," *Journal of Muslim Philanthropy and Civil Society* 1, no. 1 (2018), https://scholarworks.iu.edu/iupjournals/index.php/muslimphilanthropy/article/view/1635.

Muslim Philanthropy

kitchen in Jerusalem, Muslims have been providing food, security, safe spaces, community care, and a sense of belonging through their ṣadaqa for centuries. Some of the institutions that were established so long ago are still in existence, providing ṣadaqa jāriya, or ongoing rewards, for their founders.

One such organization is the Muhammad 'Ali Benevolent Society. This organization also goes by the name Mabarrat. Established in 1901 in Egypt, it was originally a health clinic created and funded by Princess Ayn al-Hayat Rifaat.[165] This charitable women's organization was established in 'Abidīn, a poor Cairo neighborhood. The fascinating and powerful thing about this organization is that the princess mandated that the organization's president should always be a princess of the family, and that all committee members should be women.[166] Imagine writing that into a nonprofit's articles of incorporation and bylaws—in 1901! That one health clinic grew into an entire network of health care centers and hospitals. It survived the 1952 Egyptian Revolution, when many independent organizations were closed down. However, the Society's hospitals were eventually nationalized in 1964. By this time, it was calculated that the Society had treated around thirteen million women.[167] What an impact!

Let's also recognize the Süleymaniye complex (Süleymaniye Külliyesi) in Istanbul, Türkiye. It was established it in the sixteenth century by one of the most famous sultans of the Ottoman Empire, Sultan Suleiman the Magnificent.[168] The Süleymaniye complex is

---

165 Inger Marie Okkenhaug and Ingvild Flaskerud, eds., *Gender, Religion and Change in the Middle East: Two Hundred Years of History* (Bloomsbury Publishing, 2005).
166 Hassan Hassan, *In the House of Muhammad Ali: A Family Album 1805-1952* (The American University in Cairo Press, 2000).
167 Ghada Hashem Talhami, *Historical Dictionary of Women in the Middle East and North Africa* (Rowman and Littlefield, 2013), 217.
168 Iskandar Iskandar, Dadang Irsyamuddin, Esa Dwiyan, and Hidayatul Ihsan, "Waqf Substantial Contribution Toward the Public Healthcare Sector in the Ottoman Empire," *Journal of Critical Realism in Socio-Economics (JOCRISE)* 1, no. 3 (April 9, 2023): 275–94, https://doi.org/10.21111/jocrise.v1i3.21.

a vast architectural compound that includes several significant buildings and structures, all established as part of a *waqf*. The Süleymaniye Camii (mosque) is one of the most impressive and iconic in Istanbul, known for its grand dome and elegant architecture. The Süleymaniye Madrasa is an educational institution where Islamic scholars and students give and receive instruction in various disciplines. The Süleymaniye Darüşşifa (hospital) provides free health care services to the public, following the tradition of charitable health care institutions. The Süleymaniye Imaret (soup kitchen) provides food to the needy. And the Süleymaniye Yazma Eser Kütüphanesi (manuscript library) holds important collections of manuscripts and books.[169] Sultan Suleiman established a *waqf* to ensure the continued operation and maintenance of the complex. He dedicated the income from the *waqf*, which was generated from various sources, including agricultural land and properties, to supporting the mosque, educational institutions, and charitable services. I hope one day we all get to visit it!

One of the most important reminders that Dr. Haifaa shared when she spoke to us about zakat and *ṣadaqa* is that they are both purifiers and multipliers of your wealth. I had always heard that money given in zakat or *ṣadaqa* doesn't diminish your wealth. We were taught not to be afraid to give because somehow Allah ﷻ would bless us with more wealth in some other manner. Many friends and family have shared real-life examples of how they stretched themselves in giving—and then Allah ﷻ rewarded them for their generosity multiple times over. They got a promotion at work. They got the job they were interviewing for with a higher salary. The stock they donated to a nonprofit diminished the value of their portfolio temporarily, but looking at the portfolio one year later, the value had tripled! Blessings came their way. Muslims believe that the money they keep is actually what they are losing.

---

169 Hazineeditor, "Süleymaniye Library," *Hazine* (blog), October 10, 2013, https://hazine.info/suleymaniye-library/.

Because the money they give away is what receives the blessings and rewards.

AWQĀF

The Muslim community has long been a leader in philanthropy. Two hundred years after the death of Prophet Muhammad ﷺ, charitable foundations and endowments—*awqāf*—were created as financial mechanisms to support the infrastructure of the Muslim community. A *waqf* (*awqāf* is the plural) is a charitable fund that is established by an individual donor to address a specific community issue. The donation is usually quite significant and can take the form of a building, piece of land, a water well, cash, or other physical assets. The donor specifies that the principal donation is to remain untouched, and that the income generated from that principal has a specific and intended beneficiary. Examples of income generation are rent from the usage of a building, income from leasing land, or dividends from investing cash into stock. I'm sure fourteen hundred years ago, livestock was donated. If you donated two camels, then the sale of their milk would be income generated for the *waqf*. Islamic endowments are a form of *ṣadaqa jāriya*, intended to provide continuous, long-term benefits to the community and continuous, long-term rewards to the donor in the hereafter. *Awqāf* were established to ensure the necessary infrastructure for a vibrant Muslim community. Amy Singer states, "*Waqfs* were historically the means by which social and welfare services were routinely established and maintained throughout the Muslim world."[170]

Endowments, which are often perceived as a Western concept, are actually rooted in the Islamic institution of the *waqf*. This misconception highlights the importance of decolonizing wealth in the Muslim community and reclaiming our financial heritage.

---

170 Singer, *Charity in Islamic Societies*.

When we think about endowments today, examples like Harvard University's fund, valued at over $53.1 billion as of June 2021, or Oxford University's endowment, cited as the first of its kind in my history of philanthropy class, come to mind. These narratives exemplify the adage "history is written by the victors," because in reality, Islam established endowments well before the European Dark Ages and Enlightenment eras. The concept of the *waqf*, which Europeans later "borrowed" and rebranded, demonstrates the advanced financial and philanthropic systems developed in Islamic societies. By recognizing and reclaiming this history, we can better understand the depth of Islamic financial principles and their relevance to modern wealth management and philanthropy.[171]

Oxford University was first established as Merton College in 1274, at a time when there were plenty of interactions between England and the Muslim world, including Christians traveling to Jerusalem for pilgrimage and the Crusades. During these "visits," Christians interacted with and learned from Muslims about our Islamic legal institutions. Monica Gaudiosi wrote an interesting paper documenting the incredible overlap and similarities between the *waqf* and early English trusts.[172] The Europeans adopted concepts like reserving property, naming beneficiaries, and securing continuity straight from Muslim practices. So when you hear about these amazing endowments at big universities and other institutions, know that their roots lie in Islam!

Awqāf have existed since the beginning of Islam, but a tremendous rise and growth of *awqāf* occurred during the Ottoman Empire, when Muslims were thriving in an age of economic flourishing and ethnic and religious diversity. Records in Ankara, Türkiye, report

---

171 Monica M. Gaudiosi, "Influence of the Islamic Law of WAQF on the Development of the Trust in England: The Case of Merton College," *University of Pennsylvania Law Review* 136 (1988), https://scholarship.law.upenn.edu/cgi/viewcontent.cgi?article=3909&context=penn_law_review.
172 Gaudiosi, "Influence of the Islamic Law."

Muslim Philanthropy

over 26,000 *awqāf* established by the Ottoman Muslims—1,400 of them by Muslim women. Dr. Khalil Abdur-Rashid wrote a fantastic white paper at Yaqeen Institute sharing that "Muslims did not wait for governments to solve their problems but resorted to establishing *waqf*s to meet public needs."[173] A great example of this is the *ribāṭ*s, which were established to provide for the physical, emotional, and spiritual needs of single, divorced, and poor women.

Originally, *ribāṭ*s were physical fortifications on the front lines of the Muslim empire. They housed the Muslim military on the borders of the state during the eighth century in northern Africa, defending territorial borders. *Ribāṭ*s were seen as protectors of the religion. Valerie Hoffman, in her book *Sufism, Mystics, and Saints in Modern Egypt*, brings to light another form of *ribāṭ*—the safe housing and accommodations for Muslim women where female scholars, widows, and divorcées lived, dedicating themselves to worship and spiritual pursuits. Because these women didn't have family, specifically a male guardian, they often found themselves harassed, molested, and disconnected from community and spirituality.[174] The *ribāṭ*s provided these women with safety, security, companionship, community, and spiritual growth.

Most importantly, these safe houses were established by Muslim women. Unlike Western tradition and law, Islamic law stipulates that women inherit wealth left behind by family members. Muslim women who inherit properties, houses, and other assets have also always had agency over how to spend it. In fact, in eighteenth-century Aleppo, Syria, 40% of property transfers involved women and 33% of commercial property buyers were women.[175]

---

173 Khalil Abdur-Rashid, "Financing Kindness as a Society: The Rise and Fall of Islamic Philanthropic Institutions (Waqfs)," Yaqeen Institute for Islamic Research, 2019.
174 Valerie J. Hoffman, *Sufism, Mystics, and Saints in Modern Egypt* (University of South Carolina Press, 2023).
175 Leila Ahmed, *Women and Gender in Islam: Historical Roots of Modern Debate* (Yale University Press, 1992).

Dr. Tamara Gray, the founder and executive director of Rabata states, "We can identify a historical culture of women managing their own money and investing it in projects" throughout Islamic history. This autonomy is provided for in Islamic law and upheld in the Islamic economy. Muslim women identified social issues that needed to be addressed and established *awqāf* for *ribāṭ*s, schools, hostels, and hospitals for women, the poor, and the most vulnerable in their communities.

In Morocco, sisters Fatima and Mariam al-Fihri built al-Qarawiyyin Mosque in the ninth century, which eventually became the University of al-Qarawiyyin in 1963, the oldest continuously functioning university in history (see it in the Guinness Book of World Records!).[176] Ottoman Sultan Suleiman the Magnificent's wife, Haseki Hürrem, used her wealth to create a *waqf* to support the three holy places of Islam: al-Quds, Mecca, and Medina.[177] And she didn't stop there. In Palestine, Haseki Hürrem endowed villages, farmlands, mills, and other properties for the establishment and perpetual support of a mosque, a public soup kitchen, and an inn for Muslim pilgrims on their way to Mecca.[178] There are so many wonderful and powerful examples of Muslim women leading in the establishment of *awqāf*, inspiring me to grow my wealth so I, too, can contribute more to the Muslim community!

Today, the concept of protecting our Islamic borders and taking care of our Muslim women has evolved into "education as the front line of the cultural battle of *adab* and culturalism."[179] The *ribāṭ* has, over time, developed into nonprofits. Muslim women have new challenges of misogyny, colonialism, and racism that have eroded

---

176 Rafiuddin Siddiqi, "Oldest Library of University of Al-Qarawiyyin in Fez, Morocco," *Pakistan Library and Information Science Journal* 49, no. 3 (2018).
177 Abdul Azim Islahi, "The Role of Women in the Creation and Management of Awqāf: A Historical Perspective," *Intellectual Discourse* 26 (July 2, 2018): 1025–46.
178 Islahi, "Role of Women."
179 Tamara Gray, "Ethical Dilemma of Zakat and Nonprofit Funding," November 27, 2023.

their Islamic rights in cultures that do not promote power over their finances. Muslim women are organizing and addressing their needs—from a lack of physical space in the mosque to gendered Islamophobia in mainstream society—through the establishment of nonprofits. Rabata, Muslim Women's Organization in Florida, and Texas Muslim Women's Foundation, for example, are new versions of the *ribāṭ* that Muslim women have created to care for the mind, body, and soul, so they can continue their role as guardians of the faith, develop healthy citizenry, and maintain human connectedness.

Although not financed by endowments or *awqāf*, women donors now support organizations for women and girls through charitable annual gifts.[180] Many of these donors share the opinion that the culture of Muslim women having autonomy over their finances has been eroded over the years. This has led Muslim women to shy away from investing and taking financial risks. Instead, they continue to donate their time and small monetary gifts. Additional data and research are needed to understand this paradigm shift.

Muslim philanthropy has broadened our understanding of traditional definitions of charitable giving. Rooted in justice, compassion, and equity, Muslim philanthropy attempts to address and alleviate societal issues at their root causes through zakat, *ṣadaqa*, and *awqāf*. Due to their God-given inheritance rights, and for many other reasons, Muslim women have been philanthropists since the early centuries of Islamic history. Their generosity allowed for the building of infrastructures that played a critical role in supporting vulnerable women while building community. Muslim women continue to play a vital role in community building through the nonprofit sector and continue to be the backbone of the Muslim community.

---

180   Debra Mesch, Eileen L. O'Gara, Una Osili, Andrea Pactor, and Jon Bergdoll, "Do Women Give More?," Women Philanthropy Institute, September 2015, https://philanthropy.indianapolis.iu.edu/doc/institutes/wpi-give-more.pdf.

Although the research is limited and doesn't provide a full picture of Muslim women philanthropists, we know anecdotally that Muslim women are continuing to build infrastructure for the most vulnerable in our communities. Domestic violence shelters like Minnesota's Sisters Need a Place, Florida's Muslim Women's Organization, Chicago's Apna Ghar, and Houston's Peaceful Families Project exist because of Muslim women's philanthropy. Empowerment organizations like Minnesota's Ayada Leads, Chicago's Muslim Women Alliance, and North Carolina's Muslim Women For are additional examples of Muslim women not waiting around for someone else to help them or save them. These and many other philanthropists come together to change their community for the better.

In 2023, I started my doctoral program at Indiana University in philanthropic leadership. My applied research project will tell the story of Muslim women's philanthropy and nonprofit leadership. Currently, very limited data and research are available on this, and I want to be able to tell our story of philanthropy and generosity.

Studying Muslim philanthropy is important for several compelling reasons. First, it allows us to gain a deeper understanding of the values and principles that drive charitable actions within the Muslim community. By examining the various forms of philanthropic practices, such as zakat, *ṣadaqa*, and *awqāf*, we can uncover the cultural, religious, and social motivations that shape the giving patterns of Muslims. This knowledge fosters greater intercultural awareness and empathy, promoting a more inclusive and harmonious society.

Second, studying and researching Muslim philanthropy provides valuable insights into the broader landscape of global giving and social impact. Muslims constitute a significant portion of the world's population, and their philanthropic activities have far-reaching effects on societal challenges, from poverty alleviation to health care and education. By understanding the strategies and priorities of Muslim philanthropists, we can collaborate more effectively to tackle shared global issues while creating positive change.

Furthermore, studying Muslim philanthropy offers a unique lens through which we can analyze the intersection of faith, ethics, and social responsibility. (My research will also examine intersections with gender.) Many Muslims view philanthropy as a direct expression of their religious beliefs—seeking to fulfill their duty to help those in need and promote justice. By delving into the philosophical motivations of Muslim giving, we can foster meaningful dialogue on the role of spirituality in philanthropic endeavors and cultivate a greater appreciation for diverse approaches to making a difference. Personally, I have found that studying Muslim philanthropy enriches our understanding of human compassion, cooperation, and generosity across cultures. By recognizing the significance of this form of giving, I aim to bridge gaps, challenge stereotypes, and work together toward a more equitable and compassionate world. Please, keep me in your *dua*s as I work to reclaim our financial narrative and tell the truly powerful story of Muslim women philanthropists!

Reflection Exercise

1. Imagine poverty as a tree. What are the root causes of poverty, and do you think zakat addresses them? Or do you think zakat just temporarily "trims the branches" of the poverty tree?

2. Does *ṣadaqa* address the root causes of poverty by eliminating inequities (racism, educational disparities, lack of affordable housing, and health care disparities)? What role do you see *ṣadaqa* playing in contemporary society?

3. How do you see your economic stability as contributing to making the world a better place?

4. After reading about Muslim philanthropy, the historical impact Muslim women have made, and the establishment of *awqāf*, what went through your mind? How did it make you feel?

5. What role do you see yourself playing in Muslim women's legacy of philanthropy?

Chapter 18

My DAF as My Philanthropic Tool

I wrote this piece for RISE in 2021 and it can be found on their website. It has been edited to reflect changes in the economy and new findings I've learned since.

During the 2020 presidential election, taxes were a hot topic on every candidate's policy platform. I heard candidates reference lowering taxes, raising taxes, and eliminating taxes altogether. The conversation around taxes was not unique to that election, but 2020 was the year I started to pay more attention to taxes beyond the income taxes I pay. As you invest and build your wealth, you will need to understand capital gains taxes, estate taxes, and maybe even property taxes. When you file your taxes every year, you will need to understand how to claim exemptions and deductions in order to avoid paying higher taxes. It's such a complex system, and one that frustrates me, because every time I learn something new, it either changes again or leads to more new things to learn!

One particular moment that piqued my interest during the 2020 presidential election was when I learned of Senator Elizabeth Warren's proposal to tax a person's wealth. In Islam, taxing wealth is not a foreign concept. As discussed in Chapter 17, zakat, often described as a tax, almsgiving, or charity, is a 2.5% "tax" on excess wealth that you have held in your possession for at least one year. Zakat excludes wealth that is used on a regular basis, such as your house, car, or everyday jewelry. It is a beautiful concept because it's not just a tax but also an act of worship, a social justice strategy, and an economic equalizer. It functions as a social safety net for Muslims, wherein those with financial privilege are commanded to share their wealth with those in need because those in need have a right to it.

Back to the elections. During discussions of economic inequality and tax reform, we constantly heard from candidates that the rich don't pay their fair share. I have heard people in lower income brackets say they pay more taxes than large companies like Amazon. I have seen my middle-class friends upset because they are in a higher tax bracket than most billionaires. How is all this possible? The rich stay rich because they exploit the tax loopholes that the average American is simply unaware of—or doesn't even qualify for—and that's by design. Let's talk about two of those loopholes.

The first tax loophole is salary and compensation. Billionaires' compensation consists of salary, stock, equity, and a host of other benefits. But income tax is only paid on one's salary. For example, a CEO of a company can have a salary of $250,000 and receive 100,000 shares in stock options. She pays a 37% income tax on the $250,000, but let's say the shares are valued at $100,000 and the CEO sells them a year later, when they are valued at $250,000. She would only have to pay a capital gains tax, which is "a levy on the profit from an investment that is incurred when the investment is sold," according to Investopedia.com. In this example, the CEO would pay 25% on the $150,000 increase in the shares' value. Thus, she pays a lower tax on a lower amount of capital than what she actually earned. It is these types of tax structures and laws that contribute to the economic inequality we are experiencing across the nation. Imagine if we told the nonprofit we are working for to pay us in stock, any stock, instead of a salary.

The second loophole is a dark chasm known as donor-advised funds (DAFs). The infamous DAFs are financial tools that I am still trying to wrap my mind around. During the pandemic, when I started my journey in taking stock (pun intended!) of my financial situation, I evaluated my income, my wealth, and my giving, which led me to learn about donor-advised funds. The American Muslim Community Foundation (AMCF) defines a DAF as "a giving vehicle that provides you with immediate tax benefits." Through AMCF you can create a DAF, which provides a flexible way to manage your charitable giving to organizations of your choice. "You can invest your balance, name the fund after a loved one, and pass it on generation to generation."

While I was evaluating my personal income and giving, RISE was in the process of creating a brokerage account. During this time, I kept running into DAFs. I learned, to my astonishment, that people who donate stock to a nonprofit do not have to pay any capital gains tax on the growth of the value of the stock, AND they can take a tax deduction for the donation! DAFs give the donor a tax deduction and they allow the nonprofit to benefit from the gain. No one pays any taxes on the sale of the stock. This is why I wanted to open a DAF to fund my favorite nonprofits.

At the same time, I also learned that the wealthy can put their assets into a DAF and defer their taxes while paying out only 5%. The 5% payout rule states that by law, DAFs must distribute 5% of the value of their net investment assets annually in the form of charitable giving. Originally, this rule was created to prevent foundations from receiving assets but never actually making charitable distributions with them. The criticism of DAFs comes from the fact that many rich people use them to grow their wealth by hoarding the remaining 95% in their funds. Ostensibly, tax laws and tax incentives were created so that the wealthy would have agency in their charitable giving and, hopefully, increase it. But is that what's really happening? Are billionaires actually giving more? And in my own position of relative privilege, how can I leverage these laws and incentives to benefit my community?

I decided to look more into these questions, so I contacted my friend Muhi Khwaja at AMCF. He helped me understand the inner workings of a DAF and the benefits of utilizing this vehicle to distribute my zakat to my favorite nonprofits and give more. Remember, I worked for two corporations before I transitioned to the nonprofit sector. I earned stock and purchased stock through the employee stock purchase programs, so I've held some stocks for almost twenty years and others for ten years. Both companies are doing well—so well that the capital gains on those stocks would be significant and so would the capital gains tax.

Now here's where zakat and taxes intersect for me. After calculating my zakat this past Ramadan, I opened up a DAF at AMCF with my husband, and we named it after our moms. The Razia Asghar Foundation. (May they be rewarded for the charitable giving we are able to contribute. *Ameen.*) I transferred stock equivalent to the amount of my zakat into my DAF. Then I chose my favorite causes—nonprofits that are zakat-eligible—to distribute my zakat to. I was able to claim the tax deduction on my 2021 taxes, and by the end of Ramadan, all my zakat was distributed and I had donated all of my DAF—not just the required 5%.

This is one example of how a DAF can be leveraged. You can transfer cash and other assets into a DAF as well. Maybe you came into a large inheritance or the company you work for has just given you $100,000 in stock. You may not know exactly which charity or nonprofit to donate that to. You want to be thoughtful and create a plan in order to have the biggest impact, but paying 40% income tax on this windfall doesn't sound very exciting. Moving the money into a DAF is an option. The entity that holds your DAF can invest that money on your behalf until you are ready to distribute. But be careful. Make sure it's sharia-compliant investing. You don't want your DAF invested into the market of haram businesses or companies. (I recently learned that Azzad Wealth Management offers sharia-compliant DAFs. So much to learn!)

When I calculate my zakat right before Ramadan, like many Muslims do so we can give it in Ramadan and double its blessings, I dream of giving hundreds of thousands of dollars to charity. I dream of donating the entirety of a nonprofit's Ramadan goal by writing just one check. I'm not a billionaire; I'm not Melinda Gates or Mackenzie Scott, but I'm a philanthropist nonetheless. After learning about the benefits of DAFs, I have made a conscientious decision to utilize them to avoid capital gains taxes. This allows me to give more to organizations that are providing zakat to the people who need it.

Senator Warren didn't win the presidential election, and unfortunately her proposal to tax wealth hasn't seen the light of day. While we learn about these tax loopholes and leverage them in funding the nonprofit sector, we need to consider systemic tax reform that provides for a more equitable structure. I believe that we can make progress toward a society that funds social impact work equitably, with organizations not just relying on generous individuals but also receiving their share of the wealth they deserve. For now, I invite you to consider opening a DAF and exploring different types of tax laws to see how they can enhance your philanthropic giving.

Reflection Exercise

1. Are the economic or philanthropic advantages of having a DAF enough to make you want to open one? Why or why not?

2. If you have a DAF, reflect on your journey of how and why you started it, what you learned along the way, and what you would have done differently.

3. What other tax laws do you know of that might help your philanthropy?

Chapter 19

Giving Circles

I wrote this piece for RISE in 2017 and it can be found on their website. It has been edited to reflect changes in the economy and new findings I've learned since.

Two months before the holy month of Ramadan begins, my mailbox, inbox, and messaging groups swell with invitations to fundraising dinners from all across the Twin Cities metro. Typically, a renowned speaker flies in, gives a keynote at a semiformal dinner, and a familiar face challenges us to dig deeper into our pockets with a starting bid to donate $25,000! While these events often support worthy causes, I've noticed a concerning trend in how some organizations present their case for support. For instance, I've attended dinners where the exact same slides with the exact same statistics were presented three years in a row. This lack of updated information raises questions about the organization's progress, impact, and transparency in how they're using the funds raised. As donors, we should expect clear, current information about how our contributions are making a difference.

Most of our 501(c)3 organizations are required by law to provide a Form 990. This form allows the IRS and the general public to evaluate a nonprofit's operations; it includes information on the nonprofit's mission, programs, and finances. As a best practice, an annual report is typically created as well. However, I rarely see this offered by our Islamic organizations. While some organizations might lack the talent or resources to create an annual report, an alternative approach could be to create a financial transparency page on their website and post the previous years' Form 990s there. My mind is boggled by the lack of transparency and accountability about the sustainability of many organizations.

Confused about what my donations were accomplishing, I started to explore what it means to give. What is a gift? How do I donate my time, talent, treasure, ties, and testimony?

I especially wanted to learn about giving circles. Wikipedia's definition: "A giving circle is a form of participatory philanthropy by a group of individuals who form a voluntary association to donate their money or time." The group then decides how to allocate these resources to charitable organizations or community projects. After speaking to a few Muslim sisters in my community, I found that giving circles have been around in our tradition long before they were given that name.

A community member shared with me the concept of *afusha* that exists in her Oromo[181] community. The *afusha* builds economic strength through sisterhood. It's a pay-it-forward model. Women come together on a monthly basis, using a notebook to register and sign in. The membership fee can be $30–$200 per person, per month. It's an intimate setting, usually at someone's home. The women bring cash and give it to their treasurer. The women then decide where the greatest need is in their network, and the treasurer passes it along. A wedding, a funeral, the birth of a child, a mosque, an illness, or an emergency back home…But the *afusha* is more than a giving circle of emergency funding. It's a true model of time, talent, and treasure. These women volunteer their time to cook for weddings, set up for events, bring food to sick neighbors, and continue to check up on them. They are known to partake in the festivities of weddings by dressing up in the same color, dancing, singing, and celebrating. I found that the *afusha* model

---

181 The Oromo people are a Cushitic ethnic group native to the Oromia region of Ethiopia and parts of northern Kenya.

embodies a sense of collective community care. And as the elders of the *afusha* age, the younger women, fresh college grads and new moms, are stepping up and evolving the *afusha* to meet the needs of their generation.

I spoke to another sister who introduced me to *ayuuto* (or *hagbad*), a savings model found in the Somali community. *Ayuuto* predates, but addresses, the injustices that Muslims are facing in banking because of false terrorism charges and narratives. Often members of the Somali community in the US are unable to get loans from banks, open checking or savings accounts, or transfer money because of false allegations of funding terrorists. Even if they do qualify for loans, the interest rates are exorbitantly high and clash with Islamic principles. And let's not ignore the problematic use of credit scores, which forces poor people to pay higher rates of interest, disqualifies them from home or auto loans, and exacerbates the cycle of poverty.

To combat this, ten to fifteen Somali women will pool a significant amount of money, around $1,000 each month, for about one year. Each month, one woman from the group receives the entire amount in that pool to apply toward the purchase of a car or to start a new business. *Ayuuto* is a culturally sensitive alternative lending model that aims to create economic stability.

The *ayuuto* concept, familiar to me from Indian culture, where it's known as *chiti*, also resembles the Pakistani version known as "committee." In my mom's family's practice of *chiti*, her siblings would contribute a set amount monthly. They would write their names on small slips of paper—the *chiti*s—and place them in a circle. Names were drawn to determine the order in which each sibling would receive the pooled funds each month. This system allowed each participant to anticipate a larger sum at a specific time, useful for major expenses, while continuing to contribute throughout the year. My Arab friends have shared with me that this exists in their culture as well.

Kaltun Karani, founder and executive director of Hikma Academy, helped me understand the Somali practice of *qaaraan*. The Somali community is tribe-based, which can be complicated and contentious. But during times of emergencies and crises, the tribes come together. *Qaaraan* is a form of responsive philanthropy. A few years back, a brother was arrested on false pretenses, and his mother and brother needed to raise $100,000 in legal fees. They traveled from city to city, tribe to tribe, and clan to clan, requesting support. When they received funds from Tribe A, they shared this news with other tribes, which inspired those tribes to contribute their own support. The tribes were competing to support and unite around a genuine need for this family and their brother. The family was able to raise enough money to cover the legal fees. Alhamdulillah, he is a free man now!

Finally, I learned about the co-op model of *qubi* found in Somali culture. It's also a payback model for investing in a new business, with the intention of a return on that investment (ROI). The *qubi* participants are like shareholders of a new business. They help the new entrepreneur get started, giving the entrepreneur the motivation to succeed and remain accountable to her shareholders. These are business loans for new startups outside of the traditional banking route. We take care of our own.

The above giving models are all examples of giving circles. They consist of a group of people coming together as a voluntary association. They donate their money and their time. Together, they decide how to distribute their resources to people in need. Perhaps the Western vernacular "giving circle" is new to us, but we've been giving in circles for years, if not centuries.

I had never been a part of a giving circle before. My friend from the In Faith Foundation invited me to sit in on a giving circle session she was conducting at the Chain of Lakes Church. I watched and listened as thirty to forty women came together to give. Each woman introduced herself, sharing a story about the boldest, most meaningful gift she had ever given (donated), followed by describing the difference she wanted to make in the world. My friend guided them through conversations on the power of the purse and how women have the power to make a difference. She wove stories from the Christian faith throughout the session. There were activities related to scarcity and abundance mindsets and a quiz to help each attendee understand her giving style. Like a true democracy, the women nominated three causes they wanted to support. Representatives of these three groups presented a pitch, and the women voted on which group would receive the $1,450 they had collected. It was such a powerful moment for me to see these women collectively, democratically, and through sisterhood, give a substantial amount to a charity they believed in.

I was determined to apply this model in our community and start a Muslim women's giving circle at RISE. I did some research to see if there were any giving circles organized by Muslim women in the US. I was pleasantly surprised to find one in California. I called up the sister and picked her brain on how she started it and how to get Muslim sisters involved. Her advice to me was to make it fun— invite people to an in-person event with food.

I decided to test the concept with a pilot giving circle, and the first session was a resounding success. I reached out to a handful of women and invited them over for brunch. Eight women showed up, enjoyed the food and the company, and each contributed $100 to the circle. We conversed, shared, nominated nonprofits, and voted on where to donate our pooled resources. The experience felt empowering and inspiring.

Encouraged by this positive start, I organized a second session with six different women, replicating the format of the first. This circle also saw initial success, with each participant again donating $100. We were able to make a small but meaningful donation to a nonprofit supporting women facing domestic violence and displacement. However, maintaining momentum proved challenging. As the perceived convener, when my capacity became limited and I couldn't organize a third circle, the group's activities naturally slowed. This experience highlighted the importance of shared leadership and consistent engagement in sustaining such initiatives.

Reflecting on other giving circles I've been involved with, I noticed similar patterns of ebb and flow. The circle in California faced difficulties, and another I joined through AMCF in 2021 also struggled to maintain long-term momentum after initial success. Interestingly, the AMCF circle was revived in 2023, with invitations extending into 2024, demonstrating the resilience and enduring appeal of the giving circle concept.

These experiences led me to ponder: What factors contribute to the sustainability of giving circles, and how can we address these challenges to create lasting impact? The revival of the AMCF circle offers hope and suggests that with the right approach, giving circles can overcome obstacles and continue to make a difference in their communities.

During the COVID-19 pandemic and the uprising after the murder of George Floyd in 2020, I revisited the idea of giving circles because I saw them morph into mutual aid groups. I watched Muslim women gather their sisters from the masjids through WhatsApp groups, organize supply runs, and take care of those most impacted by the pandemic. After the murder of George Floyd and the subsequent protests against police brutality and the killing of unarmed Black men, the community faced white supremacists in our neighborhoods, violent racism in our cities, and so much more. And yet I found Muslim sisters organizing mutual aid. My heart swelled watching my sisters make an ask and find donors instantly through CashApp, Zelle, and Venmo. Those sisters took their Costco memberships and bought food, hygiene products, diapers, and formula and delivered the supplies to the mutual aid sites. They didn't just drop them off, though. They helped organize the sites. Seeing our sisters in the middle of their communities reminded me that we are the center of collective care.

It was when we professionalized giving circles that they seemed to come to halt. But when someone was in need—a crisis was happening—Muslim women became responsive philanthropists. They showed up.

Whenever I'm asked to give, I believe I am being invited to *khayr*, goodness. Had I not worked on my finances, invested, and become a conscious spender, I wouldn't be able to give as generously as I'm able to. When we make a more conscious effort in our finances, our giving and its impact can be tremendous. When we look past the terminology or the formality, we see Muslim women often moving money and redirecting resources to where they belong.

Reflection Exercise

1. Do you have a giving circle concept (whether similar or different) in your family or community?

2. Describe a time when you may have pooled resources together in your family or friend network to help someone. How did you feel doing that?

3. If you could organize a giving circle in your community, who would you invite, what causes would you consider supporting, and how much would you give?

Chapter 20

Muslim Women Philanthropists

Just to recap: Philanthropy is the act of using one's time, talent, treasure, testimony, ties, or other resources to promote the welfare of others, especially through charitable or voluntary activities. Philanthropy can take many forms, including donating money to a charity, volunteering time to a community organization, or providing expertise or resources to support a social cause. The goal of philanthropy is to improve the well-being of others, especially those who are disadvantaged or in need, and to promote positive social change.

The Indiana University definition of philanthropy as "voluntary action for the public good, including giving of time, talent, and treasure for charitable purposes"[182] emphasizes that philanthropy involves not just monetary donations but also the contribution of personal skills and expertise, as well as the willingness to engage in time- or labor-consuming voluntary activities that promote the public good. This definition also highlights the idea that philanthropy is a form of action, driven by a desire to make a positive impact on society, and is characterized by a sense of altruism and concern for others.

How is Muslim philanthropy different? Muslim philanthropy is charitable giving that is informed by Islamic values and principles. It is guided by the religious obligation of zakat, which requires Muslims to donate a portion of their wealth to those in need, as

---

[182] Robert L. Payton and Michael P. Moody, *Understanding Philanthropy: Its Meaning and Mission,* (Indiana University Press, 2008).

well as by the broader concept of ṣadaqa, which refers to voluntary giving for the sake of God and for the benefit of others.

One key difference between Muslim philanthropy and mainstream philanthropy is the emphasis on giving as an act of worship and spiritual fulfillment. In Islam, giving is seen as a means of seeking the pleasure of God and earning spiritual reward; it is not solely motivated by the desire to do good or make a social impact. Additionally, Muslim philanthropy often places a greater emphasis on supporting causes and organizations that are aligned with Islamic values and principles, such as those that promote social justice, education, and humanitarian relief.

A unique aspect of Islamic philanthropy is the concept of zakat, which is both obligatory and philanthropic. While zakat is a mandatory form of giving for those who meet certain wealth criteria, it still falls under the umbrella of philanthropy because it serves the public good and addresses societal needs. Its obligatory nature doesn't diminish its philanthropic essence; rather, it underscores the importance Islam places on systematic and regular giving as a means of wealth redistribution and community support.

I want to share something Dr. Shariq Siddiqui once told me. Dr. Siddiqui's research on Muslim philanthropy in the global context revealed an interesting insight. He found that one of the biggest motivators of generosity was the desire to prevent harm. This expands our understanding of philanthropy beyond just voluntary action for the public good to include actions taken to avoid public harm, emphasizing the holistic approach Islam takes to social responsibility and community well-being.[183] This is reflected in the use of Islamic financial instruments such as awqāf, which can be used to generate funds for charitable purposes in perpetuity. Awqāf

---

183 Shariq Ahmed Siddiqui and David A. Campbell, eds., *Philanthropy in the Muslim World: Majority and Minority Muslim Communities,* (Edward Elgar Publishing, 2023).

Muslim Women Philanthropists

are important mechanisms for Muslim philanthropy as they allow for the creation of sustainable sources of funding for charitable causes that both meet current needs and prevent future harm.

ISLAM'S PHILANTHROPIC ROOTS

Let's take a step back in Islamic history and view the beginning of Islam through the eyes of philanthropy. When I started to reread certain passages of the *sīra*,[184] I came to realize that Islam was built on philanthropy. The *ṣaḥāba*[185] were philanthropists, and that legacy continues today—with women playing an integral role.

Abū Bakr ﷺ, one of the Prophet Muhammad's closest companions and the first man to accept Islam, was known for his philanthropy and generosity. As a successful entrepreneur and skilled trader, he became a very wealthy person. During the early years of Islam, Abū Bakr used his money to buy the freedom of enslaved Muslims who were being tortured and persecuted by the Quraysh—most famously, Bilāl ﷺ.[186] Abū Bakr was at once saving the lives of these enslaved new Muslims and emancipating them.[187] And while freeing slaves would become one of the eight zakat-worthy categories, this occurred during a time when the commandment of zakat had not yet been revealed and required of the Muslims.

'Uthmān ibn 'Affān ﷺ, another of the Prophet Muhammad's companions, was also known for his philanthropy and charitable work—the most famous act of which was when he purchased a well in Medina. According to the *sīra*, a man by the name of Rūma

---

184 A word meaning "biography," *sīra* usually refers to the traditional biography of the Prophet Muhammad ﷺ.
185 The companions of the Prophet were the disciples and followers of Prophet Muhammad ﷺ who saw or met him during his lifetime and remained Muslim until their deaths.
186 Meraj Mohiuddin, *Revelation: The Story of Muhammad: Peace and Blessings Be upon Him* (Whiteboard Press, 2015), 132.
187 Muhammad Habibur, Rahman Khan Sherwani, and Syed Moinul Haq, *Hadrat Abu Bakr: The First Caliph Of Islam* (Literary Licensing, 2011).

owned a well in Medina and sold its water for profit. When the Muslims migrated to Medina from Mecca, they had very limited resources, especially financial, and they were often unable to afford the water. ʿUthmān ibn ʿAffān, through his wealth and generosity, purchased the well and made the water free for both Muslims and non-Muslims alike.[188] This well still exists today, and its *waqf* has expanded to provide water to date farms as well as people.[189] Half of the profits from sales of the dates are given to charity, mainly to widows and orphans, and the other half are reinvested.[190] The impact of this *waqf* as a continuous charity continues to benefit ʿUthmān ibn ʿAffān over 1,400 years later.

ʿAbd al-Raḥmān ibn ʿAwf ﷺ was another philanthropic companion of the Prophet Muhammad ﷺ. He was a self-made man. After his migration to Medina, he quickly began to trade in the market, doing so well that he became wealthy. But he never allowed his wealth to corrupt him.

ʿAbd al-Raḥmān ibn ʿAwf ﷺ consistently answered the Prophet's call to fund the Muslim army, which, when it was forming, had very few resources to fight the Quraysh. He gave two thousand dinars in support of an expedition that the Prophet ﷺ needed to dispatch. He provided two hundred *uqiyya*[191] of gold during the Tabuk expedition. But what really touched my heart was his generosity toward the family of the Prophet Muhammad ﷺ after his passing. ʿAbd al-Raḥmān ibn ʿAwf took on the responsibility of taking care of the widows of the Prophet Muhammad ﷺ. He provided for them financially and accompanied them on their travels for safety

---

188 Md. Mokhter Ahmad and Md. Safiullah, "Management of Waqf Estates in Bangladesh: Toward a Sustainable Policy Formulation," *Waqf Laws and Management* (With Special Reference to Malaysia) (2012): 229–62.

189 Hasanain Abdullah, "The Caliph Uthman bin Affan (R.A) and the Well," Awqaf SA, August 17, 2020, https://awqafsa.org.za/the-caliph-uthman-bin-affan-r-a-and-the-well/.

190 Abdullah, "Caliph Uthman bin Affan."

191 An *uqiyya* is a historical unit of weight equivalent to forty dirhams.

and security reasons. He once sold a piece of land and distributed the profits to the relatives of the Prophet Muhammad's mother and wives, and included the poor as well.[192]

Khadīja bint Khuwaylid

For me, the most important female philanthropist was our mother, Khadīja bint Khuwaylid ﷺ. She was the first wife of the Prophet Muhammad ﷺ, a successful businesswoman who owned a caravan trade, and a person of astute business acumen.

Khadīja used her wealth to support charitable causes and to help those in need. She would often donate money to the poor and needy, support widows and orphans, and provide for the needs of travelers and pilgrims. One particular story from her biography is her care for Ḥalīma al-Saʿdiyya ﷺ, the wet nurse of Prophet Muhammad ﷺ. (Bedouin women were hired to nurse and care for Meccan children during this time, and it was quite normal for parents to send their children off to more rural areas to provide them with a quieter, safer environment and exposure to classical Arabic. Ḥalīma al-Saʿdiyya and her husband provided that for the Prophet Muhammad ﷺ).

When Khadīja and the Prophet Muhammad ﷺ were wed, she invited Ḥalīma al-Saʿdiyya to the wedding to rejoice with them. Khadīja gifted her forty sheep at the wedding to thank her for nursing her beloved husband.[193]

However, her most notable act of philanthropy was that she used her wealth to help fund the entire movement known as Islam. Khadīja's philanthropy supported not just her husband ﷺ but the new Muslims during the beginning years of Islam's formation as

---

192 Abdul Wahid Hamid, "'Abdur-Rahman Ibn 'Awf,'" in *Companions of the Prophet* (MELS, 1998), 49–56.
193 Haylamaz Reşit and Coşar Hülya, *Khadija: The First Muslim and the Wife of the Prophet Muhammad* (Tughra Books, 2014).

well. Those who embraced Islam were often cut off by their families and/or persecuted. As we saw, some of the first Muslims were slaves of the elite, and most of the elite did not accept Islam, nor did they want others to. They were violently adamant about this. Khadīja used her wealth to help emancipate enslaved Muslims.

Many people who joined the faith early on were from the lower socioeconomic classes. Khadīja supported their conversions and made sure they were welcomed into the community.[194] Her actions helped establish a tradition of charity and social justice within the Muslim community. Her legacy as a philanthropist and supporter of charitable causes set an example for Muslim men and women throughout history. She was the first in a long line of Muslim female philanthropists who have funded Islam and built movements.

Fāṭima bint Muḥammad

Fāṭima bint Muḥammad ﷺ, the youngest daughter of the Prophet Muhammad ﷺ, stands as a timeless exemplar of philanthropic generosity and compassion. Born into a family that would reshape the course of history, Fāṭima carried forward her father's legacy of kindness and selflessness, embodying the essence of Islamic charity in her daily life. Despite her esteemed lineage, Fāṭima led a life of remarkable simplicity and humility. Her household was not one of material abundance; rather, it was rich in faith, love, and generosity. This humble lifestyle, however, did not hinder her philanthropic spirit. On the contrary, it seemed to fuel her empathy and drive to help others. Fāṭima was known to frequently give away her own food and clothing to those in greater need, even when she herself had little to spare.[195] Her actions serve as a powerful reminder that true philanthropy is not measured by the quantity of what is given, but by the spirit in which it is offered.

---

194 Syed Razwy, *Khadijatul kubra* (Tahrike Tarsile Quran, n.d.).
195 Hamid, *Companions of the Prophet*, 21.

One of the most significant beneficiaries of Fāṭima's generosity was Ahl al-Ṣuffa,[196] a group of impoverished Muslims who lived just outside the Prophet's mosque in Medina. These individuals, having left behind their homes and possessions for the sake of their faith, dedicated their lives to the pursuit of knowledge and the preservation of the Prophet's teachings.[197]

The Ahl al-Ṣuffa lived in challenging conditions, often going without basic necessities. Fāṭima, recognizing their dedication and sacrifice, took it upon herself to support them however she could. She would often prepare meals, mend clothes, or provide whatever assistance was within her means to ensure their well-being. Her support for the Ahl al-Ṣuffa went beyond mere material provision though. Fāṭima understood the importance of their work preserving and disseminating Islamic knowledge. By caring for their basic needs, she indirectly contributed to the preservation of her father's teachings and the foundations of Islamic scholarship.

Fāṭima's life teaches us several profound lessons about philanthropy and generosity. She proves that one does not need to be wealthy to be philanthropic. Even with limited means, she found ways to help others, demonstrating that generosity is more about the willingness to give than the amount given. Her regular acts of kindness, though often small in scale, had a significant cumulative impact. This reminds us that though we have dreams of writing that big check at the fundraiser, philanthropy need not consist of grand gestures. Consistent small acts of kindness can create lasting change. Despite her own modest circumstances, Fāṭima often prioritized the needs of others over her own comfort. She gave her time, effort, and compassion, reminding us that philanthropy can take many forms. Islamic teachings emphasize

---

[196] The hijra was the journey of the Prophet Muhammad ﷺ and his followers from Mecca to Medina.
[197] Mohiuddin, *Revelation*.

that acts of generosity carry immense spiritual rewards. Fāṭima's life exemplifies the belief that what we give in this life is not lost, but rather invested in our eternal afterlife.

In an era where philanthropy is often associated with wealthy individuals or large organizations, Fāṭima bint Muḥammad stands as a timeless reminder that true generosity stems from the heart, not the wallet. Her life demonstrates that anyone, regardless of their financial status, can be a philanthropist. As we reflect on Fāṭima's example, we are challenged to reconsider our own approach to giving. In a world that often measures worth by material possessions, her legacy calls upon us to open our hearts, extend our hands, and touch the lives of those around us with whatever means we have at our disposal. In doing so, we not only honor her legacy but also contribute to building a more compassionate and generous world.

Rufayda al-Aslamiyya

Rufayda al-Aslamiyya —Islam's first nurse and surgeon—was a woman![198] Her expertise was in medical treatment, especially emergency medicine. Her generosity is seen in her establishment of a field hospital using her own personal wealth. During the early Muslim battles, including the Battle of Badr (624 CE) and the Battle of Uhud (625 CE), Rufayda set up a tent near the battlefield to treat and care for wounded soldiers. Known as "Rufayda's tent," this makeshift facility provided medical care free of charge.

Her hospital was an act of charity in and of itself, and it also provided opportunities for others to give as well. Rufayda trained a team of volunteers—all women—who gave their time and skills in

---

198 Khalid Muhammed Khalid, *Women Around the Messenger* (Light Publishing, 2015).

health care and medicine to care for the wounded.[199]

When not in battle, Rufayda tended to the medical needs of the growing Muslim community by providing medical care and hygiene and disease prevention education to the community, never forgetting the orphans, the disabled, or the poor. Her tent was what we would today consider a not-for-profit organization or a nongovernmental organization.

Imagine the next time you're at a family gathering, and the inevitable conversation about career choices arises. As aunties and uncles wax poetic about the prestige of medical degrees, picture yourself leaning in with a twinkle in your eye. "Did you know," you might say, "that the first person to create a field hospital in Islamic history was a woman?" Watch as eyebrows raise and curiosity piques. "Her name was Rufayda al-Aslamiyya, and she wasn't just a doctor—she was a pioneering nurse, a surgeon, and a health care nonprofit entrepreneur!" Now, as you share Rufayda's story, see how it transforms the conversation. Suddenly, it's not just about prestigious careers, but about innovation, compassion, and breaking barriers. Let Rufayda's legacy inspire our daughters to dream beyond conventional paths and to see medicine not just as a career, but as a calling—a way to serve, to lead, and to change the world, just as this remarkable woman did centuries ago.

'A'isha bint Abū Bakr

'A'isha bint Abū Bakr ﷺ was a beloved wife of the Prophet Muhammad ﷺ and the daughter of the caliph Abū Bakr ﷺ. She gave generously to the poor and needy and would support widows and orphans in need. She was also known for her knowledge and wisdom and was a prominent scholar in her own right.

---

199 Rafat Jan, "Rufaida Al-Asalmiya: The First Muslim Nurse," *Image: The Journal of Nursing Scholarship* 28, no. 3 (September 1996): 267–68.

'A'isha was known for her deep knowledge and understanding of Islam as well as her strong leadership qualities. She played a significant role in the early development of Islam and was a trusted source of wisdom and guidance for both men and women.

One of 'A'isha's most important contributions was in the area of education. She recognized the need to educate Muslim women about Islam and its teachings so they could become active participants in the community and fulfill their roles as wives, mothers, and leaders.

'A'isha took on the task of educating Muslim women with great enthusiasm and dedication. She held regular gatherings in her home where women could come to learn about Islam, ask questions, and discuss matters of concern. These gatherings became known as *ḥalaqa*s and were a vital part of the early Islamic community. 'A'isha's teachings focused on a wide range of topics, including the Quran, the Prophet Muhammad's teachings and actions, and the principles of Islamic jurisprudence. She also emphasized the importance of personal piety, good character, and social justice.[200]

Under 'A'isha's guidance, Muslim women delved into the intricacies of Islamic jurisprudence and spirituality, and many went on to become influential leaders and scholars themselves.[201] 'A'isha's commitment to education helped further empower Muslim women and gave them the tools they needed to actively participate in the community and contribute to its growth and development.

'A'isha's example reminds us of the importance of education in empowering individuals and communities, and of the critical role that women have played in preserving and transmitting Islamic knowledge. As she teaches us, aside from donating

---

200 Saiyid Sulaiman Nadvi, *Hadhrat Ayesha Siddiqui: Her Life and Works* (Islamic Book Publishers, 1982).

201 Muḥammad Akram Nadwī, *Al-Muḥaddithāt: The Women Scholars in Islam*, 2nd ed. (Interface Publications, 2013).

wealth or treasure, we can give our time and our talent as forms of philanthropy. 'A'isha made it her primary mission to impart knowledge, utilizing her exceptional talents as a teacher and scholar. Her days were structured around this noble pursuit, as she tirelessly shared her deep understanding of Islam with those eager to learn.

When I helped organize RISE's first Economic Empowerment workshop, I realized I was giving my time and talent in training Muslim women on financial literacy and economic stability. I was channeling my inner 'A'isha.

The Two Zaynabs

Two other wives of the Prophet ﷺ known for their exceptional generosity were Zaynab bint Khuzayma ؓ and Zaynab bint Jahsh ؓ.

Zaynab bint Khuzayma, known as "the Mother of the Poor," was renowned for her generosity even before her marriage to the Prophet ﷺ, and her charitable nature intensified after their marriage. Once, when a poor man came to her door asking for food, she gave him her last bit of flour, choosing to go hungry herself. Although she was married to the Prophet ﷺ for only eight months before his passing, scholars suggest that Zaynab's generosity likely extended her time as his wife.[202]

Zaynab bint Jahsh was known as a person with "the longest arms," a phrase with both literal and metaphorical meanings. 'A'isha ؓ narrated an incident where the Prophet ﷺ said the first of his wives to join him after death would be the one with "the longest arms." The wives initially interpreted this literally, measuring their arms.[203] However, he meant it metaphorically, as a reference to

---

202 Khalid, *Women Around the Messenger.*
203 *Ṣaḥīḥ al-Bukhārī*, no. 1420.

charitable giving. Zaynab bint Jaḥsh was the first to pass away after the Prophet ﷺ, confirming her exceptional generosity.

Zaynab bint Jaḥsh was skilled in leatherwork, tanning hides, and weaving clothes. She dedicated all her handiwork to supporting the most vulnerable in the Muslim community, embodying the principle that work done by hand is among the purest sources of income. Upon her death, ʿAʾisha eulogized her, saying, "A grateful and devout person and a haven for orphans and widows has passed away," highlighting Zaynab's lasting impact through her charitable work and dedication to those in need.

MUSLIM FEMALE PHILANTHROPISTS

The above examples were of women around the Prophet Muhammad ﷺ. Now let's look at their legacy—ways that Muslim women have continued their philanthropy.

Princess al-Bandarī al-Fayṣal was the CEO of the King Khalid Foundation (KKF) and advocated against domestic violence in Saudi Arabia. In 2013, KKF advocated for a Women and Child Abuse Prevention Law, which was subsequently adopted and passed by the government. Al-Fayṣal passed away in 2019.[204] May Allah ﷻ elevate her to the highest Janna for her monetary generosity and her tireless public policy work. *Ameen*.

Shaykha Lubna Al Qasimi was ranked by *Forbes* in 2017 as the thirty-sixth most powerful woman in the world. During her time as the Minister of International Cooperation and Development for the United Arab Emirates, she moved the country's philanthropic dollars into various avenues of foreign humanitarian and development aid. And we're talking a *lot* of

---

204 Tamara Abueish, "Saudi Princess al-Bandari: A Lifetime Dedicated to Philanthropy, Women's Rights," *Al Arabiya English*, March 16, 2019, https://web.archive.org/web/20190322095049/https://english.alarabiya.net/en/features/2019/03/16/Saudi-Princess-Al-Bandari-A-lifetime-dedicated-to-philanthropy-women-s-rights.html.

dollars. She increased the UAE's donations from $1.6 billion to $5.4 billion in 2013 and maintained a high level of $4.9 billion in 2014. Currently, she volunteers at the Friends of Cancer Patients Society and serves on the board of the Dubai Autism Center.[205]

Dr. Nisreen El-Hashemite is known as "the Science Princess." She is the granddaughter of the first king of Iraq, King Faisal I Hussein. Told when she was young that "science is not for royalty," she defied royal protocol to become a medical doctor, and she also holds a PhD in genetics.[206] She advocates for gender equality, gender pay equity, and women's participation in science and established the Royal Academy of Science International Trust (RASIT) and the Women in Science International League program within RASIT. She is committed to empowering girls and young women to shape their own futures.[207]

Dr. Rola Hallam is a Syrian-British medical doctor and philanthropist who has supported various initiatives related to health care and humanitarian aid. She is the founder of CanDo, a social enterprise that enables local, frontline health care workers to provide health care to their own war-affected communities.[208]

I realize that these women are privileged—some are even royalty—and they have access to tremendous amounts of money and power. But they are also all leaders in their own fields who use their wealth and power to make the world a better place. I hope they

---

205 "Sheikha Lubna Al Qasimi," *Forbes*, accessed April 30, 2023, https://www.forbes.com/profile/sheikha-lubna-al-qasimi/?sh=7a0372bd640e.

206 Adeline Loh, "Meet Dr Nisreen El-Hashemite, the Iraqi Princess Who Overturned Convention to Pursue Medicine," *The Peak Magazine*, May 12, 2017.

207 "In the Words of HRH Dr. Nisreen El-Hashemite: 'We Need to Encourage Girls and Young Women to Pursue Science and Stay in Science Careers,'" UN Women – Europe and Central Asia, accessed April 30, 2023, https://eca.unwomen.org/en/news/stories/2018/02/in-the-words-of-dr-nisreen-el-hashemite.

208 Learn more at https://www.candoaction.org/.

inspire you like they inspire me. I may not be a princess, but it is affirming to learn about Muslim women who have made significant contributions to philanthropy and humanitarian work.

My heritage is Indian, so naturally I wanted to learn about Indian Muslim women philanthropists and their charitable contributions. I found that they have contributed to various causes, including education, health care, women's empowerment, and community development. Their philanthropic contributions include time, talent, treasure, testimony, and ties, as they have established charitable organizations, provided funding and resources, and advocated for social causes. And as a Hyderabadi Indian Muslim woman, I feel a sense of pride and a responsibility to continue their legacy. Here are a few of them:

> **Rubina Nafees Mazhar** is the founder and president of SAFA, which focuses on providing opportunities for education and employment to Hyderabad's disadvantaged women and girls. Mazhar believes that empowering women is empowering families.[209] She focuses on upskilling women and educating girls living in Hyderabad's slums. SAFA provides training on skills like tailoring, embroidery, cooking, beauty, and wellness. But that's not all—SAFA also offers advanced training in computers, nursing, Information Technology Enabled Services (ITES), advanced ITES, and retail management. SAFA also manages a microenterprise development program. Disrupting the cycle of poverty by empowering underprivileged women and survivors of domestic violence, Rubina has established an organization that uplifts entire families.[210]
>
> **Jameela Nishat** is the founder of the Shaheen Women's

---

[209] Nikat Fatima, "This Muslim-Run NGO Run in Hyderabad Helps Women Build Sustainable Livelihoods," *TwoCircles.Net* (blog), November 7, 2022, https://twocircles.net/2022nov07/447386.html.

[210] Learn more at https://www.safaindia.org/.

Resource and Welfare Society.[211] Domestic violence and child marriages run rampant in Hyderabad, as young girls are married off to rich men to escape poverty. The abuse is heartbreaking. Shaheen helps girls complete their education and pursue higher degrees by providing tuition assistance and financial aid. Her journey reflects my own transition from the corporate world to nonprofits, as she left her governmental job to focus on empowering young girls and women.

But I was born in the United States! So here are some examples of Muslim women philanthropists in the States. Remember, not all of these women are giving away millions of dollars, but they are part of the ecosystem of nonprofits, foundations, and government organizations.

Dilnaz Waraich is president of the WF Fund (formerly the Waraich Foundation). I first met Dilnaz as a student at Indiana University, as we were both Zakat Foundation Institute fellows in the Muslim Philanthropy Initiative. While I was leading RISE, Dilnaz invited me to a conversation, after which she committed to providing funding for our programs. And she continued to increase that giving over subsequent years. RISE was also invited to participate in the Community Collaborative Initiative (CCI),[212] where Dilnaz played a crucial role. She was able to raise over $1 million from the philanthropic community, enabling the funding of Muslim-led and Muslim-serving nonprofits. The cohort RISE belonged to received $200,000!

Faria Abedin, managing partner at the property management firm Abedin Enterprises, joined her husband in founding

---

211 "Journeys for Change - Alice Chou on Shaheen, Bringing Muslim and Hindu Women to Empower Themselves," Journeys for Change, December 10, 2009, https://web.archive.org/web/20161005094019/http://www.journeysforchange.org/node/121.

212 Community Collaborative Initiative: https://philanthropy.iupui.edu/institutes/muslim-initiative/programs/cci/index.html.

the Shakil Ahmed and Faria Abedin Family Foundation to help them reach their philanthropic goals. The foundation grants nearly $100,000 annually to nonprofits that are helping facilitate access to basic health care, providing justice and legal services, supplying emergency relief, and, my favorite, promoting women's mental and physical health. Faria serves on the boards of numerous organizations, including Women for Women International, Trenton Area Soup Kitchen, Ta'leef Collective, and the Inner-City Muslim Action Network (IMAN).

These are just a few examples of Muslim women philanthropists in the United States. There are many others who have made significant contributions to various fields and causes. I invite you to learn more about them, be inspired by their journeys, and begin your own journey toward becoming a philanthropic leader.

But wait—who inspires me in Minnesota? Two women come to mind: Johanna Osman and Nahid Murad.

> **Johanna Osman** is a trustee at the Wege Foundation and the founder and executive director of Sakan Community Resource. Due to the US's predatory, interest-based banking system, many Muslims struggle to find affordable housing. Johanna established Sakan to make sharia-compliant, zero-interest loans available. And not just loans for homes—loans for education and businesses too. I love that they provide financial acumen training, offer down payment assistance, and imagine a future where all Minnesotans have access to stable homes and financial tools that align with their faith and values.[213]
>
> **Naheed Murad** is a pathologist, but she left her medical career and transitioned into public health. Not only is she an MD, but she also holds a master's in public health from the University

---

213 Learn more at sakanresources.org.

of Minnesota. Naheed is the cofounder and treasurer for Zakat, Aid and Charity Assisting Humanity (ZACAH).[214] ZACAH first began as ZACAH Transitional Home to shelter women who were refugees, victims of domestic violence, or who had been evicted due to loss of income. During the pandemic, homelessness escalated exponentially, and Naheed responded by moving the unsheltered from hotels to stable housing. Soon after, ZACAH was faced with the resettlement of Afghan refugees and stepped up to the challenge. And if that wasn't keeping her busy enough, Naheed is also the cofounder and director of clinical operations for Rahma Heart Care,[215] which provides cardiology consultative and diagnostic services to the uninsured, underinsured, and undocumented populations of Minnesota. All services are 100% free of cost, making Rahma Heart Care the only clinic of its kind in the US. She works tirelessly to serve our community, and not just through these two organizations. She serves on several boards and, together with her family, generously supports multiple nonprofit organizations in Minnesota. She truly is an inspiration!

THE REST OF THE TS

The women above gave generously of their treasure! But as we know, Muslim women give in all kinds of ways. Let's look at women who give of their time, talent, testimony, and ties.

Here are some examples of Muslim women philanthropists who have given of their time to different causes:

> **Wafa Omran-Elhindi** is one of Islamic Relief USA's prized volunteers. She lost her five-year-old son to a rare brain tumor and turned her grief into an opportunity to serve as a sponsor mom to as many children as she could. In communities struck

---

214 Learn more at https://www.zacah.org/.
215 Learn more at https://mccminnesota.org/rahmaclinic/.

by natural disasters, Wafa has devoted her time to restoring damaged houses and providing essential care packages and food parcels to affected residents. Her impact extends beyond disaster relief, as evidenced by one of her most memorable experiences. In September 2019, Wafa and a group of fifty Islamic Relief volunteers prepared an impressive 25,000 meals, which were distributed to disaster sites in the United States and various countries in Africa. Throughout all her efforts, Wafa is guided by a powerful mantra: to serve Allah by serving the community. This principle fuels her tireless dedication to making a difference in the lives of others.[216]

Sana Fatima Farooqi's volunteer time is dedicated to washing the bodies of deceased women in the Muslim ritual of *ghusl*, which is performed before each woman is shrouded and laid to rest. Sana manages a loose coalition of about ten women who volunteer their time for this noble duty in New Haven, Connecticut. Not everyone has female relatives or friends around to perform this sacred duty. The gap that Sana and her group of volunteers fills helps prepare a Muslim sister to meet her Lord.[217]

Here are some examples of Muslim women philanthropists who have donated their talent and expertise to better their communities:

Na'ima B. Robert is an author and was founding editor of the UK-based Muslim women's publication, *SISTERS Magazine*. Dedicated to supporting and promoting Muslim women writers, Na'ima has donated her talent as a writer and her leadership skills to the Muslimah Author Project, which has helped elevate the voices of Muslim women in the literary

---

216 Learn more at https://irusa.org/volunteer/volunteer-spotlight/.
217 Learn more at http://features.yaledailynews.com/blog/2019/11/22/after-life-muslim-deathcare-in-new-haven/.

world.²¹⁸ I definitely want to send her my book once it's published!

You know **Munira Ahmed** as "the Face of Resistance." Remember in 2017, during the Women's March and subsequent rallies and protests, when a series of "We the People" posters was produced featuring diverse women? Do you remember a woman wrapped in the American flag as her hijab? That was Munira. The photo was originally taken in 2007 by New York–based photographer Ridwan Adhami for the cover of a publication geared toward Muslim-Americans called *Illume Magazine*. In 2016, the photo was selected by the Amplifier Foundation and rendered into a graphic image by artist Shepard Fairey. Munira didn't get paid for this or receive any royalties. Her talent was to simply be a subject for the photography. And for once, a hijabi woman was seen in a positive light—the face of resistance—and as part of the American people.

All of us have talents—baking, sewing, creating slides, event planning, running social media campaigns. I had two women volunteers help me collate all the results and feedback from over two hundred surveys after our second annual women's leadership conference. The reporting and evaluation they provided helped us improve our next conference. They donated their talent because they believed in the empowerment of women. Use your talent to make the world a better place.

Here are some examples of Muslim women philanthropists who have used their voices and platforms to provide testimony in support of social justice:

Ilhan Omar. When Trump won the presidential election in 2016, I cried myself to sleep. I was so devastated. But when Ilhan Omar was elected to the Minnesota legislature, I found

---

218 Learn more at https://www.naimarobert.com/.

the silver lining I needed to continue organizing. And two years later, watching her be elected as a United States Representative from Minnesota solidified my need to continue showing up and participating in democracy. But what inspired me most was that Representative Omar consistently and courageously speaks out. She is the only elected official from my state who I have seen supporting the Palestinian cause—the only elected official who spoke out and gave them a voice. She has also advocated for a number of public policies, including refugee rights, public education, and criminal justice reform.

Linda Sarsour is a Palestinian-American activist who has provided testimony in support of a number of causes, including advocating for the rights of immigrants and refugees, supporting racial justice initiatives, and promoting women's rights. I first met Linda when she was challenging the FBI's surveillance of Muslim Student Associations in New York, post-9/11. She was front and center, using her voice to condemn the FBI's Islamophobia and othering.[219] Through her work with MPower Change,[220] she made sure we used our voices to show up in the democratic process. She was also one of the cofounders of the 2017 Women's March. Linda has used her platforms to raise awareness around police brutality, the Keystone XL Pipeline construction through Native land, and women's rights over their bodies.

Dalia Mogahed was the director of research at the Institute for Social Policy and Understanding, where she led the organization's pioneering research and thought leadership programs on American Muslims.[221] Her research provides

---

219 "Othering" refers to the process of treating or perceiving someone as intrinsically different or alien. In this context, it involves viewing Muslims as fundamentally separate from mainstream society, often leading to discrimination and marginalization.

220 Learn more at www.mpowerchange.org.

221 Learn more at www.ispu.org.

testimony in support of causes related to Muslim communities, including promoting interfaith understanding and combating Islamophobia. Dalia's 2016 TedTalk, "What's It Like Being Muslim in America?"[222] has over 8.6 million views. This, coupled with her interview on *The Daily Show with Trevor Noah*, has provided mainstream America with an accurate, inside perspective on Muslims in America and has done more to bridge gaps between communities than many interfaith dialogue efforts. She uses her research to provide fact-based, evidence-based testimonies that effectively combat anti-Muslim hate.

Amani Al-Khatahtbeh, an American author and activist who has provided testimony by advocating for the rights of Muslim women and promoting interfaith understanding, is the founder of MuslimGirl.com, which aims to amplify the voices of Muslim women and promote their inclusion in society. Al-Khatahtbeh has spoken at various events and forums to share her experiences and advocate for the rights of Muslim women, particularly in the areas of representation and equality.

In 2019, RISE collaborated with the Coalition of Asian American Leaders to advocate for a public policy that would secure funding from the State of Minnesota to support nonprofit organizations led by and supporting people of color. The funds would support capacity-building and the strengthening of infrastructure. We asked that $1 million be appropriated from the state's budget. During multiple days at the Capitol, we spoke to our elected officials, sharing our stories of struggle and the need for this funding. That year, $500,000 was allocated and distributed in our communities. The following year, we advocated for more. The nonprofits that had received these grants shared the impacts

---

222 Find the TedTalk here: https://www.ted.com/talks/dalia_mogahed_what_it_s_like_to_be_muslim_in_america.

that the previous year's funding had made, and the results were phenomenal. In fact, we were brought back into the legislative session to provide our testimonies. We showed how we used the funding, how it strengthened our systems, and how this benefited our communities and Minnesota as a whole. When we have stronger processes and systems in place, we can achieve our goals and realize the work of our various missions, making Minnesota a better place. In 2021, the state appropriated $1 million.

Here are some more examples of Muslim women philanthropists who have used their ties—relationships and social capital—to raise awareness and invite others to the work:

> **Queen Rania Al Abdullah of Jordan** has used her royal connections and visibility to raise money for various charitable causes in Jordan, specifically for children. You want to know how many ties she has? Well, if thirty-three million followers on social media is any indication, then you could say a lot of people know her and will answer her calls to action. For example, in 2017 she launched the Madrasati Palestine campaign, which raised funds to renovate schools in Palestine. She has also worked with international organizations such as UNICEF and the World Economic Forum to raise awareness and support for education and child welfare programs.
>
> **Sharmeen Obaid-Chinoy** uses her connections in the film and media industries to raise awareness and funds to combat the horrific practice of honor killings. When she produced her documentary *A Girl in the River: The Price of Forgiveness*, she organized a screening at the United Nations, which raised funds for the victims of honor killings in Pakistan. She has also partnered with organizations such as the United Nations Population Fund to raise awareness of gender-based violence and reproductive health issues.

Again, I know we aren't all queens or filmmakers, but we do have friends and family who listen to us. Sometimes they believe in the same causes and will answer our call to philanthropy. Lean into those ties.

HOW AM I A PHILANTHROPIST THROUGH THE FIVE TS?

When I first learned about the five T's of philanthropy, I was hopeful and inspired. It made me feel like I already was a philanthropist! I took time to journal about the many ways I give back to our society.

Treasure

Through my annual zakat distribution and additional *ṣadaqa* monetary giving, I try to donate to causes I care about and help people directly. I donate locally to help people in my own community. Sometimes people need help with rent or when their car breaks down, and it's a blessing that they can turn to their community for help.

The Muslim nonprofit sector is growing, and in order to be sustainable, these nonprofits rely on donors. There are so many wonderful causes, from supporting women's and girls's education to protecting our civil rights, and I want to be a part of all of it. And by donating to organizations that are addressing these issues—especially ones that are good stewards of their donors' money—I'm taking part in that *khayr*. My favorite nonprofits are the ones that build a relationship with me, invite me to get to know the organization, and make me feel like part of their nonprofit. I appreciate the transparency, accountability, and relationships.

Time

Are you time-wealthy? What I mean is, do you feel like you have an abundance of time? Volunteering my time has made me feel wealthy. I am a cofounder and board member of the Brooklyn Park Islamic Center. Nonprofit startups are a lot of work, and establishing a masjid is no different. It involves organizing the community, finding a building, raising money, and then making Allah's home inviting to others—all of which require dedicated time. One of my favorite things to do is spring-cleaning right before Ramadan starts. I love vacuuming the *muṣallā* (the prayer hall) so there's a clean prayer space to focus on one's relationship with Allah. Decorating the masjid to welcome Ramadan is exciting and joyful too!

I have also done volunteer work at food shelves for the Muslim American Society. Bagging groceries and distributing them to neighbors really gives you pause to count your food security blessings. During the pandemic, I helped the Dr. Shabaz Charity Group create iftar boxes for fasting Muslims who needed meals to break their fast.

Talent

With almost twenty-five years of work experience and three college degrees (two of them master's degrees), I have a lot to offer in terms of knowledge. I've mentored people, and I also offer free coaching from time to time. One Ramadan, I chose a nonprofit to advise on their fundraising campaign and helped them with their grants.

People ask me how I started a nonprofit, how to write grants, and how I transitioned from the corporate sector to the nonprofit sector. I take those calls, and I share my lived experience with them while giving advice and recommending action steps.

I serve on the board of a foundation, and you might classify that as volunteering my time, but really I was invited to serve because of my talent and experiences. I advise on different strategies and programs and am asked for my opinions and feedback.

Testimony

Your voice is your power. I felt this firsthand when I started doing advocacy work. There was a time when I was afraid to talk to politicians and elected officials—but then I was trained! I received training from Vote.Run.Lead. and also from the Joint Religious Legislative Coalition. These two organizations helped me understand that talking to elected officials is a storytelling process. My job was to help them understand how an issue affected me personally. I went with Protect MN to their Day at the Capitol and shared my story about how gun violence affected my family and me. I asked my legislators to pass sensible gun legislation. Next, I went back to the Minnesota State Capitol with my fellow nonprofit organizations and testified for the Nonprofit Infrastructure Grant Program, asking legislators to designate funding for nonprofits that serve communities of color. I used my experiences with these elected officials to tell my community members who I was voting for and why. I was able to share stories of who supported the Muslim community and how. I became a trusted source in the community. My testimony was a form of philanthropy.

Ties

I describe myself as a network weaver because I love connecting people to others. The relationships I build and the conversations I have always inspire me to connect people on one side of my network with those on another side. It's incredibly powerful to see mentoring relationships blossom, donors connecting with new nonprofits, and collaborations occurring between organizations. One year, I was volunteering with the Minnesota Deaf Muslim Community, helping with their fundraising plans. Part of their fundraising involved a dinner, and I requested three tables to fill for that fundraiser. I asked my close circle of friends to join me. The three tables were filled and we helped raise money for the organization. Without a long-nurtured network, I wouldn't have been able to fill those tables with eager donors that night.

I might not look like the billionaires typically seen as philanthropists, but through the five Ts, I know I am a philanthropist day in and day out.

Reflection Exercise

1. Who are some Muslim women, past and present, you admire as philanthropists?

2. What are the ways you donate your five T's in philanthropy?

    a. Time

    b. Talent

    c. Treasure

    d. Testimony

    e. Ties

3. Are there other ways not listed here?

Chapter 21

Transfer of Wealth to Women in 2030

An unprecedented amount of assets will shift into the hands of U.S. women over the next three to five years, representing a $30 trillion opportunity by the end of the decade.[223]

A great wealth transfer is coming, passed down from the baby boomer generation, and women may emerge as the biggest beneficiaries. Approximately $30 trillion in wealth is set to change hands in the next decade and women are poised to inherit a sizable share.[224]

So, does this wealth transfer include me? Or you? McKinsey and Company is considered one of the top global management consulting firms. Yet their research did not break down who these women are who are set to inherit this great wealth. I wish this data showed me demographics by race or ethnicity, age, religion, or even generational information. How long has the baby boomer's family been in the United States? Were they new immigrants, second generation, or more? My mom would be considered a baby boomer, but she already gave me everything I

---

223 Pooneh Baghai, Olivia Howard, Lakshmi Prakash, and Jill Zucker, "Women as the Next Wave of Growth in US Wealth Management," McKinsey, July 29, 2020, https://www.mckinsey.com/industries/financial-services/our-insights/women-as-the-next-wave-of-growth-in-us-wealth-management.

224 Rebecca Lake, "Women and the Great Wealth Transfer," Investopedia, December 11, 2023, https://www.investopedia.com/financial-advisor/women-and-great-wealth-transfer/.

would've inherited when I got married. She has a few pieces of jewelry left that my siblings and I will inherit, but my parents have no other assets.

The Federal Reserve Bank, the central bank of the United States, conducts a periodic Survey of Consumer Finances. The latest survey, conducted in 2019, shows that the typical white family has eight times the wealth of the typical Black family and five times the wealth of the typical Hispanic family. In terms of dollars, white families have an average $983,400 in wealth, Black families have $142,500, and Hispanic families have $165,000. The Other category includes, well, everyone who doesn't identify as white, Black, or Hispanic. This includes South Asians like Indians, Pakistanis, or Bangladeshis and Southeast Asians like Malaysians, Chinese, and Indonesians. This data clearly needs to be disaggregated, but we can see that the Other category holds significantly less wealth—roughly $600,000—than white families, but more than Black or Hispanic families.[225] This wealth gap affects the transfer of wealth across different racial and ethnic groups. While white women may benefit from intergenerational wealth transfer, women from marginalized communities often have less access to inheritance and other forms of wealth accumulation due to historical and systemic inequalities.

Dear Muslim women, we are the generation that must build wealth so that we can transfer it by 2050 to our next generation. The first part of this book illustrated some ways you can start to understand your current finances, what your relationship to money is, and some practical actions you can take to begin your wealth-building plan. Now I want to talk about building generational wealth for our daughters, our granddaughters, and our *ummah*.

---

225 Board of Governors of the Federal Reserve System, "Federal Reserve Board - Survey of Consumer Finances (SCF)," accessed July 27, 2023, https://www.federalreserve.gov/econres/scfindex.htm.

We are a people of *iḥsān*. Allah ﷻ wants us to exhibit excellence in everything we do—including our financial acumen and philanthropic giving. We need to strive to establish a base of financial stability so that we can build our institutions and sustain them for generations to come until the Day of Judgment.

It took centuries for white women to reach the point where they will see such a significant transfer of wealth, but access to wealth was the norm for Muslim women when Islam was first established. Colonization, Western influences, wars, and global anti-Muslim hate came in and ruined that for us. Now it's time to reclaim our heritage, take control over our money, and direct our giving.

I'm going to watch this wealth transfer and the data that gets collected around it and try to parse out what it means for Muslim women of color. I want to inspire my generation to build wealth and give hope to our future granddaughters' generation for their own wealth. I envision my wealth to be a source of *khayr* for issues that Muslim women are facing and will face. I hope that my daughter and her future daughters can build on my wealth to continue that *khayr*. Will you join me in securing this financial future for our sisterhood?

Reflection Exercise

1. What wealth will you leave behind for your children?

2. What would it take for Muslim women to be part of a great wealth transfer to our next generation?

3. What institutions are we building and sustaining for our girls?

4. If you are a mother, mother figure, auntie, *khaltu*, or mentor to youth, how might you begin communicating this knowledge to them?

Conclusion

Now that you're at the end of this book, I ask you once again to reflect on what you want to do in life and how you will make it happen.

When I first started my journey in economic empowerment, I had to do an assessment of my current financial situation. I got a notebook, which I divided up into different sections, and broke down the different facets of my finances. I took stock of my credit cards. I looked at my credit report. I examined my annual Social Security report. I looked at my monthly income, which included salary and other assets that were generating revenue for me, and then I started to plan my next steps.

I had a to-do list. I spoke to financial advisers. I met with people who I knew had some sort of financial savviness and investment experience—people I could get reliable advice from. This is what the hadith about "tying your camel" is about. You have to put time, effort, and work into this. You have to prioritize managing your finances and growing your wealth. You have to consistently make *dua* for your *rizq*. And then you leave the rest to Allah.

I started out strong, on top of my game in the beginning. I was monitoring my financial situation every day, then once a week, and then slowly once a month, until things felt like they were in "set it and forget it" mode. Except that I forgot it for a little too long. A year later, I picked up the notebook and went back and reviewed things. It hit me that the steps I had taken the year before had been successful. From Ramadan 1442 to Ramadan 1443, my wealth increased, and I had to recalculate and distribute a higher amount of zakat. Alhamdulillah. I couldn't have been more pleased.

My savings went up, and I transferred those savings into my

investment account. I was able to give larger donations to some of my favorite charities through stock transfers. I added new charities into my donation portfolio. I accidentally hit the "make this a monthly donation" on one of my larger donations, and let's just say I am a top donor of that organization now. They are stewarding me quite nicely, and I thought it was just because I'd been giving for so long—not because I gave ten times more than I meant to. Clearly, that money was not meant for me, and Allah ﷻ sent it on its way to its rightful owners.

I also enjoyed life more. Assessing my credit cards made me realize which of them weren't providing me with any benefits, and I closed them down. My new credit card with the travel benefits is the best thing ever. I love traveling and can't wait for my next adventure!

When I did my first financial assessment, I figured out how to reduce my hours at work so I could take more graduate classes. I was able to complete my second master's and eventually resign from my job. I'm writing this book on my radical sabbatical. Reducing my hours and leaving my job did not kill me financially, and it was assessing my financial situation a year and a half ago that allowed me to do these things that are important to me.

When I was learning all these things, I asked myself, "Why didn't anybody tell me this earlier?" What would life have been like had I known these things in my twenties? But I don't want any of us to dwell on the past. Instead, I want to help you take what I learned and apply it now. Have you heard the phrase "cash is king"? Well then, my Investing Queens, go out there and rule your finances!

While I was figuring out my finances, the changes I made saw my wealth grow, alhamdulillah. My zakat obligation grew; I was purifying my wealth by giving away more. It felt so good! Helping others is pleasing Allah! As a household, our *ṣadaqa* grew too. To not think twice when being asked to give is such a privilege,

Conclusion

subhanallah. I want that for you too!

I know that some of you will embark on a journey similar to mine. Some of you will look at your finances and realize you need to take different steps than I did at first. And perhaps there are some of you who are going to just hate on me and criticize this book. Share it all with me. I would love to know what resonated with you, what actions you took, and what resulted. What didn't resonate with you and why? Tell me what you learned and teach me something new and amazing. Email me at nausheena@nausheena.com.

Take your money, invest it, calculate zakat, include your *ṣadaqa*, become a philanthropist, and change the world for the *ummah* and all of humanity. Reap the benefits in the *akhira*.

Acknowledgments

Abū Hurayra reported: The Prophet, peace and blessings be upon him, said, "Whoever does not thank people has not thanked Allah."[226] So many people helped me write this book. First, thank you to my wonderful anse, Dr. Tamara Gray, for planting the seed that, as part of our leadership development, Muslim women need to write and be published. Thank you for always inspiring me, motivating me, and believing in me. Thank you to my entire team at RISE, but specifically Zaynab Abdi. You are the one that made the Economic Empowerment Series come to life, providing the backdrop for this book. I hope you still have your cryptocurrency and launch the symposium. Ashfaq Mohiuddin and Nazia Sharif, my favorite cousin and cousin-in-law, who provided me with the week-long writing retreat in their beautiful San Francisco home. Ashy, you've always been a brother, adviser, and confidant to me. To Sarah Abe for volunteering to be the content editor and accepting payment in coffee. To Annie Qaiser, a Shero copyeditor, who not only did my first round of editing, but pushed me to expand the chapters and the storytelling. I told Daybreak to hire you. Ustadha Kaltun Karani, who guided me to intentionally rise. Dr. Shariq Siddiqui, my first Muslim professor, who encouraged me to pursue the master's and the doctorate in philanthropy. I wish I had a Muslim teacher and mentor like you when I was a kid. Shafaq Kazi, my first financial adviser, for guiding me on this wealth-building journey to become a smarter investor. Amina Iqbal, I met you at a time when Muslim women were being asked to influence and educate philanthropic advisers. How powerful! Afshan Malik, thank you for being a great steward, for reading

---

226 *Sunan Abū Dāwūd*, no. 4811.

Sethi's book and putting it on your Instagram, and for being my CFRM classmate. Make those rotis, sis! To Ustadha Aatifa Shareef for fact-checking the references to hadith and Quran—I hope to join you on a Sisters' Suhbah soon! To Sarah Gruidl who has always been my content and copyeditor since I first began writing for *Expressions*. Cat moms united. Anse Najiyah, the Rabata family, and Daybreak Press team, your guidance during this journey has helped produce an incredible opportunity for Muslim women to rise and reclaim their economic power. May your organizations continue to be filled with *baraka*. To Imteyaz, my Allah-given soulmate, you've always been supportive and sometimes quite shocked at everything I go out and do. Arshia and Ayaz, my legacy, for whom this book was written with the hope you'll actually take action. To all my Muslim sisters, who for the past decade have helped me transition into the nonprofit sector and build a sisterhood that I can proudly lean on.

$$\text{وَمِنْهُم مَّن يَقُولُ رَبَّنَآ ءَاتِنَا فِى ٱلدُّنْيَا حَسَنَةً وَفِى ٱلْءَاخِرَةِ حَسَنَةً وَقِنَا عَذَابَ ٱلنَّارِ ۝}$$

Yet there are others who say, "Our Lord! Grant us the good of this world and the Hereafter, and protect us from the torment of the Fire."

Quran 2:201

Ameen!

Resources

Books and websites

1. *The Latte Factor* by David Bach and John David Mann
2. *Smart Women Finish Rich* by David Bach
3. *7 Daily Rituals for Gratitude* by Federica Avanzi and Simone Masserini
4. *I Will Teach You to Be Rich* by Ramit Sethi
5. Ellevest | ellevest.com
6. Learn more about *sukūk* | https://shariaportfolio.com/5-key-differences-between-sukuk-and-conventional-bonds/
7. Why you should hold cash in your investment portfolio | https://www.investopedia.com/articles/investing/072316/3-reasons-cash-smart-position-your-portfolio.asp
8. Dollar-cost averaging (DCA) | https://www.investopedia.com/terms/d/dollarcostaveraging.asp
9. Learn more about REITs and SPRE | https://www.sp-funds.com/spre/

Investment accounts

ShariaPortfolio | www.shariaportfolio.com

Saturna Capital | www.saturna.com

Azzad | https://azzadasset.com/

Wahed Invest | https://www.wahed.com/

Hoopoe Advisors | https://www.hoopoeadvisors.com/

Fidelity | fidelity.com

Stock screener tools

Wahed Invest | https://www.wahed.com/

Musaffa | https://musaffa.com/

Zoya | https://zoya.finance/

Islamicly | https://www.islamicly.com/

Finispia | https://finispia.com/halal-stock-screener/

DAFs

American Muslim Community Foundation | amcf.org

The St. Paul and Minnesota Foundation | spmf.org

ShariaPortfolio | www.shariaportfolio.com

Wills

My Wassiyah | mywassiyah.com

Shariawiz | https://www.shariawiz.com/

IRUSA (powered by Shariawiz) | https://irusa.org/wills/

Glossary

NON-ENGLISH TERMS

ﷻ *(subḥāna wa taʿāla):* This phrase is used by Muslims after mentioning Allah's name as a way of showing reverence and respect. It translates as "the Most Glorified, the Most High."

ﷺ *(ṣallā Allāhu ʿalayhi wa sallam):* This phrase is used by Muslims after mentioning the Prophet's name as a way of showing respect. It means "Peace and blessings be upon him [the Prophet Muhammad]."

◈ *(raḍī Allāhu ʿanhu):* This phrase is used by Muslims after mentioning the name of a male companion of the Prophet ﷺ as a way of showing respect. It means "May Allah be pleased with him."

◈ *(raḍī Allāhu ʿanha):* This phrase is used by Muslims after mentioning the name of a female companion of the Prophet ﷺ as a way of showing respect. It means "May Allah be pleased with her."

abaya: A long, flowing robe worn by Muslim women.

adab: Prescribed Islamic etiquette, including good manners, morals, good character, decency, and humaneness.

Ahl al-Ṣuffa: A group of impoverished Muslims who lived near Prophet Muhammad's mosque in Medina; known for their dedication to Islamic knowledge and often supported through acts of charity.

akhira: The Arabic phrase referring to the hereafter.

Al-Ghazālī, Imam: A Muslim scholar and Sufi philosopher known for his influential works on spirituality, Islamic theology, and philosophy who died in 1111.

al-fuqarāʾ: Arabic for "the poor."

alhamdulillah: A phrase meaning "all praise be to Allah," which is sometimes used to thank God.

al-masākīn: Arabic for "the needy."

ʿ*aqiqa:* An Islamic tradition involving the sacrifice of animals to celebrate the birth of a child, with the meat distributed to the poor.

awqāf: (plural of *waqf*) An Islamic endowment fund where assets are allocated to religious, educational, or charitable causes, providing continuous benefit (*ṣadaqa jāriya*).

aya: A verse of the Quran; translates literally to "a sign."

baraka: A term meaning blessing or divine grace, often associated with acts of charity and good deeds in Islamic tradition.

bismillah: A phrase meaning "in the name of Allah," which is often recited when beginning a task.

dawat: A gathering or feast in South Asian cultures, often for family or community celebrations.

deen: The comprehensive way of life that Islam prescribes, encompassing beliefs, character, and deeds.

dua: A personal prayer or supplication made by Muslims to Allah, seeking guidance, assistance, or forgiveness.

dunyā: This world, this life (as opposed to the hereafter).

Eid: A significant Islamic celebration marking either the end of Ramadan (Eid al-Fitr) or the completion of the Hajj pilgrimage (Eid al-Adha).

farḍ: Required or obligatory for a Muslim.

fiqh: The body of Islamic law that governs daily life, including marriage, business, inheritance, and worship.

hadith: A collection of traditions relating the sayings and actions of the Prophet Muhammad ﷺ.

Hajj: The major pilgrimage to Mecca that Muslims are required to perform at least once in their lifetime if financially and physically able.

halal: Permissible or lawful in Islam, often used to describe food or financial transactions that adhere to Islamic principles.

ḥalaqa: A group of students who come together to study Islam.

haram: Something which is unlawful or prohibited in Islam.

iftar: Refers to breaking of the fast, typically in the month of Ramadan.

iḥsān: The Islamic concept of striving for excellence in all deeds and actions, particularly in one's relationship with Allah.

imān: Faith and belief in Allah.

inshallah: A phrase meaning "with the will of Allah," or "God willing."

janimaz: A prayer rug used by Muslims during the five daily prayers.

Janna: Paradise.

jazākum Allāhu khayran: A phrase meaning "May Allah reward you with good," which is often said to express thanks or gratitude.

Jumuʿa: The Friday prayer, and also used as the word for the day of Friday itself.

khayr: Goodness; often used to describe the positive impact of charitable giving or philanthropy.

Maghrib: The fourth of the five daily prayers performed by Muslims at sunset.

mahr: A mandatory bridal gift provided by the husband to the wife at the time of marriage, ensuring her financial security.

masjid: A place of worship and ritual prayer.

mirchi ka salan: A traditional Hyderabadi dish made with chili peppers in a spicy curry sauce.

nafs: An Islamic term referring to the self or ego, representing various stages of spiritual development.

nafs al-ammāra: The commanding self, which inclines toward desires and evil actions.

nafs al-lawwāma: The self-accusing soul, which is aware of its mistakes and seeks to correct them.

nafs al-muṭma'inna: The soul at peace, content and aligned with the will of Allah.

niṣāb: The minimum threshold of wealth that a Muslim must possess before being obligated to pay zakat.

niyya: The intention behind an action in Islam, which determines its religious or spiritual significance.

Quran: The holy book of Islam; the word of Allah as revealed to the Prophet Muhammad ﷺ.

Ramadan: The holy month of prescribed fasting for the Muslims. It was during this month that the revelation of the Quran began.

Glossary

ribā: Refers to usury or interest.

ribāṭ: Hospice, hostel, base, or retreat.

rizq: The Islamic concept of sustenance or provision, encompassing all forms of blessings provided by Allah, including wealth, health, relationships, etc.

ṣadaqa: Voluntary charitable giving in Islam, distinct from zakat, and given to seek blessings or support those in need.

ṣadaqa jāriya: A form of continuous charity in Islam where the benefits of a good deed continue to accrue even after the giver has passed away.

sharia: Islamic law.

sharia-compliant: Financial products or investments that adhere to Islamic law, avoiding interest and activities that conflict with Islamic values.

sīra: Biography of the Prophet ﷺ.

sukūk: Sharia-compliant bonds used in Islamic finance, structured to avoid interest by linking returns to asset ownership rather than debt repayment.

sunna: The way of life of the Prophet Muhammad ﷺ; constitutes the second foundation of Islamic law, after the Quran.

tahajjud: An optional prayer performed at night after sleeping for a while and before Fajr.

takhat: An Indian daybed, traditionally intricately carved and covered with luxurious fabrics and pillows.

tarāwīḥ: An optional night prayer performed during Ramadan after Isha.

thawb: A long, flowing garment traditionally worn by men in Arab countries, often made from cotton or wool.

***ummah*:** The worldwide community of Muslims.

'umra: The lesser pilgrimage to Mecca, which can be performed at any time of the year.

***waqf*:** An endowment made by a Muslim to a religious, educational, or charitable cause.

zabiha: Meat that has been slaughtered according to Islamic guidelines, making it halal.

zakat: A mandatory form of charitable giving in Islam, calculated as 2.5% of a Muslim's wealth, and one of the five pillars of Islam.

Glossary

FINANCIAL TERMS

401(k): A retirement savings plan offered by employers in the United States that allows employees to contribute a portion of their pretax salary to an investment account, often matched by employers.

529 plan: A 529 plan is a tax-advantaged savings plan designed to encourage saving for future education costs; usually not sharia-compliant.

Accounting and Auditing Organization for Islamic Financial Institutions (AAOIFI): A global, independent, Islamic nonprofit organization that sets accounting, auditing, governance, ethics, and sharia standards for Islamic financial institutions and the industry.

annual fee: A yearly charge imposed by some credit card companies for the use of their card.

annual percentage rate (APR): The annualized interest rate charged on outstanding credit card balances or loans.

asset: Something you own that has monetary value, generates income, or increases in value.

asset allocation: The process of dividing your investments among different asset classes, such as stocks, bonds, and cash, to achieve a balance of risk and return.

automation: The process of setting up automatic payments or investments to simplify financial management and ensure timely contributions.

autopayment: An arrangement where your bills, such as credit card payments, are automatically deducted from your checking account on a specified date each month.

balance transfer: The process of moving a credit card balance from one card to another, often to take advantage of lower interest rates or promotional offers.

bank statement: A monthly summary provided by your bank that shows all transactions in your account, including deposits, withdrawals, and any fees.

bonds: Bonds are debt securities issued by governments or companies to raise capital. When an entity issues a bond, they are essentially borrowing money from investors.

budget: A financial plan that outlines your income and expenses, helping you allocate your resources to meet your financial goals.

capital fund: A fund established by organizations, including nonprofits, to generate income while preserving the principal amount.

capital gains tax: A tax levied on the profit made from selling an asset, such as stocks or real estate, for more than its purchase price.

car loan: A loan taken to purchase a car, which is repaid with interest in monthly installments until the loan is fully paid off.

checking account: A bank account that allows you to deposit and withdraw money easily.

company stock: Shares of ownership in a specific company.

compound interest: Interest that is calculated on both the initial principal and the accumulated interest from previous periods.

cost of living adjustment (COLA): An adjustment made to income or benefits, typically to account for inflation and changes in the cost of living.

Coverdell education savings account (ESA): Another tax-

Glossary

advantaged education savings account that can be used for educational expenses.

custodial account: A financial account held in the name of a minor but managed by an adult custodian until the minor reaches a certain age.

credit card: A plastic card issued by a financial institution that allows you to borrow money up to a certain limit to make purchases.

credit card statement: A monthly statement from your credit card issuer that details your transactions, balances, minimum payment due, and the due date.

credit limit: The maximum amount of credit extended to you by a credit card issuer.

credit score: A numerical representation of a person's creditworthiness based on their credit history.

credit utilization: The percentage of your available credit limit that you are currently using.

debt: Money owed to creditors or lenders.

deferred payment plan: A credit card feature that allows you to make purchases and pay for them at a later date, typically within a specified grace period.

digital wallet: A digital tool or application that allows you to store and manage your payment information, such as credit card details and bank account numbers, for online and mobile transactions.

diversification: A strategy that involves spreading your investments across various types of assets to reduce risk.

dollar-cost averaging (DCA): Dollar-cost averaging is an investment strategy where you invest a fixed amount of money at regular intervals, regardless of market conditions.

dual-income households: Families in which both partners work and contribute financially, leading to shared responsibility for managing household expenses and savings.

economic constraints: Limitations imposed by financial circumstances that affect spending, investment, or other financial decisions.

economic empowerment: The process of increasing an individual's or community's capacity to make financial decisions, control resources, and manage assets to achieve personal and communal advancement.

employee stock purchase plan (ESPP): An employee benefit plan that allows employees to purchase company stock at a discounted price, typically through payroll deductions.

endowment fund: A fund established by an institution, organization, or individual through donations of money or property.

exchange-traded funds (ETFs): An investment fund that holds a diversified portfolio of assets, such as stocks or bonds, and is traded on a stock exchange.

financial goals: Specific objectives you set for your financial future, such as saving for retirement, buying a home, or paying off debt.

financial literacy: The knowledge and understanding of financial concepts that enable individuals to make informed decisions about budgeting, investing, and managing debt.

financial plan: A comprehensive strategy for managing your finances, including saving, investing, budgeting, and achieving your financial goals.

Glossary

FIRE (financial independence, retire early): A movement aimed at achieving financial independence and early retirement by saving aggressively and living frugally.

fraud: Deceptive or illegal activities intended to result in financial gain, often involving misrepresentation or theft.

generational wealth: Assets and resources that are passed down from one generation to the next, including money, property, education, and skills.

giving circle: A group of individuals who pool their resources to collectively support a cause or charity, emphasizing collaborative philanthropy.

grace period: This term has two common uses in credit and finance:

1. For credit cards: The period during which you can pay your credit card balance in full without incurring interest charges. It typically spans from the end of the billing cycle to the due date.

2. For loan payments: The amount of time after a payment due date during which a payment can be made without incurring a late fee or being reported as late to credit bureaus.

halal investing: Investing in assets and companies that comply with Islamic laws, particularly those related to interest (*ribā*) and unethical products or services.

identity theft: The fraudulent use of someone else's personal information, such as their name, Social Security number, or credit card details, to commit financial crimes.

individual retirement account (IRA): A tax-advantaged retirement savings account that individuals can set up independently to save for retirement.

inflation: The rate at which the general level of prices for goods and services rises, leading to a decrease in the purchasing power of a currency.

interest (*ribā*): A charge for borrowed money that is generally a percentage of the amount borrowed.

interest rate: The percentage charged by a lender for borrowing money (e.g., on loans and credit cards) or earned on investments (e.g., savings accounts and bonds).

investment account: An account that allows individuals or organizations to buy and sell various types of investments, such as stocks, bonds, mutual funds, and ETFs. It is used for saving, growing wealth, or achieving financial goals.

late fees: Charges imposed by creditors when a payment is not made on time.

minimum payment: The smallest amount you must pay on your credit card balance each month to keep the account in good standing. Paying only the minimum can result in high interest charges and a longer repayment period.

mutual aid: A form of community care where individuals pool resources to support those in need, often in response to crises or emergencies.

mutual funds: An investment vehicle that pools money from multiple investors to purchase stocks, bonds, or other securities, managed by professionals.

net worth: The difference between your assets (what you own) and your liabilities (what you owe).

pink tax: The price disparity where products marketed to women are often more expensive than those marketed to men.

portfolio: The collection of investments, such as stocks, bonds, real estate, and precious metals, held by an individual or entity.

Glossary

principal amount: The original amount of money borrowed or invested, before interest or other charges are applied.

profit-sharing contracts: Agreements in Islamic finance where profits and losses are shared between parties.

real estate investment trust (REIT): A company that owns or finances income-generating real estate, allowing investors to earn dividends from properties without owning them directly.

rollover IRA: A retirement account that allows the transfer of funds from a 401(k) or other retirement accounts without paying taxes on the transfer.

Roth IRA: An individual retirement account that allows after-tax contributions to grow tax-free.

savings account: A bank account designed for saving money.

self-directed brokerage account (SDBA): An option within a retirement plan, such as a 401(k), that allows participants to choose and manage their own investments.

sharia-compliant investments: Investments that adhere to Islamic principles and are considered halal (permissible) in accordance with sharia.

simplified employee pension individual retirement account (SEP IRA): A retirement account that allows self-employed individuals or small business owners to contribute toward their retirement.

stocks: Shares of ownership in a company.

stock market: A marketplace where stocks (shares of ownership in companies) are bought and sold.

stock screener: A financial tool or application that helps investors identify stocks and investment opportunities that align with specific criteria, such as sharia compliance in the case of Islamic investors.

student loans: Loans specifically designed to help students pay for education expenses.

testimony: Using one's voice or platform to advocate for social justice or raise awareness about important causes.

Uniform Gift to Minors Act (UGMA) and Uniform Transfers to Minors Act (UTMA): Custodial accounts that allow an adult to hold assets on behalf of a minor until they reach the age of maturity, at which point the assets are transferred to the minor.

Bibliography

AAUW. "The STEM Gap: Women and Girls in Science, Technology, Engineering and Mathematics." Accessed June 19, 2023. https://www.aauw.org/resources/research/the-stem-gap/.

Abdullah, Hasanain. "The Caliph Uthman bin Affan (R.A) and the Well." Awqaf SA, August 17, 2020. https://awqafsa.org.za/the-caliph-uthman-bin-affan-r-a-and-the-well/.

Abdur-Rashid, Khalil. "Financing Kindness as a Society: The Rise and Fall of Islamic Philanthropic Institutions (Waqfs)," Yaqeen Institute for Islamic Research, 2019.

Abueish, Tamara. "Saudi Princess al-Bandari: A Lifetime Dedicated to Philanthropy, Women's Rights." *Al Arabiya English*, March 16, 2019. https://web.archive.org/web/20190322095049/https://english.alarabiya.net/en/features/2019/03/16/Saudi-Princess-Al-Bandari-A-lifetime-dedicated-to-philanthropy-women-s-rights.html.

Adams, Tom, Melanie Herman, and Tim Wolfred. "Exit Agreements for Nonprofit CEOs: A Guide for Boards and Executives." *Nonprofit Quarterly*, January 13, 2020. https://nonprofitquarterly.org/exit-agreements-nonprofit-ceo-guide-for-boards-and-executives/.

"Adolescent Income and Financial Literacy." Giftcards.com, accessed August 18, 2023. https://www.giftcards.com/adolescent-income-and-financial-literacy?utm_source=rakuten&utm_medium=affiliate&utm_campaign=2116208&utm_content=686295&ranMID=4443 2&ranEAID=TnL5HPStwNw&ranSiteID=TnL5HPStwNw-GYenFuvsd1Ee79UsNbOcVA.

Ahmad, Md. Mokhter, and Md. Safiullah, "Management of Waqf Estates in Bangladesh: Toward a Sustainable Policy Formulation." *Waqf Laws and Management (With Special Reference to Malaysia)* (2012): 229–62.

Ahmed, Leila. *Women and Gender in Islam: Historical Roots of Modern Debate*. Yale University Press, 1992.

Al Maddah, Fatemah A. "Islamic Finance and the Concept of Profit and Risk Sharing." *Middle East Journal of Entrepreneurship, Leadership and Sustainable Development* 1, no. 1 (2017): 89–95.

Aladangady, Aditya, and Akila Forde. "Wealth Inequality and the Racial Wealth Gap." Federal Reserve System, October 22, 2021. https://www.federalreserve.gov/econres/notes/feds-notes/wealth-inequality-and-the-racial-wealth-gap-20211022.html.

Albrecht, Leslie. "Who Donates More Time and Money to Charity—Men or Women? Here's Your Answer." MarketWatch, accessed September 2, 2023. https://www.marketwatch.com/story/wealthy-women-give-away-their-money-and-time-more-than-rich-men-2018-10-24.

al-Kāsānī, Masʿūd ibn Aḥmad. *Badāʾiʿ al-ṣanāʾiʿ fī tartīb al-sharāʾiʿ*. Edited by ʿAlī Muḥammad Muʿauwaḍ. Dār al-Kutub al-ʿIlmīya, n.d.

Avanzi, Federica, and Simone Masserini. *7 Daily Rituals for Gratitude*. VMB Publishers, 2021.

Azid, Toseef, and Jennifer L. Ward-Batts, eds. *Economic Empowerment of Women in the Islamic World: Theory and Practice*. World Scientific, 2020.

Bach, David, and John David Mann. *The Latte Factor: Why You Don't Have to Be Rich to Live Rich*. Atria Books, 2019.

Backman, Maurie. "Women and Investing: Key Findings and Opportunities." The Motley Fool, accessed August 18, 2023. https://www.fidelity.ca/en/investor/investorinsights/womenandinvesting/.

Baghai, Pooneh, Olivia Howard, Lakshmi Prakash, and Jill Zucker. "Women as the Next Wave of Growth in US Wealth Management," McKinsey, July 29, 2020. https://www.mckinsey.com/industries/financial-services/our-insights/women-as-the-next-wave-of-growth-in-us-wealth-management.

Barone, Adam. "What Is an Asset? Definition, Types, and Examples." Investopedia, accessed September 4, 2023. https://www.investopedia.com/terms/a/asset.asp.

Bertrand, Marianne, Jessica Pan, and Emir Kamenica. "Gender Identity and Relative Income within Households." National Bureau of Economic Research, May 2013. https://doi.org/10.3386/w19023.

Board of Governors of the Federal Reserve System. "Federal Reserve Board - Survey of Consumer Finances (SCF)." Accessed July 27, 2023. https://www.federalreserve.gov/econres/scfindex.htm.

Bouderbala, Sobhi. "Al-Ḥabasha in Miṣr and the End of the World: Early Islamic Egyptian Apocalypse Narratives Related to Abyssinia." *Northeast African Studies* 19, no. 1 (April 1, 2019): 9–22. https://doi.org/10.14321/nortafristud.19.1.0009.

Bradford, Joe. "Video: Is Life Insurance Halal?" Joe Bradford, April 10, 2019. https://joebradford.net/video-is-life-insurance-halal/.

Brown, Joshua, and Joel Wong. "How Gratitude Changes You and Your Brain." Greater Good, June 6, 2017. https://greatergood.berkeley.edu/article/item/how_gratitude_changes_you_and_your_brain.

Center for American Progress. "The Basic Facts About Women in Poverty." August 3, 2020. https://www.americanprogress.org/article/basic-facts-women-poverty/.

Clark, Jeffrey. "Comparing the Savings Behaviors of Women and Men in DC Plans." Vanguard, n.d. https://institutional.vanguard.com/content/dam/inst/iig-transformation/insights/pdf/2022/comparing-the-saving-behaviors-of-women-vs-men-in-dc-plans.pdf.

Clarke, Anthony. "Islamic Finance: Unlocking Opportunities Beyond Religious Boundaries." Nasdaq, July 11, 2023. https://www.nasdaq.com/articles/islamic-finance-unlocking-opportunities-beyond-religious-boundaries.

"Consumer Expenditure Surveys: Tables." U.S. Bureau of Labor Statistics, accessed September 2, 2023. https://www.bls.gov/cex/tables.htm.

Copur-Gencturk, Yasemin. "'Girls Can't Do Math' and Other Myths: How Unconscious Bias Leads to Gender Gaps in STEM." USC News, July 26, 2021. https://news.usc.edu/trojan-family/girls-learn-math-bias-gender-ability-stem/.

Deahl, Jessica. "Countries Around the World Beat the U.S. on Paid Parental Leave." *NPR*, October 6, 2016. https://www.npr.org/2016/10/06/495839588/countries-around-the-world-beat-the-u-s-on-paid-parental-leave.

Desouky, Tamer. "The Art of Gratitude: Quranic Themes on Shukr." Yaqeen Institute for Islamic Research, April 20, 2022. https://yaqeeninstitute.org/read/paper/the-art-of-gratitude-quranic-themes-on-shukr.

De Waal, Alexander, ed. *Islamism and Its Enemies in the Horn of Africa*. Indiana University Press, 2004.

DOL. "Continuation of Health Coverage (COBRA)." Accessed September 2, 2023. http://www.dol.gov/general/topic/health-plans/cobra.

Education Data Initiative. "Student Loan Debt by Gender [2023]: Men vs Women." Accessed September 2, 2023. https://educationdata.org/student-loan-debt-by-gender.

Elias, Abu Amina. "Sharia, Fiqh, and Islamic Law Explained," September 7, 2021. https://www.abuaminaelias.com/sharia-fiqh-qanun/.

"Expressing Gratitude Can Improve Mood, Reduce Stress." Purdue Today archive, Purdue University, October 19, 2022. https://www.purdue.edu/newsroom/purduetoday/releases/2022/Q4/expressing-gratitude-can-improve-mood,-reduce-stress.html.

Fatima, Nikhat. "This Muslim-Run NGO Run in Hyderabad Helps Women Build Sustainable Livelihoods." *TwoCircles.Net* (blog), November 7, 2022. https://twocircles.net/2022nov07/447386.html.

Feldblum, Chai R., and Victoria A. Lipnic. "Select Task Force on the Study of Harassment in the Workplace: Report of the Co-Chairs of the EEOC." Equal Employment Opportunity Commission, June 2016. https://www.eeoc.gov/select-task-force-study-harassment-workplace.

Fidelity Investments. "2021 Women and Investing Study." https://www.fidelity.com/bin-public/060_www_fidelity_com/documents/about-fidelity/FidelityInvestmentsWomen&InvestingStudy2021.pdf.

Gaudiosi, Monica M. "Influence of the Islamic Law of WAQF on the Development of the Trust in England: The Case of Merton College." *University of Pennsylvania Law Review* 136 (1988). https://scholarship.law.upenn.edu/cgi/viewcontent.cgi?article=3909&context=penn_law_review.

Gerdeman, Dina. "Bad at Math: How Gender Stereotypes Cause Women to Question Their Abilities." *Forbes*, March 8, 2019. https://www.forbes.com/sites/hbsworkingknowledge/2019/03/08/bad-at-math-how-gender-stereotypes-cause-women-to-question-their-abilities/.

GhaneaBassiri, Kambiz. "U.S. Muslim Philanthropy After 9/11." *Journal of Muslim Philanthropy and Civil Society* 1, no. 1 (2018). https://scholarworks.iu.edu/iupjournals/index.php/muslimphilanthropy/article/view/1635.

Giftcards.com. "Adolescent Income and Financial Literacy." Accessed June 19, 2023. https://www.giftcards.com/adolescent-income-and-financial-literacy.

Gratton, Peter. "Real Estate Investment Trust (REIT): How They Work and How to Invest." Investopedia, July 19, 2024. https://www.investopedia.com/terms/r/reit.asp.

Gray, Tamara. "Ethical Dilemma of Zakat and Nonprofit Funding." November 27, 2023.

Guess, Ben. "Women Pay up to $37,000 More than Men to Own a Car and Home." Jerry, May 24, 2023. https://getjerry.com/studies/women-pay-up-to-usd37-000-more-than-men-to-own-a-car-and-home.

Habibur, Muhammad, Rahman Khan Sherwani, and Syed Moinul Haq. *Hadrat Abu Bakr: The First Caliph Of Islam*. Literary Licensing, 2011.

Hamid, Abdul Wahid. "'Abdur-Rahman Ibn 'Awf." In *Companions of the Prophet*, pp. 49–56. MELS, 1998.

Bibliography

Hanson, Melanie. "Student Loan Debt by Gender." EducationData.org, July 16, 2023. https://educationdata.org/student-loan-debt-by-gender.

Hassan, Hassan. *In the House of Muhammad Ali: A Family Album 1805–1952*. The American University in Cairo Press, 2000.

Hazineeditor. "Süleymaniye Library." *Hazine* (blog), October 10, 2013. https://hazine.info/suleymaniye-library/.

Her Culture. "The Importance of Women in STEM: Why Diversity Matters." March 2, 2022. https://www.herculture.org/blog/2022/3/2/the-importance-of-women-in-stem-why-diversity-matters.

Hill, Evan, Ainara Tiefenthäler, Christiaan Triebert, Drew Jordan, Haley Willis, and Robin Stein. "How George Floyd Was Killed in Police Custody." *The New York Times*, June 1, 2020. https://www.nytimes.com/2020/05/31/us/george-floyd-investigation.html.

Hoffman, Valerie J. *Sufism, Mystics, and Saints in Modern Egypt*. University of South Carolina Press, 2023.

Houston, Melissa. "Women and Money: Busting the Money Myths." *Forbes*, accessed June 19, 2023. https://www.forbes.com/sites/melissahouston/2021/10/06/women-and-money-busting-the-money-myths/.

International Crisis Board. "Crisis Group Welcomes Lubna Olayan to Its Board." January 19, 2022. https://www.crisisgroup.org/crisis-group-welcomes-lubna-olayan-its-board.

"In the Words of HRH Dr. Nisreen El-Hashemite: 'We Need to Encourage Girls and Young Women to Pursue Science and Stay in Science Careers,'" UN Women – Europe and Central Asia, accessed April 30, 2023. https://eca.unwomen.org/en/news/stories/2018/02/in-the-words-of-dr-nisreen-el-hashemite.

Iskandar, Iskandar, Dadang Irsyamuddin, Esa Dwiyan, and Hidayatul Ihsan. "Waqf Substantial Contribution Toward the Public Healthcare Sector in the Ottoman Empire." *Journal of Critical Realism in Socio-Economics (JOCRISE)* 1, no. 3 (April 9, 2023): 275–94. https://doi.org/10.21111/jocrise.v1i3.21.

Islahi, Abdul Azim. "The Role of Women in the Creation and Management of Awqāf: A Historical Perspective." *Intellectual Discourse* 26 (July 2, 2018): 1025–46.

Jan, Rafat. "Rufaida Al-Asalmiya: The First Muslim Nurse." *Image: The Journal of Nursing Scholarship* 28, no. 3 (September 1996): 267–68. https://doi.org/10.1111/j.1547-5069.1996.tb00362.x.

Jonsson, David. *Islamic Economics and the Final Jihad.* Salem Publishing, 2006.

Journeys for Change. "Journeys for Change - Alice Chou on Shaheen, Bringing Muslim and Hindu Women to Empower Themselves." December 10, 2009. https://web.archive.org/web/20161005094019/http://www.journeysforchange.org/node/121.

Kashani-Sabet, Firoozeh. "Who Is Fatima? Gender, Culture, and Representation in Islam." *Journal of Middle East Women's Studies* 1, no. 2 (2005): 1–24.

Kelly, Jack. "Former Wells Fargo Executives Could Face Serious Criminal Charges." *Forbes*, January 7, 2020. https://www.forbes.com/sites/jackkelly/2020/01/07/former-wells-fargo-executives-could-face-serious-criminal-charges/.

Khalid, Khalid Muhammed. *Women Around the Messenger.* Light Publishing, 2015.

Khan, Ibrahim. "Are Credit Cards Haram or Halal? - Islamic Finance." Islamic Finance Guru, May 31, 2022. https://www.islamicfinanceguru.com/articles/are-credit-cards-haram-or-halal.

Khan, Mustafa. "How to Buy Halal Stocks - Stock Screening Method." IFG, May 31, 2022. https://www.islamicfinanceguru.com/articles/investment/how-to-screen-for-halal-sharia-compliant-shares.

Khorrami, Najma. "Gratitude Helps Minimize Feelings of Stress." *Psychology Today*, July 7, 2020. https://www.psychologytoday.com/us/blog/comfort-gratitude/202007/gratitude-helps-minimize-feelings-stress.

Krawcheck, Sallie. "8 Myths That Hold Women Back from Investing." August 9, 2023. https://www.ellevatenetwork.com/articles/7138-8-myths-that-hold-women-back-from-investing.

Krawcheck, Sallie. "Just Buy the F...... Latte." *Ellevest*, January 24, 2024. https://www.ellevest.com/magazine/personal-finance/just-buy-the-f-ing-latte.

Lake, Rebecca. "Women and the Great Wealth Transfer." Investopedia, December 11, 2023. https://www.investopedia.com/financial-advisor/women-and-great-wealth-transfer/.

Lambert, Emily. "When Women Earn More Than Their Husbands." Chicago Booth, February 18, 2013. https://www.chicagobooth.edu/media-relations-and-communications/press-releases/when-women-earn-more-than-their-husbands.

Bibliography

Lindner, Jannik. "Struggles and Solutions: Two Income Families Statistics Unveiled." *Gitnux*, July 7, 2024. https://blog.gitnux.com/two-income-families-statistics/.

Lindzon, Jared. "How Parents Talk about Money Differently to Their Sons and Daughters." Fast Company, January 14, 2019. https://www.fastcompany.com/90283344/how-parents-talk-about-money-differently-to-their-sons-and-daughters.

Loh, Adeline. "Meet Dr Nisreen El-Hashemite, the Iraqi Princess Who Overturned Convention to Pursue Medicine." *The Peak*, May 12, 2017. https://www.thepeakmagazine.com.sg/interviews/meet-dr-nisreen-el-hashemite-iraqi-princess-overturned-convention-pursue-medicine/.

McCraty, Rollin, and Doc Childre. "The Grateful Heart: The Psychophysiology of Appreciation." In *The Psychology of Gratitude*. Edited by R. A. Emmons and M. E. McCullough. Oxford University Press, 2004.

McGurran, Brianna. "Women and Credit 2020: How History Shaped Today's Credit Landscape." *Experian* (blog), February 28, 2020. https://www.experian.com/blogs/ask-experian/women-and-credit/.

Menk, Mufti. "Mufti Menk - Sūrat Nuh Part One." Muslim Central, audio lecture, posted May 8, 2016. https://muslimcentral.com/mufti-menk-surah-nuh-part-one/.

Mesch, Debra, Eileen L. O'Gara, Una Osili, Andrea Pactor, and Jon Bergdoll. "Do Women Give More?" Women Philanthropy Institute, September 2015. https://philanthropy.indianapolis.iu.edu/doc/institutes/wpi-give-more.pdf.

Mirza, Younus Y. "The Deputy of Maryam – The Mystic Rābi'a al-'Adawiyya in Light of the Quranic Mary." *Maydan* (blog), August 15, 2023. https://themaydan.com/2023/08/the-deputy-of-maryam-the-mystic-rabia-al-adawiyya-in-light-of-the-quranic-mary/.

Mogahed, Dalia. "Five Surprising Facts about Divorce in American Muslim Communities." ISPU, January 7, 2021. https://www.ispu.org/five-facts-about-divorce/.

Mohiuddin, Meraj. *Revelation: The Story of Muhammad: Peace and Blessings Be upon Him*. Whiteboard Press, 2015.

Moss, Emily, Kriston McIntosh, Wendy Edelberg, and Broady Kristen. "The Black-White Wealth Gap Left Black Households More Vulnerable." Brookings Institution, December 8, 2020. https://www.brookings.edu/articles/the-black-white-wealth-gap-left-black-households-more-vulnerable/.

Munir, Hassam. "Did Islam Spread by the Sword? A Critical Look at Forced Conversions." Yaqeen Institute for Islamic Research, May 12, 2018. https://yaqeeninstitute.org/read/paper/did-islam-spread-by-the-sword-a-critical-look-at-forced-conversions.

Muslim Women Mathematicians. Accessed June 19, 2023. https://muslimwomenmathematicians.org/home.html.

Nadvi, Saiyid Sulaiman. *Hadhrat Ayesha Siddiqui. Her Life and Works*. Islamic Book Publishers, 1982.

Nadwī, Muḥammad Akram. *Al-Muḥaddithāt: The Women Scholars in Islam*. 2nd ed. Interface Publications, 2013.

Nietzel, Michael T. "Women Continue to Outpace Men in College Enrollment and Graduation." *Forbes*, August 7, 2024. https://www.forbes.com/sites/michaeltnietzel/2024/08/07/women-continue-to-outpace-men-in-college-enrollment-and-graduation/.

Nisa, Eva. "Networking Humanity: Women, Piety, and Philanthropy." *Middle East Insights* 198 (January 15, 2019).

Okkenhaug, Inger Marie, and Ingvild Flaskerud, eds. *Gender, Religion and Change in the Middle East: Two Hundred Years of History*. Bloomsbury Publishing, 2005.

Orem, Tina, and Ramona Paden. "Tax Deductible Donations: Rules for Charitable Giving." NerdWallet, July 11, 2023. https://www.nerdwallet.com/article/taxes/tax-deductible-donations-charity.

Paderbornersj. "Who Was Rufayda Al Aslamiya the First Muslim Female Nurse, given Tributes by Aga Khan University during Oath Taking Ceremonies." *Paderborner "SJ" Blog* (blog), May 27, 2012. https://sjpaderborn.wordpress.com/2012/05/27/who-was-rufayda-al-aslamiya-the-first-muslim-female-nurse-given-tributes-by-aga-khan-university-during-oath-taking-ceremonies/.

Payton, Robert L., and Michael P. Moody. *Understanding Philanthropy: Its Meaning and Mission*. Indiana University Press, 2008.

Pierre, Kathy. "Women Aren't Bad with Money. Society Just Made Them Think They Were." *Relevant*, March 16, 2018. https://relevantmagazine.com/life5/career-money/women-arent-bad-money-society-just-made-think/.

Purtill, Corinne, and Dan Kopf. "The Reason the Richest Women in the US Are the Ones Having the Most Kids." *Quartz*, November 11, 2017. https://qz.com/1125805/the-reason-the-richest-women-in-the-us-are-the-ones-having-the-most-kids.

Quṭb, Muḥammad ʿAlī. *Women Around the Messenger*. International Islamic Publishing House, 2008.

Razwy, Syed. *Khadijatul kubra*. Tahrike Tarsile Quran, n.d.

Reşit, Haylamaz, and Coşar Hülya. *Khadija: The First Muslim and the Wife of the Prophet Muhammad*. Tughra Books, 2014.

Robinson, Carly, Matthew A. Kraft, Susanna Loeb, and Beth E. Schueler. "Accelerating Student Learning with High-Dosage Tutoring." EdResearch for Recovery, February 2021.

Sahadi, Jeanne. "More Women Now Make as Much as Their Husbands, but Still Do More at Home." CNN Business, April 16, 2023. https://www.cnn.com/2023/04/16/success/husbands-wives-earning-division-of-labor-pew-survey/index.html.

Shaikh, Ahmed. "Zakat Is Not for Hors d'Oeuvres." *Islamic Horizons*, July 2021. https://issuu.com/isnacreative/docs/ih_july-august_21/s/12706310.

Sharma, Ritu. *Teach a Woman to Fish: Overcoming Poverty around the Globe*. Palgrave Macmillan, 2014.

"Sheikha Lubna Al Qasimi," *Forbes*, accessed April 30, 2023, https://www.forbes.com/profile/sheikha-lubna-al-qasimi/?sh=7a0372bd640e.

Shook, R. J. "Women Feel Ignored By Advisors, Study Says." *Forbes*, August 7, 2020. https://www.forbes.com/sites/rjshook/2020/08/07/woman-feel-ignored-by-advisors-study-says/.

Siddiqi, Rafiuddin. "Oldest Library of University of Al-Qarawiyyin in Fez, Morocco." *Pakistan Library and Information Science Journal* 49, no. 3 (2018).

Siddiqui, Shariq Ahmed, and David A. Campbell, eds. *Philanthropy in the Muslim World: Majority and Minority Muslim Communities*. New Horizons in Nonprofit Research Series. Edward Elgar Publishing, 2023.

Siddiqui, Shariq, Raheel Wasif, Micah Hughes, Afshan Paarlberg, and Zeeshan Noor. *Muslim American Zakat Report 2022*. Muslim Philanthropy Initiative at Indiana University Lilly Family School of Philanthropy, 2022.

Singer, Amy. *Charity in Islamic Societies*. Cambridge University Press, 2008.

Smith, Bonnie G., ed. *The Oxford Encyclopedia of Women in World History*. Oxford University Press, 2008.

Smith, Tim. "Understanding Endowments: Types and Policies That Govern Them." Investopedia, July 9, 2022. https://www.investopedia.com/terms/e/endowment.asp.

Stamm, Sonia J., and Ted LeBow. "The Ideal Exit of the Nonprofit Executive." *BoardEffect* (blog), February 25, 2016. https://www.boardeffect.com/blog/the-ideal-exit-of-the-nonprofit-executive/.

Suleiman, Omar. "Maximize Your Wealth - Omar Suleiman - Quran Weekly," Quran Weekly, posted August 8, 2014, YouTube. https://www.youtube.com/watch?v=yAPoLDfiRBs.

Suleiman, Omar. *40 on Justice: The Prophetic Voice on Social Reform.* Kube Publishing, 2021.

Sullivan, Julie. "Comparing Characteristics and Selected Expenditures of Dual- and Single-Income Households with Children," Monthly Labor Review, U.S. Bureau of Labor Statistics, September 2020. https://www.bls.gov/opub/mlr/2020/article/comparing-characteristics-and-selected-expenditures-of-dual-and-single-income-households-with-children.htm.

"Sūra Al-Insan Chapter 76." Al-Islam.org, January 24, 2014. https://www.al-islam.org/enlightening-commentary-light-holy-quran-vol-19/surah-al-insan-chapter-76.

Tagle, Andee, and Malaka Gharib. "Want to Get Better at Being Thankful? Here Are Some Tips." NPR, November 23, 2022. https://www.npr.org/2022/11/18/1137822057/get-better-at-being-grateful.

Talhami, Ghada Hashem. *Historical Dictionary of Women in the Middle East and North Africa.* Rowman and Littlefield, 2013.

The Human Capital Hub. "Exit Packages Global Trend." Accessed September 4, 2023. https://thehumancapitalhub.com/articles/exit-packages-global-trend.

The Sincere Seeker. "What Is Istikhara Prayer and How to Pray Istikhara?" *Medium* (blog), April 2, 2023. https://thesincereseeker.medium.com/what-is-istikhara-prayer-how-to-pray-istikhara-e73d4e1e6cdc.

Twin Cities Habitat for Humanity. "How to Build Generational Wealth Through Homeownership." October 17, 2022. https://www.tchabitat.org/blog/how_to_build_generational_wealth_through_homeownership.

"Umrah 2023." Dar El Salam, accessed September 4, 2023. https://dstworldtravel.com/umrah2023/.

Bibliography

US Inflation Calculator. "Current US Inflation Rates: 2000–2023." September 13, 2023. https://www.usinflationcalculator.com/inflation/current-inflation-rates/.

Villanueva, Edgar. *Decolonizing Wealth: Indigenous Wisdom to Heal Divides and Restore Balance*. Berrett-Koehler Publishers, 2018.

von Benda-Beckmann, Franz, and Keebet von Benda-Beckmann. *Social Security between Past and Future: Ambonese Networks of Care and Support*. LIT Verlag, 2007.

"Well of Rumah." Madain Project, accessed September 23, 2023. https://madainproject.com/well_of_rumah.

Wiepking, Pamala. "The Global Study of Philanthropic Behavior." *VOLUNTAS: International Journal of Voluntary and Nonprofit Organizations* 32, no.

Women Champions: The Changing Face of Philanthropy." Salaam Gateway - Global Islamic Economy Gateway, accessed August 21, 2023. https://salaamgateway.com/story/women-champions-the-changing-face-of-philanthropy. 2 (2021): 194–203.

Yousef, Jinan, and Mohamad Zaoud. "Trusting God, The Provider with Dr. Jinan Yousef." DoubleTake Podcast, February 8, 2023. https://yaqeeninstitute.org/jinan-yousef/trusting-god-the-provider-with-dr-jinan-yousef-doubletake-podcast.

Zaman, Hasan. "Historical Origins of Sukuk." *International Journal of Sukuk and Waqf Research* 1, no. 1 (2020): 27–29. http://cribfb.com/journal/index.php/IJSWR/article/view/1145.

Index

Numbers

401(k) *23, 24, 30, 96, 113, 161, 164, 192, 209, 211, 227, 228, 229, 230, 231, 242, 355, 361*

529 plan *224, 355*

A

abundance mindset *16, 70, 71, 130, 134, 135, 136, 140, 141, 142, 144, 145, 146, 252*

Accounting and Auditing Organization for Islamic Financial Institutions (AAOIFI) *208, 355*

annual fee *172, 173, 355*

annual percentage rate (APR) *355*

assets *35, 77, 111, 117, 153, 158, 159, 163, 191, 206, 212, 213, 216, 218, 225, 235, 236, 237, 283, 287, 289, 297, 298, 337, 338, 341, 350, 357, 358, 359, 360, 362*

automation *175, 246, 247, 355*

autopayment *355*

awqāf *285, 287, 289, 290, 291, 292, 294, 310, 350*

B

balance transfer *355*

bank statement *183, 356*

baraka *126, 139, 345, 350*

Bollywood *13*

bonds *23, 82, 157, 199, 205, 206, 214, 215, 224, 254, 347, 353, 355, 356, 358, 360*

budget *5, 7, 10, 16, 23, 27, 28, 29, 30, 43, 46, 56, 57, 60, 65, 78, 95, 97, 103, 105, 106, 116, 118, 133, 161, 198, 241, 244, 245, 273, 329, 356*

C

camel milk *112, 113*

capital fund *199, 200, 356*

capital gains tax *296, 297, 298, 356*

car loan *356*

checking account *26, 161, 163, 183, 185, 199, 355, 356*

company stock *209, 212, 356, 358*

compound interest *187, 356*

conscious spending *244, 245, 246, 247, 249, 250, 251*

cost of living adjustment (COLA) *194, 356*

credit card *26, 27, 82, 138, 161, 163, 170, 171, 172, 173, 174, 175, 176, 178, 179, 180, 181, 182, 213, 245, 342, 355, 357, 359, 360*

credit limit *357*

credit score *30, 166, 171, 175, 177, 178, 179, 180, 181,*

182, 246, 357

credit utilization 180, 357

custodial account 225, 357

D

debt 70, 82, 88, 99, 129, 134, 155, 163, 164, 169, 179, 180, 181, 213, 215, 223, 225, 250, 277, 278, 279, 353, 356, 357, 358, 365, 367

deferred payment plan 174, 357

digital wallet 357

diversification 357

dollar-cost averaging (DCA) 211, 357

dua 61, 107, 116, 119, 124, 125, 126, 139, 252, 266, 341, 350

dual-income households 149, 358

E

economic constraints 147, 358

economic empowerment 1, 17, 33, 147, 158, 189, 237, 261, 270, 280, 341, 358

education savings account (ESA) 356

Eid 8, 15, 158, 228, 350, 351

employee stock purchase plan (ESPP) 209, 358

endowment fund 198, 199, 350, 358

F

financial goals 33, 34, 36, 40, 41, 42, 52, 58, 59, 65, 69, 70, 88, 134, 140, 171, 244, 356, 358, 360

financial literacy 2, 5, 31, 62, 71, 79, 81, 153, 159, 177, 319, 358

financial plan 35, 41, 356, 358

five T's 263, 331, 335

fraud 172, 359

G

generational wealth 112, 114, 115, 156, 159, 224, 338, 359

giving circle 302, 304, 305, 306, 308, 359

grace period 357, 359

H

hajj 8, 61, 88, 115, 139, 207, 223, 235, 350, 351

halal investing 2, 39, 205, 209, 218, 359

I

identity theft 172, 180, 183, 359

India 7, 8, 9, 14, 17, 21, 22, 49, 111, 113, 248, 268, 282

individual retirement account (IRA) 230, 359

inflation 79, 80, 105, 194, 195, 196, 203, 207, 217, 231, 242, 356, 360, 373

interest rate 172, 176, 177, 183, 355, 360

Index

interest (*ribā*) 190, 206, 359, 360

investment account 42, 80, 92, 116, 185, 199, 200, 202, 209, 210, 211, 224, 226, 242, 247, 342, 355, 360

IRA 77, 161, 164, 211, 212, 224, 230, 231, 232, 233, 242, 246, 256, 359, 361

Islamic finance 189, 190, 191, 192, 201, 206, 208, 218, 222, 229, 353, 361

L

late fees 13, 161, 174, 175, 183, 246, 247, 360

M

Maghrib 17, 352

minimalist lifestyle 135, 140, 141, 142, 144, 146

minimum payment 357, 360

mirchi ka salan 14, 352

Muslim philanthropy 54, 55, 274, 275, 284, 291, 292, 293, 294, 309, 310, 311

mutual aid 269, 270, 306, 307, 360

mutual fund 216, 218, 224

N

nafs 132, 133, 134, 136, 140, 144, 145, 146, 352

net worth 159, 360

P

philanthropy 3, 40, 45, 47, 48, 54, 55, 62, 98, 117, 261, 263, 274, 275, 280, 283, 284, 287, 288, 291, 292, 293, 294, 300, 302, 304, 309, 310, 311, 313, 314, 315, 316, 319, 320, 322, 323, 331, 333, 335, 344, 352, 359, 363, 369, 373

pink tax 91, 92, 360

portfolio 41, 42, 81, 155, 185, 196, 201, 202, 205, 206, 207, 210, 211, 212, 213, 214, 216, 217, 218, 247, 287, 342, 347, 358, 360

principal amount 200, 242, 356, 361

profit-sharing contracts 361

Q

Quran 3, 14, 39, 87, 120, 124, 125, 126, 127, 128, 132, 133, 134, 137, 138, 139, 141, 148, 149, 154, 155, 156, 187, 188, 189, 191, 219, 235, 236, 262, 265, 266, 270, 277, 280, 314, 318, 345, 350, 352, 353, 371, 372

R

real estate investment trust (REIT) 216, 361

rizq 4, 39, 87, 108, 123, 124, 125, 126, 131, 133, 134, 139, 145, 170, 220, 231, 233, 248, 265, 341, 353

rollover IRA 231, 361

Roth IRA 164, 232, 233, 361

S

ṣadaqa 139, 294

savings account 23, 26, 27, 30, 79, 80, 111, 116, 121, 161, 163, 166, 171, 195, 196, 207, 216, 224, 356, 357, 359, 361

scarcity mindset 16, 18, 70, 71, 129, 130, 131, 132, 144, 146

self-directed brokerage account (SDBA) 228, 361

SEP IRA 77, 164, 230, 231, 232, 242, 361

sharia compliance 215, 228, 231, 362

simplified employee pension individual retirement account (SEP IRA) 361

sīra 311, 353

stock market 26, 35, 80, 81, 196, 205, 206, 207, 208, 210, 211, 216, 217, 361

stocks 26, 29, 42, 72, 74, 80, 82, 153, 161, 165, 196, 199, 201, 202, 205, 207, 208, 210, 212, 213, 214, 216, 218, 222, 242, 247, 298, 355, 356, 358, 360, 361

stock screener 201, 213, 214, 361

stock split 243

student loans 15, 26, 99, 129, 161, 223, 362

sukūk 205, 206, 212, 215, 216, 347, 353

T

takhat 8, 11, 353

testimony 263, 274, 283, 302, 309, 322, 325, 327, 328, 329, 333, 362

thawb 142, 353

U

ʿumra 115, 354

Uniform Gift to Minors Act (UGMA) and Uniform Transfers to Minors Act (UTMA) 224, 362

W

waqf 283, 286, 287, 288, 290, 312, 350, 354

Z

zabiha 13, 354

zakat 2, 17, 31, 39, 60, 97, 112, 116, 124, 140, 161, 209, 262, 273, 275, 276, 277, 278, 279, 280, 281, 282, 283, 284, 285, 286, 291, 292, 294, 295, 298, 299, 309, 310, 311, 331, 341, 342, 343, 352, 353, 354

www.ingramcontent.com/pod-product-compliance
Ingram Content Group UK Ltd.
Pitfield, Milton Keynes, MK11 3LW, UK
UKHW041303180426
11947UKWH00009B/659